The Impact of 9/11 on Politics and War

Also by Matthew J. Morgan

A Democracy Is Born

The American Military after 9/11: Society, State, and Empire
The Impact of 9/11 on Business and Economics
The Impact of 9/11 and the New Legal Landscape
The Impact of 9/11 on the Media, Arts, and Entertainment
The Impact of 9/11 on Psychology and Education
The Impact of 9/11 on Religion and Philosophy

The Impact of 9/11 on Politics and War

The Day that Changed Everything?

Edited by
Matthew J. Morgan

With a Foreword by
R. James Woolsey, Jr.

palgrave
macmillan

First published in 2009 by
PALGRAVE MACMILLAN®
in the United States—a division of St. Martin's Press LLC,
175 Fifth Avenue, New York, NY 10010.

Where this book is distributed in the UK, Europe and the rest of the
world, this is by Palgrave Macmillan, a division of Macmillan Publishers
Limited, registered in England, company number 785998, of Houndmills,
Basingstoke, Hampshire RG21 6XS.

Palgrave Macmillan is the global academic imprint of the above companies
and has companies and representatives throughout the world.

Palgrave® and Macmillan® are registered trademarks in the United States,
the United Kingdom, Europe and other countries.

ISBN: 978–0–230–60763–7

Library of Congress Cataloging-in-Publication Data

The impact of 9/11 on politics and war : the day that changed
everything? / edited by Matthew J. Morgan; with a foreword by R. James
Woolsey, Jr.
    p. cm.
Includes bibliographical references and index.
ISBN-13: 978–0–230–60763–7 (alk. paper)
ISBN-10: 0–230–60763–2 (alk. paper)
 1. September 11 Terrorist Attacks, 2001. 2. War on Terrorism, 2001–
3. United States—Foreign relations—2001– I. Morgan, Matthew J.

HV6432.7.I44 2009
973.931—dc22   2008051800

A catalogue record of the book is available from the British Library.

Design by Newgen Imaging Systems (P) Ltd., Chennai, India.

First edition: August 2009

10 9 8 7 6 5 4 3 2 1

Printed in the United States of America.

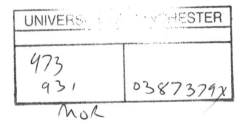

For all those who have lost their lives in today's wars

Contents

Part II   The Impact on War, Peace, and Security

Part III   Regional Impacts

Part IV   The Future after 9/11

Foreword

R. James Woolsey, Jr.

On January 25, 1993, five days into the new Clinton administration, an Islamist terrorist, Mir Aimal Kasi, killed two CIA employees just outside the CIA entrance and wounded three others. We had of course begun the manhunt for Kasi, which was ultimately successful four years later, but given how little we knew of him in 1993, we expected the search to be a long one. This terrible terrorist attack was of course very much on my mind a short time later at my confirmation hearings to be director of Central Intelligence where I said of the new post–cold war period, "We have slain a large dragon, but we now live in a jungle full of a bewildering variety of poisonous snakes. And, in many ways, the dragon was easier to keep track of."

When we saw the first attack on the World Trade Center less than a month later—followed by bin Laden's 1996 move from Sudan to Afghanistan, his fatwa declaring war on the United States later that year, and the series of subsequent attacks over the next few years—we should have had no doubt that we were in a battle with at least one snake that continued to coil and strike.

But the snake's essential character eluded the United States far longer than it should have. Americans have three propensities when faced with seemingly senseless violence against them: (1) to defer to law enforcement authorities to solve the problem by capturing and punishing the perpetrators and thus deterring others; (2) to assume that the perpetrators are "crazy" and, by implication, to have motives that cannot be understood; and (3) to assume that the perpetrators' claims of having been wronged by us may be, at least in part, true. Very few have the initial instincts of the cabdriver whom I asked, just after 9/11, if he agreed with a front-page story in the newspaper that day reporting some prominent figures' views that 9/11 had been "payback" for America's history of slavery and wars against the American Indians. "Nope," he said, "we have to take these guys out—they don't hate us for what we've done wrong, they hate us for what we've done right."

There were, sadly, not enough Americans with that cabdriver's insight to affect government policy after 9/11. We continued to emphasize the law enforcement route over more effective counterterrorist steps and we continued to assume either that our enemies were ranting goofballs or, alternatively, that we were to some degree at fault for the attacks.

We made another major mistake: we ignored the important close relationship in ideology between our enemies and our sometime-allies, the Saudis. Both al Qaeda and Saudi Arabia's Wahhabis hold views that lie somewhere between murderous and genocidal with respect to Shi'ites, Jews, homosexuals, and apostates and are massively repressive of everyone else, particularly women. Both dream of a worldwide Caliphate, a theocratic totalitarian dictatorship. They differ only on the question of who should be in charge of moving the world toward this goal; this is somewhat like the lethal rivalry in the 1920s and 1930s between the Trotskyites and the Stalinists. And as Lawrence Wright points out in *The Looming Tower*, with a little over 1 percent of the world's Muslims, the Saudis control around 90 percent of the world's Islamic institutions.

We were thus insufficiently attentive to the fact that the chance was about nine out of ten that any given madrassa in Pakistan or the West Bank that was teaching hatred and the undermining of religious freedom, either through jihad or propaganda (da'wa), was funded by our own purchases at the gasoline pump.

Finally, the administration's tactics in fighting the war in Iraq, for over three years until January of 2007, used the same "search and destroy" approach that had failed so miserably in Vietnam until it was changed in early 1968. The administration's recapitulation, until the surge and strategy change in early 2007, of the failed tactics used in Vietnam had the effect of poisoning the public discourse and bringing a huge condemnation of the only approach that will, over the long run, succeed in bringing about a more peaceful world: the spreading of democracy and the rule of law.

On this point consider a few numbers from Freedom House's *Freedom in the World 2008* report. There are 121 electoral democracies in the world, approximately 63 percent of the world's governments—an increase of about 100 since the end of World War II. Ninety of these are rated "free" by Freedom House and another 31 "partly free" (e. g., substantial corruption). Democracies very rarely fight one another. The establishment of democratic governments operating under the rule of law is, of course, no panacea—but no one has found a better long-term recipe for peace and justice in the world.

The work of Professors Paul Collier of Oxford and Michael L. Ross of UCLA, among others, makes a persuasive case that the dominance of an autocratic state's economy by oil is one of the major barriers to such a state's moving toward democracy and the rule of law. And the events of the last decade—including both Wahhabi influence around the world and the efforts of Messrs. Putin, Chavez, and Ahmadinejad to undermine democracy in their own countries and among their neighbors—give real resonance to Thomas L. Friedman's First Law of Petropolitics: "As the price of oil goes up, the pace of freedom goes down, and as the price of oil goes down, the pace of freedom goes up."

The pages that follow are, happily, quite far from offering a single approach to this extremely important issue. The distinguished group of authors featured in this volume, instead, sets out a full, fascinating, and multifaceted interdisciplinary assessment of what we have learned about "The Day that Changed Everything." Whatever your view of the implications of that day, be prepared to have your assumptions challenged.

Acknowledgments

The terrorist attacks on September 11, 2001, were an event that for most Americans will be remembered for a lifetime as a pivotal moment in history. As in the case of the Kennedy assassination a generation before, on November 22, 1963, Americans share a collective memory and trauma of the event, often asking each other and reminiscing about what one was doing during that fateful moment. Now, with several years having passed since 9/11, this series reflects on that event by bringing together from a broad spectrum of disciplines the leading thinkers of our time.

In undertaking such an ambitious project as this, appreciation must go to a wide range of people. First and foremost are the distinguished and skillful writers who have contributed to the series. Their willingness to share their talents and follow through with their commitment to this effort made all the difference. I cannot thank them enough for the sacrifices they have made to contribute their work to this series.

As I thank the many authors from such diverse backgrounds, perspectives, and even countries, I should caution readers that opinions expressed in this series reflect the views of each contributing author of each chapter and should not be contrived to represent views of the contributing authors generally or even my own views. The series has self-consciously attempted to include a "big tent" of different perspectives, some highly critical of policy decisions, others supportive of government actions in difficult times, some dubious of the significance of 9/11, others finding it a disruptive event that "changed everything." I have tried to reserve my own views to allow this series to collect these perspectives.

I would like to thank several people who have made special contributions to this process. First, two friends have proven themselves adept at finding my errors and improving my work, which is an invaluable skill for an author to find in a trusted colleague. These two distinguished professionals—Jennifer Walton of JPI Capital and Linda Nguyen of Deloitte Consulting—have taken time out of their busy schedules to review the manuscripts, and I am eternally grateful to them. Second, many of our authors are extremely busy top leaders at the pinnacle of their careers. In these cases, their professional assistants and staff have been incredibly helpful in managing correspondence and facilitating the timely completion of these contributions. Among these helpful professionals are Flip Brophy of Sterling Lord Literistic, Minna Cowper-Coles, Chip Burpee, Sarah Neely, Toni Getze, Nancy Bonomo, Elizabeth Ong Baoxuan, Brooke Sweet, and Janet Conary. I also owe gratitude to institutions with colleagues very supportive of my writing during my time with them: Bentley College of Waltham, Massachusetts, and McKinsey & Company.

Finally, I owe a debt of gratitude to several members of the publishing community to bring this massive effort to fruition. First, Hilary Claggett of Potomac Books, my editor at Greenwood/Praeger for my first book (*A Democracy Is Born*, 2007), envisioned an interdisciplinary series reflecting on the national tragedy that was 9/11. This concept was initially to be set out in four volumes, but owing to the enthusiastic response from the scholarly and writing communities, the series expanded to six, allowing for a full treatment of each major area we have undertaken. Next, Toby Wahl of Westview Press, and former Political Science Editor at Palgrave Macmillan, supported me with my publication of *The American Military after 9/11: Society, State, and Empire* at Palgrave (2008) and provided energy and commitment in the initial stages of the development of *The Day that Changed Everything?* After his departure, Farideh Koohi-Kamali, Editorial Director at Palgrave, assumed Toby's responsibilities and provided excellent advice and support, taking the series through its last stages in the summer of 2008. Those dedicated professionals who completed the production process, including Allison McElgunn of Palgrave Macmillan and the team at Newgen Imaging Systems led by Maran Elancheran, deserve my gratitude as well as that of our contributing author team. Finally, Editorial Assistants Asa Johnson and Robyn Curtis deserve heartfelt appreciation for their efforts to bring the book to publication in its final form, exceeding all expectations. In my experience as an author, I have never before demanded nor received the kind of support that Asa and Robyn mustered for this massive series. Working with both of them was an absolute pleasure and they reflect great credit upon Palgrave Macmillan.

MATTHEW J. MORGAN
White Plains, New York

Contributors

Foreword. R. James Woolsey, Jr., former Director of Central Intelligence, is the Annenberg Distinguished Visiting Fellow at Stanford University's Hoover Institution. He is also a Venture Partner at Vantage Point Venture Partners and Chairman of the Strategic Advisory Group of the Paladin Capital Group.

Christopher Ankersen is Course Tutor at King's College London and editor of two books, *Civil-Military Cooperation in Post-Conflict Operations* and *Understanding Global Terror.*

David J. Betz is Senior Lecturer of War Studies at King's College London, where he heads the Insurgency Research Group and is Academic Director of the online master's degree, War in the Modern World. He is the author of *Civil-Military Relations in Russia and Eastern Europe, Army and State in Post-Communist Europe,* and numerous journal articles.

Stephen J. Cimbala is Distinguished Professor of Political Science at Penn State Brandywine and the author of numerous works in national security policy, nuclear arms control, defense studies, and other fields. Cimbala is a past winner of the University's Eisenhower award for teaching, has served as a consultant to various government agencies and think tanks, and is a frequent media commentator on national security topics.

Lamont Colucci, a former diplomat with the U.S. State Department, is Assistant Professor of Politics and Government at Ripon College. He is the coordinator for an interdisciplinary national security studies program and teaches courses on national security, foreign policy, intelligence, terrorism, and international relations.

Karin K. De Angelis is a doctoral student in military sociology at the University of Maryland.

Bruno S. Frey is Professor of Economics at the University of Zurich. He received honorary doctorates in economics from the University of St. Gallen and the University of Goeteborg. He is the author of numerous articles in professional journals and books, including *Not Just for the Money* (1997), *Economics as a Science of Human Behaviour* (1999), *The New Democratic*

Federalism for Europe (1999), *Arts & Economics* (2000), *Inspiring Economics* (2001), *Successful Management by Motivation* (2001), *Happiness and Economics* (2002), and *Dealing with Terrorism: Stick or Carrot?* (2004).

F. Lincoln Grahlfs is Professor Emeritus at the University of Wisconsin Colleges, where he served as chairman of the Department of Anthropology and Sociology for the thirteen campus system at the time of his retirement, in 1988. He is a veteran of World War II and taught sociology and anthropology for 32 years. He is the author of two books, *Voices From Ground Zero: Recollections and Feelings of Nuclear Test Veterans* and *Undaunted: The Story of a United States Navy Tug and Her Crew in World War II.*

Marc Grossman is a Vice Chair of the Cohen Group and former Undersecretary of State for Political Affairs.

Rohan Gunaratna is Head of the International Center for Political Violence and Terrorism Research, Nanyang Technological University, Singapore and author of 12 books, including *Countering Terrorism* and the *New York Times* best seller *Inside Al Qaeda.*

Sohail Inayatullah is Professor at the Graduate Institute of Futures Studies, Tamkang University, Taipei, and the author of 18 books, including *Questioning the Future* and *Macrohistory and Macrohistorians.*

Robert G. Kaufman is Professor of Public Policy at Pepperdine University and author of *In Defense of the Bush Doctrine.*

Sarwar A. Kashmeri, strategic communications consultant and Fellow of the Foreign Policy Association, has been recognized on both sides of the Atlantic as an observer and commentator on U.S.-European business and foreign policy issues for over a decade. He is the author of *America and Europe after 9/11 and Iraq: The Great Divide*, which recently released its third printing.

Simon Luechinger is a postdoctoral research fellow at the London School of Economics.

Peter Marcuse is Professor Emeritus of Urban Planning at Columbia University and author of several books.

John Mueller holds the Woody Hayes Chair of National Security Studies and is Professor of Political Science at Ohio State University. His book *Overblown* (2006) was called by the *New York Times* "important" and "accurate, timely, and necessary." Mueller is the author of the prize-winning *War, Presidents and Public Opinion* (1973) ("a classic" according to the *American Political Science Review*), *Atomic Obsession: Nuclear Alarmism from Hiroshima to Al Qaeda.* (2009), and several other books.

Takuya Murata completed graduate work in political science at the University of Hawai`i.

Saul Newman is Reader in Political Theory at the University of London and author of three books, including *Unstable Universalities*.

Anders Nielson is a Research Associate at the International Center for Political Violence and Terrorism Research, Nanyang Technological University, Singapore.

Paul S. Oh is Instructor of American Politics, Policy, and Strategy at the U.S. Military Academy at West Point and is the Course Director of the senior seminar, Intelligence and Policy. He has been an officer in U.S. Army intelligence for 12 years, including service in Iraq as a commander and intelligence staff officer.

J. Peter Pham is Associate Professor of Justice Studies, Political Science, and Africana Studies and Director of the Nelson Institute for International and Public Affairs at James Madison University as well as Senior Fellow in Africa Policy Studies at the Foundation for the Defense of Democracies. The author of three books and over two hundred articles on Africa, Dr. Pham has advised both the U.S. government and private sector on political and security issues affecting relations with the continent.

Jerrold M. Post is Professor of Psychiatry, Political Psychology, and International Affairs at George Washington University. He is the author of ten books, including *Political Paranoia* and *The Mind of the Terrorist: The Psychology of Terrorism from the IRA to al Qaeda*.

David R. Segal is Professor of Sociology and Director of the Center for Research on Military Organization at the University of Maryland and the author of several books, including *The Postmodern Military* and *Recruiting for Uncle Sam*.

William L. Waugh, Jr., is Professor of Public Administration and Urban Studies at Georgia State University. He is the author of seven books, including *Living with Hazards, Dealing with Disasters*, and *International Terrorism*.

Introduction

Matthew J. Morgan

This book is the first volume of the six-volume series *The Day that Changed Everything?* With some time having passed now since the attacks of September 11, 2001, it is possible to reflect upon the attacks and assess their impact. The series brings together from a broad spectrum of disciplines the leading thinkers of our time to reflect on one of the most significant events of our time. This first volume is devoted to the impact of 9/11 on war and politics, perhaps among the most obvious areas of human society affected by the attacks.

When the French daily *Le Monde* announced on its September 12 headline, "*nous sommes tous américains,*" it seemed that a transformative moment in world politics had occurred. The North Atlantic Treaty Organization invoked, for the first time in the half century of the alliance's history, the collective security principle that an attack against one is an attack against all. In the United States, terrorism and security came to the fore of policy discussions and election campaigns. More specifically, President Bush experienced a distinct change in perspective. Before 9/11, the president had argued in October 2000 at a presidential debate at Wake Forest University, "I am worried about over-committing our military around the world. I want to be judicious in its use. I don't think nation-building missions are worthwhile." By June 2002, President Bush was articulating a need for "preemptive action when necessary" in a speech at West Point that would eventually evolve into the 2002 *National Security Strategy* that came to be called the "Bush Doctrine." American wars in Afghanistan and Iraq promised to transform the Middle East as well as reconstruct relationships with American allies around the world. With the change of administration in 2009, President Obama has inherited the long-term ramifications of these decisions. As of this writing, there has been a turnaround in Iraq with a dangerously deteriorating situation in Afghanistan. The new administration seems to remain committed to an American grand strategy centered on intervention in those two countries.

Joseph Nye used a compelling metaphor to describe the change ushered in on September 11. Rather than creating change in itself, the event illuminated developments that had taken place over the years before. Nye argued that "the world changed in profound ways during the last decades of the twentieth century. September 11, 2001, was like a flash of lightning on a summer evening that displayed an altered landscape, leaving U.S. policymakers and analysts still groping in the dark, still wondering how to understand and respond."[1] Whether the attacks were the originator of the change or a sudden and graphic indicator, it is a fairly accepted truism that a revolutionary step in world affairs took place. Financier George Soros argued it was not so much the attacks themselves, but the American administration's response to them that was significant:

> It is generally agreed that September 11, 2001, changed the course of history. But we must ask ourselves why that should be so. How could a single event, even one involving 3,000 civilian casualties, have such a far-reaching effect? The answer lies not so much in the event itself as in the way the United States, under the leadership of President George W. Bush, responded to it.[2]

In *Foreign Affairs*, former secretary of state Madeleine Albright blended Nye's and Soros's perspectives of events by suggesting that the attacks were revelation of global change in addition to leading to a significant departure of the status quo in American foreign policy:

> For President Bush, September 11 came as a revelation, leading him to the startled conclusion that the globe had changed in ways gravely hazardous to the security—indeed, the very survival—of the United States. This conclusion soon led Bush to a fateful decision: to depart, in fundamental ways, from the approach that has characterized U.S. foreign policy for more than half a century.[3]

The Impact of 9/11: Politics and War explores the changes since the September 11 attacks in four main parts: (1) the impact on organizations and institutions, (2) the impact on war, peace, and security, (3) regional impacts, and (4) the future after 9/11. Following this introduction is an overview chapter by John Mueller, who has for decades been one of the great thinkers in the fields of political science and security studies. Mueller's overview sets the context for all four of the following parts as he argues that the threat has been "overblown." If 9/11 changed everything, perhaps it is policy makers' reactions that are responsible for this.

The first part explores important political and military organizations and institutions. In the United States, our major policymaking institutions have been transformed by the attacks. The diplomatic arm of the United States, the State Department, faces new challenges. The Bush administration had already been a target of criticism for practicing cowboy diplomacy and needlessly snubbing allies. Detractors thus energetically questioned the decision in 2001 to invade Afghanistan with an ad hoc coalition rather than accepting the offer of NATO allies to mobilize the collective security alliance for the invasion. The more difficult call for allies in Iraq might have gone down with them more easily had there been a greater sense of cooperation in Afghanistan when it had been offered. Ambassador Marc Grossman, the former undersecretary of state for Political Affairs, had previously served as the U.S. ambassador to Turkey and was tapped to help coordinate authorization for American forces to invade Iraq from the north. With his senior position and experience, his chapter is uniquely positioned to reflect on changes to the State Department and the practice of diplomacy brought about by 9/11.

An army intelligence officer, Major Paul Oh of the Department of Social Sciences at West Point, explains the reorganization of the U.S. intelligence community in the aftermath of the attacks. Given the 9/11 Commission's findings that the attacks represented a massive intelligence failure, those various agencies that constitute the intelligence community have been one of the major constituencies affected by 9/11. The false prediction of and failure to find weapons of mass destruction in Iraq only raised continued questions about the efficacy of the U.S. government intelligence services. The American military is another institution greatly impacted by September 11. My own *The American Military after 9/11: Society, State, and Empire*, published in 2008, is based upon this premise. David Segal, one of the world's leading military sociologists, and coauthor Karin De Angelis explore changes to the U.S. armed forces.

William Waugh, an internationally known scholar in disaster studies and emergency management, assesses the impact of the terrorist attacks on the nation's capacity to deal with catastrophic disasters. Peter Marcuse of Columbia University, a leading urban planning expert, reflects on New York City after the attacks. This is a particularly apt topic from his vantage point in New York, where almost a decade after the destruction of the World Trade Center, there has been little progress made on Ground Zero. The section ends with two chapters on the terrorist organizations rather than those combating terrorism in America. Rohan Gunaratna, best-selling author of *Inside Al Qaeda*, writes with one of his colleagues from the International Center for Political Violence and Terrorism Research, Anders Nielson, on al Qaeda's post-9/11 activities. Jerrold Post, a leading political psychologist and founder of the CIA's Center for the Analysis of Personality and Political Behavior, concludes the section with his exposition on al Qaeda 2.0, the next evolution of the terrorist organization.

Part II focuses on the impact of the attacks on war, peace, and security. During the cold war, the superpowers engaged in limited wars that left them both bloodied: the Soviets, withdrawing beaten from Afghanistan, and the Americans, pulling out in stalemate from Korea and strategic defeat from Vietnam. In the aftermath of these setbacks in low-intensity conflict, a doctrinal focus emerged on high-intensity combat such as was fought in the

Second World War. By the end of the 1990s, American strategists were arguing against the military's failure to establish effective doctrine and tactics for peacekeeping. By the end of this decade, the failure to establish any clear counterinsurgency doctrine has now become the theme of current strategists.[4] Both failings have the same root cause: a strategic culture focused on the objective of total victory. Some have argued that this culture has its roots in Vietnam, a strategic fiasco that led leaders of the military establishment to avoid low-intensity warfare in any form. But American culture, with its foundations in absolutist ideologies and unprecedented industrial and political accomplishments, has much deeper roots. The strategic trauma of Vietnam, rather than shaping the culture, was unable to change it. Iraq and Afghanistan, however, as a second chance at adaptation, may prove different.

Part II kicks off with a chapter by Bruno Frey, an internationally renowned economist, and one of his colleagues from the University of Zurich, Simon Luechinger. They explore how 9/11 has led to the salience of other strategic responses besides deterrence. Next, Stephen Cimbala, a prolific author on security and defense, looks at the developing nuclear threat. Robert Kaufman, a political scientist who has established himself as a persuasive apologist for the Bush Doctrine, explores the lasting implications of that response to 9/11 on U.S. grand strategy. Lamont Colucci, a former diplomat in the U.S. State Department, has developed a theory of Crusading Realism, a new approach to international relations that Dr. Colucci believes has emerged in the aftermath of 9/11. Next, security experts Christopher Ankersen and David Betz (from the London School of Economics and King's College, respectively) address civil-military cooperation after 9/11, particularly a key development, given the wars in Afghanistan and Iraq.

Next, two chapters provide critical assessments of post-9/11 security. F. Lincoln Grahlfs of the University of Wisconsin Colleges suggests that 9/11 has catalyzed rather than caused the aggressive form of warfare. Saul Newman's critical analysis of the tradeoff between liberty and security follows. Dr. Newman, a political scientist from the University of London, argues that the logic of security in the aftermath of 9/11 serves to undermine democracy. His essay is a thoughtful exposition applying to today's circumstances the logic of Ben Franklin's quotation, "Those who would give up essential Liberty, to purchase a little temporary Safety, deserve neither Liberty nor Safety." (This theme is explored in greater detail in the third volume of this series, on the new legal landscape.)

Part III explores various regional impacts of 9/11 around the world, beginning with a chapter by foreign policy expert Sarwar Kashmeri, who looks at the impact on Europe. A look at Asian politics follows with a chapter by futurist Takuya Murata, a brilliant young scholar from the University of Hawai'i, a leading academic institution in Asian political studies. Mr. Murata reflects on changing relationships with U.S. allies, Japan and India, and its strategic competitor China, arguing that 9/11 has strengthened some relationships and weakened others. Finally, J. Peter Pham of the Nelson Institute for International and Public Affairs at James Madison University looks at newly revealed strategic significance of the African continent.

The volume concludes with a one-chapter section providing a perspective of a leading scholar in the field of alternative futures studies. Sohail Inayatullah of Tamkang University in Taipei provides a provocative conclusion to the volume with his "macrohistorical perspective" to explore world futures after 9/11.

The contributing authors of this volume—and the entire series—have deliberately been assembled to bring together divergent perspectives on 9/11 and its aftermath. Some have interpreted the 9/11 attacks as a massive change in international and domestic politics; others view the attacks as accelerators of existing trends and policies. Some of the contributors are in strong agreement with the Bush administration's policies (and a few even served in the administration). Others have an equally vigorous disagreement with the administration's policies after 9/11. This series attempts to bring together leading minds from a variety of perspectives. Without any particular "ax to grind," I believe that this approach, incorporating such diverse viewpoints, is the best way to explore the question of whether September 11, 2001, was the day that changed everything.

Notes

1. Joseph S. Nye, Jr., "U.S. Power and Strategy after Iraq," *Foreign Affairs* 82, no. 4 (July/August 2003): 60–73, see 60–61.
2. George Soros, "The Bubble of American Supremacy," *Atlantic Monthly* 292, no. 5 (December 2003): 63–66, see 63.
3. Madeleine K. Albright, "Bridges, Bombs, or Bluster?" *Foreign Affairs* 82, no. 5 (September/October 2003): 2–18, see 3.
4. John Nagl's *Counterinsurgency Lessons from Malaya and Vietnam: Learning to Eat Soup with a Knife* (Westport, CT: Praeger, 2002) is now one of the most cited expositions on counterinsurgency, along with the new *Field Manual 3-07.22: Counterinsurgency Operations* (Washington, DC: Department of the Army, 2004), of which Nagl was on the author team. For two examples of the contemporary literature on counterinsurgency, see two edited volumes: *Countering Insurgency and Promoting Democracy,* ed. Manolis Priniotakis (New York: CENSA, 2007) and Daniel Marston and Carter Malkasian, *Counterinsurgency in Modern Warfare* (Oxford: Osprey Publishing, 2008). Both of these contain repeated references to Nagl's book as well as the new field manual. Nagl himself was a contributing author for the latter and provided an endorsement on the cover of the former. Interestingly, Nagl was also part of the community of scholars at the end of the interwar decade that called for greater focus on peacekeeping. See John A. Nagl and Elizabeth O. Young, "Si Vis Pacem, Para Pacem: Training for Humanitarian Emergencies," *Military Review* 80, no. 2 (March/April 2000): 31–36. The consistent theme is the failure of the conventional doctrine to adapt to the realities of the day.

Chapter 1

The Long-Term Political and Economic Consequences of 9/11

*John Mueller**

A few days after the 9/11 attacks, Vice President Dick Cheney warned that there might never be an "end date" in the "struggle" against terrorism, a point at which it would be possible to say, "There, it's all over with."

More than seven years later, his wisdom seems to have been vindicated, though perhaps not quite in the way he intended. The War on Terror at least in its domestic, homeland security aspects, has been fully launched and shows clear signs of having developed into a popularly supported governmental perpetual motion (or perpetual emotion) machine that has comfortably settled in for the long term. In Washington jargon, it has become a self-licking ice cream cone.

Actually, in some respects the closest semblance to a notable opponent the enterprise has so far generated has been George W. Bush himself. He, of course, garnered great political benefit from the terrorism scare—he consistently achieved his best ratings for his handling of the issue, and he managed to use the T-word from 20 to 36 times in each of his post-9/11 State of the Union addresses, albeit only once in January 2001 (even as the word "victory," which appeared five times in 2006, vanished altogether two years later). However, for a while there, he opposed the inefficient slapping together

*John Mueller holds the Woody Hayes Chair of National Security Studies and is Professor of Political Science at Ohio State University. His book *Overblown* (2006) was called by the *New York Times* "important" and "accurate, timely, and necessary." Mueller is the author of the prize-winning *War, Presidents and Public Opinion* (1973) ("a classic" according to the *American Political Science Review*), *Atomic Obsession: Nuclear Alarmism from Hiroshima to Al Qaeda.* (2009), and several other books.

of all sorts of disparate government agencies into the hopelessly unwieldy Department of Homeland Security, and he even suggested that letting a responsible Dubai company manage the occasional American port was not necessarily the end of the world. Eventually, of course, he buckled on both issues, but at least there were some transitory glimmers. There may not even be that much from successor administrations in the White House, whatever their party.

What has happened is that terrorism and the attendant "war" have become internalized—fully embedded in the public consciousness—with the result that politicians and bureaucrats are, or have become, as wary of appearing soft on terrorism as they are about appearing soft on drugs or as they once were about appearing soft on communism.

Essential to this dynamic is that the public apparently continues to remain unimpressed by several inconvenient truths:

1. There have been no al Qaeda attacks whatever in the United States since 2001.
2. No true al Qaeda cell (nor scarcely anybody who might even be deemed to have a "connection" to the diabolical group) has been unearthed in the country.
3. The homegrown "plotters" who have been apprehended, while perhaps potentially somewhat dangerous at least in a few cases, have mostly been flaky or almost absurdly incompetent.
4. The total number of people killed worldwide by al Qaeda types, may-bes, and wannabes outside of war zones since 9/11 stands at some 300 or so a year (300 too many admittedly, but smaller than the yearly number of bathtub drownings in the United States alone).
5. Unless the terrorists are able somehow to massively increase their capacities, the likelihood that a person living outside a war zone will perish at the hands of an international terrorist over an 80-year period is about 1 in 75,000 (by comparison an American's chance of dying in an auto accident over the same time interval is 1 in 80).

Despite all this, polls do not demonstrate all that much of a decline since 2001 in the percentage of the public anticipating another terrorist attack or expressing fear that they, themselves, might become a victim. The public has chosen, it appears, to wallow in what Leif Wenar has labeled a false sense of insecurity, and it apparently plans to continue to do so. Accordingly, it is also likely to continue to demand that its leaders pay due deference to its insecurities and to uncritically approve the huge amounts of money shelled out in a quixotic and mostly symbolic effort to assuage those insecurities.

This does not mean that people spend a great deal of time obsessing over terrorism, spooking over it, or even paying all that much attention to it: terrorism has for years now scored rather poorly on polls asking about the country's most important problem. However, people don't constantly think about motherhood either. Nonetheless, they will not look kindly upon a politician or bureaucrat who is insufficiently sentimental about that venerable institution.

An apt comparison would be with the public's concern about the threat once presented by domestic communism. Impelled by several spectacular espionage cases and by an apparently risky international environment, fears about the dangers presented by "the enemy within" became fully internalized in the years after World War II. In a famous public opinion study conducted at the height of the McCarthy period in the mid-1950s, sociologist Samuel Stouffer found that approximately 43 percent professed to believe that domestic Communists presented a great or very great danger to the United States. At the same time, however, when Stouffer asked more broadly about what their primary worries were, people mainly voiced concerns about personal matters. Unprompted, apprehensions about domestic communism (or about restrictions on civil liberties) scarcely came up in the survey. There was, Stouffer concluded, no "national anxiety neurosis" over the issue.

That conclusion probably holds for present concerns about domestic terrorism as well. There was a great deal of evasive behavior after the 9/11 attacks—indeed, several studies conclude that more than 1000 Americans died between September 11, 2001, and the end of that year, because out of fear they avoided airplanes in favor of much more dangerous automobiles. However, behavior eventually settled down and people pretty much seem now to carry on with their lives without spending much time thinking about the dangers presented by domestic terrorism. There has been no great exodus from Washington or New York, and few people seem even to have gone to the trouble of stocking up on emergency supplies despite the persistent nanny-like urgings of the Department of Homeland Security.

On the fifth anniversary of 9/11, ABC's Charles Gibson dutifully intoned, "Putting your child on a school bus or driving across a bridge or just going to the mall—each of these things is a small act of courage—and peril is a part of everyday life." However, without spending a whole lot of time thinking about it, people do seem somehow to have been able to summon the courage to carry out those perilous tasks, and if malls have now become jammed with heroes, that is a condition I imagine most Americans will be able to live with. (I, on the other hand, am determined to keep my distance.)

Problems arise, however, not from a national anxiety neurosis, but more from other results of the terrorism concern. One is that when a consensus about a threat becomes really internalized, it becomes politically unwise, even disastrous, to oppose it—or even to seem to oppose it. Another is that the internalized consensus creates a political atmosphere in which government and assorted porkbarreleers can expend, or fritter away, considerable public funds and efforts on questionable enterprises as long as they appear somehow to be focused on dealing with the threat. In the present context, the magic phrase, "We don't want to have another 9/11," tends to end the discussion.

Once again, the parallel with domestic communism is instructive. In that atmosphere politicians scurried to support the spending of billions and billions of dollars to surveil, to screen, and to spy on an ever-expanding array of individuals who had come to seem suspicious for one reason or another. Organizations were infiltrated, phones were tapped (each tap can require the full-time services of a dozen agents and support personnel), letters were intercepted, people were followed, loyalty oaths were required, endless leads (almost all to nowhere) were pursued, defense plants were hardened, concentration camps for prospective emergency use were established, and garbage was meticulously sifted in hopes of unearthing scraps of incriminating information.

At the time, critics of this process focused almost entirely on the potential for civil liberties violations. This is a worthy concern, but it is not the only one. As far as I can see, at no point during the cold war did anyone say in public "many domestic Communists adhere to a foreign ideology that ultimately has as its goal the destruction of capitalism and democracy by violence if necessary; however, they do not present much of a danger, are actually quite a pathetic bunch, and couldn't subvert their way out of a wet paper bag. Why are we expending so much time, effort, and treasure over this issue?" It is astounding, however, that that plausible, if arguable, point of view seems never to have been publicly expressed by anyone—politician, pundit, professor, editorialist—during the cold war, although some people may have believed it privately. On Stouffer's survey, only a lonely, and obviously politically insignificant share of the population—2 percent—professed to believe that domestic Communists presented no danger at all.

Something similar is now happening in pursuit of the terrible, if vaporous, terrorist enemy within. Redirecting much of their effort from such unglamorous enterprises as dealing with organized crime and white-collar embezzlement (which, unlike domestic terrorism, have actually happened since 2001), agencies like the FBI have kept their primary focus on the terrorist threat. Like their predecessors during the quest to quash domestic communism, they have dutifully and laboriously assembled masses of intelligence data and have pursued an endless array of leads; by August 2008, the agency was celebrating the receipt of its two millionth terrorism tip from the public. Almost all of this activity has led nowhere, but it will continue because, of course, no one wants to be the one whose neglect somehow led to "another 9/11"—or, as the assistant chief for the FBI's National Threat Center puts it, it's the lead "you don't take seriously that becomes the 9/11."

Criticisms of the Patriot Act focus almost entirely on civil liberties concerns, worrying that rights for innocent Americans might be trampled in the rush to pursue terrorists. No doubt this is a perfectly valid concern, but from time to time someone might wonder in public a bit about how much money the quest to ferret out terrorists and to protect ourselves is costing, as well as about how limited the results have been. Thus, in their valuable book, *Less Safe, Less Free*, David Cole and Jules Lobel ably detail and critique the process, but, as suggested in their title, the implication often is that the FBI and other agencies have failed in their well-funded quest to uncover the enemy within, not that the investigators have not found much of anything because the enemy they are questing after essentially does not exist.

We can also expect continued efforts to reduce, or to seem to reduce, the country's "vulnerability" despite at least three confounding realities: there exist an essentially infinite number of potential terrorist targets; the probability that any one of those targets will be hit by a terrorist is essentially zero; and inventive terrorists, should they ever actually show up, are free to redirect their attention from a target that might enjoy a degree of protection toward one of the many that don't. Nonetheless, hundreds of billions of dollars have been so far spent on this quest and the process seems destined to continue or even accelerate, even though, as a senior economist at the Department of Homeland Security put it in 2006, "we really don't know a whole lot about the overall costs and benefits of homeland security."

And there is more. The experience with domestic communism suggests that once a threat becomes really internalized, the concern can linger for decades, even if there is no evidence to support such a continued preoccupation. It becomes self-perpetuating.

In the two decades that followed the Stouffer survey, news about domestic communism declined until it essentially vanished altogether. In the mid-1950s, there were hundreds of articles in the *Readers' Guide to Periodical Literature* listed under the categories, "Communism-US" and "Communist Party-US." In the mid-1970s, in stark contrast, there were scarcely any. This of course reflected the fact that domestic communism really was not doing very much of anything to garner attention. The cold war continued elsewhere, but there were no dramatic court cases like the one concerning the State Department's felonious document-transmitter, Alger Hiss, and his accuser, Whittaker Chambers, or atomic spy cases like the ones involving Klaus Fuchs and Julius and Ethel Rosenberg, cases that had so mesmerized the public in the late 1940s and early 1950s.

In fact, despite huge anxieties about it at the time, there seem to have been no instances in which domestic Communists engaged in anything that could be considered espionage after World War II. Moreover, at no time did any domestic Communist ever commit anything that could be considered violence in support of the cause—this, despite deep apprehensions at the time about that form of terrorism then dubbed "sabotage." All notable terrorist violence within the United States since 2001 has taken place on television— most persistently on Fox's "24"—and the same was true about domestic Communist violence during the cold war. FBI informant Herbert Philbrick's confessional 1952 book, *I Led Three Lives*, at no point documents a single instance of Communist violence or planned violence, but violence became a central focus when his story was transmuted into a popular television series.

However, even though the domestic Communist "menace" had pretty much settled into well-deserved oblivion by the mid-1970s, surveys repeating the Stouffer questions at the time found that 30 percent of the public *still* considered internal Communists to present a great or very great danger to the country, while those who found them to be of no danger had inched up only to around 10 percent.

Some have argued that unjustified fears (or "hysteria") about the Communist enemy within was created by the media, and some now say the same thing about apprehensions about the terrorist enemy within. But the fear of domestic communism persisted long after the press had become thoroughly bored with the issue, and this development suggests that, while the media may exacerbate fears about perceived threats, they do not particularly create them. That is, fears often have an independent source, and then take on a life of their own.

Something similar may have happened with the "war" on drugs. Over the last few decades, the drug evil has so impressed itself on the American public psyche that the issue can scarcely be brought up for public discussion. At one time drugs were a big concern with the public—Ronald Reagan latched on to it, and then George H. W. Bush pushed it further, particularly after it soared into public anxiety in the first year of his presidency. Somewhere along the line it became a politically untouchable issue, and, certainly, neither Bill Clinton nor Bush the younger was tempted to tinker with, much less reexamine, the policy. In the meantime, it has picked up its own political constituency; in California the powerful prison guard lobby takes the lead.

One could, of course, suggest that the long and costly drug "war" has pretty much been a failure, particularly because drug use has scarcely plummeted and because strenuous efforts to interdict supplies have not been able to notably inflate the street price. But that discussion, considered by many to be political poison, never really happens, and the drug war and its attendant expenditures continue to ramble inexorably and consensually onward. This situation continues, despite the fact that it is severely hampering efforts to rebuild war-torn Afghanistan by seeking to cut off that struggling country's only significant source of earned revenue.

Perspectives on terror, now thoroughly internalized, seem likely to take on a similarly unexamined, self-perpetuating trajectory. Moreover, since terrorism will always be with us—like drugs, but unlike threats that were capable of dying out entirely such as communism and the threat supposedly presented by domestic Japanese during World War II—we could be in for a long siege.

This is suggested as well by the fact that routine fears and knee-jerk reactions continue to hold at impressive levels despite a notable decline in the ferocity of official warnings. Interested public officials have sometimes attempted to jigger things with various alarms and excursions, raising terror alerts from time to time, warning against "complacency," assuring all and sundry that the "war" must needs continue (and their budgets increase) because...well, because we have to do everything possible to prevent another 9/11.

However, we have been subjected to only a few such warnings lately. Early in 2007, former CIA director George Tenet did reveal on CBS' *60 Minutes* that his "operational intuition" was telling him that al Qaeda had infiltrated a second or third wave into the United States, though he added with uncharacteristic modesty, "Can I prove it to you? No." And Department of Homeland Security (DHS) Secretary Michael Chertoff informed us a few months later that his gut was telling him there would be an attack during the summer. (What his gut told him later has, as far as I can see, gone unrecorded even on the DHS Web site where the organization really might, as a public service, have used some of its ever-escalating funds to publish routine updatings— perhaps on a daily gut-o-meter. It might also, at any time, explain why airport security, elevated to the "orange" level after an airline plot in another hemisphere was rolled up years ago, remains at that level as of this writing when the extra security required by the higher rating can cost an individual airport—and therefore passengers—$100,000 per day.)

But spooky misgivings inspired by guts and intuitions are nothing compared to the colorful and unqualified fire-and-brimstone warnings issued by public officials in the past. It was in 2002 that Tenet assured us without even a wisp of equivocation that al Qaeda was not only "reconstituted," but planning in "multi-theaters of operation," and "coming after us." The next year, Chertoff's predecessor at DHS, Tom Ridge divined that "extremists abroad are anticipating near-term attacks that they believe will either rival, or exceed" those of 2001. And in 2004, Attorney General John Ashcroft, with FBI Director Robert Mueller at his side, announced that "credible intelligence from multiple sources indicates that al Qaeda plans to attempt an attack on the United States in the next few months," that its "specific intention" was to hit us "hard," and that the "arrangements" for that attack were already 90 percent complete. (Oddly enough, Ashcroft fails to mention this memorable headline-grabbing episode in *Never Again*, his 2006 memoir of the period.)

Director Mueller himself has mellowed quite a bit over time. In 2003 he assured us that, although his agency had yet actually to identify an al Qaeda cell in the United States, such unidentified (or imagined) entities nonetheless presented "the greatest threat," had "developed a support infrastructure" in the country, and had achieved "the ability and the intent to inflict significant casualties in the US with little warning." (At the time, intelligence reports

were asserting—that is, guessing—that the number of trained al Qaeda operatives in the United States was between 2,000 and 5,000, and FBI officials
were informing rapt reporters that cells were "embedded in most U.S. cities
with sizable Islamic communities," usually in the "run-down sections," that
they were "up and active," and that electronic intercepts had found some to be
"talking to each other.") In 2005, at a time when the FBI admitted it *still* had
been unable to unearth a single true al Qaeda cell, Mueller continued his dire
I-think-therefore-they-are projections: "I remain very concerned about what
we are not seeing," he ominously ruminated. However, in testimony before
the Senate Select Committee on Intelligence on January 11, 2007, Mueller
had become notably reticent, and his chief rallying cry had been reduced to a
comparatively bland "We believe al Qaeda is still seeking to infiltrate operatives into the U.S. from overseas."

Impressively, even a specific (and, it appears, unique) effort on the part of
an official to dampen terrorism fears has had no noticeable impact. In June
2007, New York Mayor Michael Bloomberg actually went so far as to urge
people to "get a life," pointing out that "you have a much greater danger of
being hit by lightning than being struck by a terrorist."

It is possible, however, that Bloomberg's glancing brush with reality
(which, most interestingly, does not seem to have hurt him politically) was
undercut by the fact that his city expends huge resources chasing after terrorists while routinely engaging in some of the most pointless security theater
on the planet. For example, New York often extracts police officers from their
duties to have them idle around at a sampling of the city's thousands of subway entrances blandly watching as millions of people wearing backpacks or
carrying parcels descend into the system throughout the city. It is also fond
of trumpeting the fact that thousands of people each year call the city's police
counterterrorism hot line—8,999 in 2006, it turns out, and more than 13,473
in 2007—while managing to neglect to mention that not one of these calls has
yet led to a terrorism arrest.

H. L. Mencken once declared "the whole aim of practical politics" to be
"to keep the populace alarmed (and hence clamorous to be led to safety) by
menacing it with an endless series of hobgoblins, all of them imaginary."
There is nothing imaginary about al Qaeda, of course, though some of the
proclaimed sightings of the group in the United States by officials do have
an Elvis-like quality to them. However, the public seems to have been able
to retain much of its sense of alarm about internal attacks even when the al
Qaeda hobgoblin doesn't actually carry any out and even when politicians
and public officials, however belatedly, temper their scary—and at times
irresponsible—bellowings.

Therefore, even without such declarations and even without further
terrorist attacks (and for that matter even without Osama bin Laden),
the War on Terror seems likely—like the ones on drugs and on domestic
Communists—to continue to grind on for a long time. Over seven years after

Cheney's declaration, there is no foreseeable time when we will be able to bring ourselves to declare it to be "all over with."

Note

This chapter draws on, develops, and updates material in John Mueller, *Overblown: How Politicians and the Terrorism Industry Inflate National Security Threats, and Why We Believe Them* (New York: Free Press, 2006).

Part I

The Impact on Organizations and Institutions

Chapter 2

Challenges to Diplomacy and the U.S. State Department

*Marc Grossman**

September 11, 2001, began as most other days had since May: we arrived at the State Department ready to promote America's agenda. But we also reported for work convinced that al Qaeda would soon attack one or more of our Missions overseas. At Secretary Powell's direction, we had reinforced security in facilities around the world to try to stop the attack that, we were sure, would come abroad.

After the morning staff meeting, chaired that day by Deputy Secretary Rich Armitage since Secretary Powell was in Peru, Rich convened another meeting in his office. Just after 9:00 a.m., news came that an airplane had hit the World Trade Center. Minutes later, the report arrived that a second aircraft had struck the second of the Twin Towers. Rich said, "This is terrorism. America is under attack." I got back to my office in time to feel the windows shake as a third airplane hit the Pentagon and watched smoke pour from the building across the river.

We evacuated most of the State Department. Rich and I moved into the Operations Center, still functioning in our building. In the first hours after the attacks, we pursued "traditional" diplomacy. We sent a short message to all U.S ambassadors, charging them to do the right thing to protect America and represent our country if Washington was taken out of action. National Security Advisor Rice asked that we inform the Russians that the president's decision to increase U.S defense readiness was solely in response to the attacks. Secretary Powell urged the Organization of American States in Lima

---

*Marc Grossman is a Vice Chair of the Cohen Group and former Undersecretary of State for Political Affairs.

to pass a strong statement on democracy in the hemisphere as one part of the answer to terror.

Secretary Powell returned late that afternoon and went to the White House. When he got back to the State Department, a group of us talked late into the evening about how best to protect America's global interests after this horrid day. Things would never be the same. Diplomacy would have to change both its substantive objectives and its professional practices to meet the challenges posed by the post-9/11 environment.

*   *   *

Although this generation of Americans will always use 9/11 as a reference point, this is not the first "revolution in diplomacy" that has been required by substance or circumstance. Historians point to a number of similar diplomatic revolutions over the centuries. Garrett Mattingly wrote of the "diplomatic revolution" in 1436, as diplomacy both shaped and reacted to changes in Renaissance Italy.[1] Henry Kissinger reviewed the ways the diplomatic profession was changed by the balance of power system and the concert of Europe in Vienna in 1814.[2] Lauren, Craig and George devoted a chapter of *Force and Statecraft* to "The Diplomatic Revolution Begins, 1919–1939."[3]

Historian John Lewis Gaddis recalled the two other times America had been forced to respond to a surprise attack on the homeland: the War of 1812 and Pearl Harbor. "Most nations," wrote Gaddis, "seek safety by withdrawing behind defenses, or making themselves inconspicuous or otherwise avoiding whatever dangers there may be. Americans, in contrast, have generally responded to threats—and particularly to surprise attacks—by taking the offensive, by becoming more conspicuous, by confronting, neutralizing, and if possible overwhelming the sources of danger rather than fleeing from them."[4]

*   *   *

While September 11 catalyzed changes in diplomacy, the simultaneous challenges of the twenty-first century were already demanding new ways to think about diplomatic goals, practices, and institutions. As Hans Binnendijk and Richard Kugler of the National Defense University put it, no single opportunity, problem, danger, or threat holds the key to the world's future—what matters is whether all of them act together and how they interact in the coming years.[5]

The challenges of simultaneity were strikingly apparent in the days after September 11; although using force was a necessity to defend our interests, terrorism and extremism would only be finally defeated by a comprehensive effort to promote pluralism and economic growth. When Secretary Powell called Pakistani leader Pervez Musharraf asking for his support to defeat al Qaeda and the Taliban, Musharraf said he would stand with the United States. Powell then asked what the United States could do immediately to show support for this decision. Musharraf said he wanted an increase in quotas on tariffs that restricted the export of textiles from Pakistan to the United States. Musharraf said that, with this rapid tariff relief, 400,000 more Pakistanis could find jobs, and people with jobs are less likely to succumb to the delusions of extremism.

Changes in the objectives and the practices of diplomacy had of course already occurred before September 11. NATO had been expanded and transformed to meet the demands of the twenty-first century. The Millennium Challenge Corporation was created as a new way to think about development assistance, supporting sustainable economic growth by investing in poor countries that rule justly, invest in their people, and promote economic freedom. The Proliferation Security Initiative is a partnership of now more than 90 countries using their own laws and resources to stop shipments of weapons of mass destruction, delivery systems, and related materials at sea, in the air, or on land. The international response to the tsunami that struck Southeast Asia in December 2004 was managed by an informal coalition of countries and international organizations that had the capacity to provide immediate assistance to the victims. Coordination was accomplished largely by conference calls and the exchange of information over the Internet; leaders of the effort consciously avoided formal international meetings and communiqués.[6]

* * *

Although there are many challenges facing the world today, this chapter highlights four key objectives for a twenty-first-century American diplomacy, necessitated not just by 9/11 but because America, its allies, and friends need to shape the global political and physical environment to promote and protect Western interests. First, diplomats need to focus on defeating violent extremism and ensuring that terrorists and extremists never acquire weapons of mass destruction. Second, diplomats need to find ways to close the gap between those who have benefited from globalization and those who have not yet done so. Third, beyond the nightmare of terrorists obtaining WMD, the world needs a modern diplomatic effort to strengthen the global commitment to nonproliferation. Finally, diplomats must join the effort to find ways to live sustainably on planet earth.

How would a twenty-first-century diplomacy meet these four challenges?

First, in the effort to defeat extremism, we should recognize that there is still work to be done that will require the use of force. However, we can begin to employ other tools by leveraging the simultaneity of the challenges: for example, more jobs and education in Pakistan, more employment and personal safety in Colombia, and addressing inequalities in Africa will help defeat extremism.

Twenty-first-century diplomats must also reverse what Ambassador Ed Djerejian called in his 2003 report on public diplomacy, "a process of unilateral disarmament in the weapons of advocacy over the last decade" that has contributed to widespread hostility toward Americans and left us vulnerable to lethal threats.[7] As Parag Khanna has written, there are millions of people in a new "second world" who are trying to decide whether America is a good or a bad thing.[8] Khanna calls for what amounts to a "rebranding" of America and for the deployment of more Foreign Service officers, more Peace Corps volunteers, and more efforts by our private sector to influence the future around the world. President Obama moved rapidly after his inauguration to pursue the vision of two states in the Middle East—one Palestinian and one Israeli—living side by side in peace. Acting on this American promise will not end terrorism in the Middle East, but it will certainly take a key argument out of the hands of those trying to convince others of America's bad faith.[9]

Second, we need to close the gap between those who benefit from globalization and those around the world—including in America—who have not yet had the chance to do so. The global economic crisis that began in earnest in late 2008 makes this imperative. To do so will require promoting and connecting accountability, transparency, the rule of law, human rights, and pluralism. American diplomats will confront skepticism after Iraq about whether the United States should promote pluralism, tolerance, and democracy around the world. Twenty-first-century diplomats will fail if they push the idea that countries will be successful only if they mimic the U.S. system. Pluralism will be promoted from the bottom up. People in other countries will choose their own ways forward. But it would be wrong to draw the lesson from Iraq that America's representatives should avoid speaking out for the rule of law, free markets, equal roles for women in society, and basic concepts of justice.

Third, America and its allies must use their unique position in the world to create a twenty-first-century nonproliferation diplomacy. Many contemporary commentators refer to President Kennedy's 1963 nightmare that, in his lifetime, 10, 15, or 20 nations would have nuclear capacity. It may be that commentators have rediscovered this comment because, 46 years later, Kennedy's prediction seems real and disturbing.

Kurt Campbell and Robert Einhorn made the point that "changes in the international system since the end of the Cold War have created an environment more favorable for nuclear proliferation. These developments include the erosion of security alliances that existed in the bipolar world; the accelerating diffusion of sensitive enabling technologies; the emergence of rogue states with ambitions to acquire weapons of mass destruction; regional instabilities in South Asia, the Persian Gulf and Northeast Asia; and the appearance of terrorist groups with apocalyptic agendas."[10]

And what if nuclear deterrence does not work as it did after World War II? In a 2007 *Wall Street Journal* column, George Shultz, William Perry, Henry Kissinger, and Sam Nunn wrote that "[t]he United States soon will be compelled to enter a new nuclear era that will be more precarious, psychologically disorienting, and economically even more costly than was Cold War deterrence."[11] Shultz, Perry, Kissinger, and Nunn went farther a year later, arguing that the world must take stronger measures to reduce nuclear dangers.[12]

There are a number of steps that can be taken to bolster nonproliferation diplomacy into the twenty-first century. The Obama administration should work with the Senate to ratify the Comprehensive Test Ban Treaty and encourage other signatories to reemphasize the importance of the Non-Proliferation Treaty (NPT) especially in advance of the NPT renewal conference in 2010. Diplomats can also reengage in the hard diplomatic work needed to solve regional conflicts because, as Campbell and Einhorn note, "[t]he main factor that could motivate a decision to pursue nuclear weapons would be an acute regional security threat."[13] The Obama administration has invited Russia to return to formal arms control negotiations; this is good not just for global nonproliferation but also as an avenue to communicate with Moscow on specific nonproliferation challenges such as Iran.

There are also economic and technological capabilities that could bolster nonproliferation diplomacy such as the Cooperative Threat Reduction Program, the Global Threat Reduction Initiative, and the U.S. Administration's Global Nuclear Energy Partnership. The International Atomic Energy Agency's (IAEA) inspection and intelligence capacities need to be strengthened. The United States should also support efforts to halt the production of fissile material for weapons and pursue missile defenses and invite other countries to join America to create and deploy this defense technology.

Fourth, twenty-first-century diplomacy must join the global conversation about living sustainably on earth. Pursuing energy independence is not realistic, but energy security is surely an achievable goal. A twenty-first-century energy security policy would rest on two principles: (1) use less energy to provide needed services and (2) pursue technologies that provide a diverse supply of reliable, affordable, and environmentally sound energy.

The level of U.S. oil imports makes U.S. adversaries including Venezuela and Iran stronger. Russian energy policies are also of vital importance, especially to U.S. allies in Europe.

The United States cannot meet the global energy challenge alone. Two diplomatic building blocks for future Western energy security will be the European Union (EU) and North Atlantic Treat Organization (NATO). Tom Friedman has asked, "What will replace the threat of Communism as the cement that holds together the Atlantic alliance?"[14] He answers that the issue that should unite the West is energy, which should be the "focus and cement of the Atlantic alliance in the 21st century."[15]

The European Union has taken steps to curb energy consumption. For example, the European Commission's "Energy Policy for Europe" includes a 20 percent reduction in greenhouse gas emissions and an increase in the share of renewable energy to 20 percent by 2020.[16] The EU can do more to move toward a common market in energy.

NATO should also play a role in energy security. As Senator Richard Lugar pointed out in a speech in Riga in December 2006, the most likely source of armed conflict in Europe and the surrounding regions in the coming decades will be energy scarcity and manipulation.[17] NATO should consider now, in consultation with the EU, what steps it will take if Poland, Germany, Hungary, Latvia, or any other member state is threatened, including consideration of whether an energy "attack" is covered by Article Five of the NATO treaty.

NATO should commit itself to preparing for and responding to attempts to use energy against its members as a matter of deterrence; attempts to manipulate energy for international political gain would not require a NATO military response if they could be deterred by preparedness and a declared will to respond. The potential threat from terrorism or national disaster to NATO member states' energy infrastructure is another reason for the organization to review what Alliance obligations would be in such cases, since sufficient investment and planning will not happen overnight.

The West must also pay renewed diplomatic attention to pipeline politics to diversify energy supplies and again actively support what was once a major Western objective: creating an East-West energy corridor. Important oil and gas pipelines that run through Turkey, like the Baku-Tbilisi-Ceyhan pipeline, which began to move Caspian oil in 2006, can further contribute to diversity of supply. The South Caucasus pipeline (Baku-Erzurum-Ceyhan) began to move natural gas that same year. The Shah Deniz project taps Azeri gas fields in the Caspian Sea and then transports the gas across Georgia and Turkey. In November 2007, Greece and Turkey inaugurated a pipeline that will bring natural gas from the Caspian Sea to Europe. Greece is already building an extension to run under the Adriatic Sea to Italy, which would give Italy and Central Europe access to Caspian Sea resources in 2012. Other lines across Turkey are also possible, and perhaps one day, for example, a Turkey-Israel oil or gas pipeline. The U.S. should continue to support the European Union's proposed Nabucco pipeline that would run from the Caucasus to Austria.

Energy security diplomacy will also require engagement with India and China on the future of coal. Governments and industry must pursue clean coal technologies as a matter of priority and diplomats must find ways to engage China and India in this collective search.

*   *   *

The modernization and reform of the diplomatic profession and its infrastructure in the United States had already begun before September 11.[18] Secretary Albright had recognized the need to change the way the department recruited and retained its personnel. Secretary Powell launched the Diplomatic Readiness Initiative, hiring almost 1,200 new State Department employees during his tenure. Secretary Rice continued to highlight diplomatic "transformation," but much more needs to be done. We should honor the courage, energy, and creativity of the men and women representing the United States today as diplomats, but to meet the new objectives of twenty-first-century diplomacy, diplomatic practice and the institutions that support it must keep changing.

There have been many studies over the years about how the State Department should change. Many of the best ideas were synthesized, and some new ones added, in a 2007 Center for Strategic and International Studies (CSIS) report, funded by the Una Chapman Cox Foundation, called *The Embassy of the Future*.[19] The CSIS Commission concluded that what we think of as traditional diplomacy—where government and social elites interact in highly formal channels—is being transformed. Even as today's diplomats continue to conduct traditional business, as we did in the hours after September 11, they must also adapt their capabilities to nontraditional settings, beyond conference rooms and offices.

Twenty-first-century diplomats will still try to influence foreign governments. But they increasingly will work directly with diverse parts of other nations' societies, including the emerging interest groups and future leaders—from business and academia, urban centers and remote villages, and religious institutions—that shape national values and actions over the long term. Twenty-first-century diplomats will also need to harness the power of private, or "Track II" diplomacy, which has begun to attract systematic interest.[20]

Today's diplomatic challenges—highlighting and demonstrating American values; strengthening the growth of civil institutions and the rule of law; promoting democracy; preventing conflicts and serving and protecting the millions of American citizens who live and travel abroad; promoting trade and investment; fighting drug trafficking; stopping the trafficking in persons; supporting sustainable development to combat poverty; preventing genocide; deterring threats to our cyber infrastructure; strengthening foreign cooperation and capacity to address global security challenges such as terrorism, weapons proliferation, international crime, disease, and humanitarian disasters—require frontline activity by skilled diplomatic professionals.

Diplomacy must be backed by credible force. If conflict does come, diplomats must support military forces before combat by making it possible—by negotiated arrangements with other countries—for United States and Allied forces to project power. During conflict, diplomacy must promote the widest possible coalition to support our efforts and when conflict ends, diplomats must be ready to lead the reconciliation and reconstruction of countries and societies. The State Department was not ready to take on postconflict leadership in Iraq and Afghanistan. It is an open question whether the Defense

Department would have allowed this even if State had been ready, but the State Department was in no position to offer the president the option of choosing a State-led operation. Secretary Powell and Secretary Rice moved to solve this problem through the creation of an Office of Post-Conflict and Reconstruction, but it is still yet to be fully tested.

The State Department, as the institution charged with carrying out the president's foreign policy, must be strengthened if America is to possess successful twenty-first-century diplomatic capacity. This is a point argued eloquently by Secretary of Defense Robert Gates in a speech given at the Center for Strategic and International Studies in January 2008.[21] President Obama's Fiscal Year 2010 budget followed President's Bush's 2009 budget in seeking substantial additional increases for State Department personnel and operations. Specific requirements include:

- The State Department needs more people. The kind of diplomacy needed for the future—active engagement across all levels of society in countries around the world—requires that the Department have adequate human resources to carry out this task. At a minimum, twenty-first-century diplomacy demands that the State Department, like the military, have a personnel "float" so that vital operations continue even while people are in necessary training and moving from assignment to assignment. A report prepared by the Stimson Center for the American Academy of Diplomacy, and also funded by the Cox Foundation, entitled *The Foreign Affairs Budget for the Future*, called for a four-year commitment to increase U.S. direct-hire staffing at the State Department and U.S. Agency for International Development by 4,733 positions to be accompanied by significant increases in training and in the number of locally employed staff overseas.[22]
- The State Department needs to make a substantial investment in new technologies to communicate both with its own employees and with target audiences around the world.
- American diplomats have a right to work in a secure, clean, modern, and environmentally friendly building in all of the countries in which the United States is represented. But the real work of a twenty-first-century diplomat will be done outside of the building. *The Embassy of the Future* concluded, "Missions should have the capacity for dispersed operations, away from the Embassy compound and toward integration with and access to key target audiences…diplomats should be able to function principally outside the Embassy in most environments. They should have the mandate, skills, communication technology and other support to operate independently and securely."[23]

American society needs to recognize the importance of diplomacy to our country's future and recognize also the increased risk to our diplomats as they pursue a twenty-first-century model of diplomacy—outside of buildings, inside of foreign societies. The State Department must shift its philosophy from risk avoidance to risk management. This is not a decision the State Department can take alone. It should be debated in society. Is America prepared to take more diplomatic casualties, considering that before September 11, more American diplomats had been killed in the line of duty than general officers in our military since World War II? As *The Embassy of the Future* report noted, "The more diplomats we have engaged further forward and deeper into societies, the more likely it is that even the best efforts to protect them will sometimes fail. Threats will be more prevalent in more places. Many American diplomats have been killed in the course of their work. They should never be forgotten. As even more of America's diplomats operate in harm's way, we will need to provide them new kinds of training and protection, the better able they are to work in troubled lands, the more secure our nation will be."[24]

* * *

We arrived at work on September 12, 2001, in a new world. The effort to protect America, its friends, and allies from further attack had become the paramount objective. The struggle for the right of people around the world to choose a life of peace, prosperity, and pluralism was fully engaged. Changes in the support and practice of diplomacy had to be accelerated. September 11 defined the stakes involved and the national security consequences of failing to increase global diplomatic effectiveness.

The United States is now more integrated into the global system than at any time in our history. Our diversity, strength, and openness have allowed the United States to be the engine, beneficiary, and benefactor of the global system. A successful diplomacy for the twenty-first century—one that takes into account the lessons of 9/11 and simultaneously recognizes the larger and related issues that will define future success—will be based on values, integration, alliances, coalitions and backed, as it must be, by military force. We should act alone if we must. But surely America can use its unique twenty-first-century diplomatic capacities to set an example for the rest of the world as an upholder of freedom, pluralism, and free markets and encourage other countries to join her to pursue these worthy objectives.

Notes

The author thanks Ms. Toni Getze and Mr. Amos Goodman for their help in preparing this chapter.

1. Garrett Mattingly, *Renaissance Diplomacy* (Baltimore: Peregrine Penguin, 1964), 47–54.

2. Henry Kissinger, *Diplomacy* (New York: Simon & Shuster, 1994), 78–102.

3. Paul Gordon Lauren, Gordon A. Craig, and Alexander L. George, *Force and Statecraft* (New York and Oxford: Oxford University Press, 2007), 47–69.

4. John Lewis Gaddis, *Surprise, Security and the American Experience* (Cambridge, MA: Harvard University Press, 2004), 13.

5. Hans Binnendijk and Richard L. Kugler, *Seeing the Elephant: The U.S. Role in Global Security* (Dulles, Virginia: Potomac Books/National Defense University Press, 2006).

6. Marc Grossman, "The Tsunami Core Group: A Step toward a Transformed Diplomacy in Asia and Beyond," *Security Challenges (Australia)* 1-1 (2005): 11–14.

7. U.S. Department of State Advisory Group on Public Diplomacy for the Arab and Muslim World, Edward P. Djerejian, Chairman, *Changing Minds, Winning Peace: A New Strategic Direction for U.S. Public Diplomacy in the Arab & Muslim World,* October 1, 2003, http://www.state.gov/documents/organization/24882.pdf (accessed May 30, 2008), 13.

8. Parag Khanna, "Waving Goodbye to Hegemony," *New York Times Magazine,* January 27, 2008.

9. Many have made similar points, including the CSIS Smart Power Commission. Richard L. Armitage and Joseph S. Nye, Jr., *CSIS Commission on Smart Power: A Smarter, More Secure America* (Washington, DC: Center for Strategic and International Studies, 2007), http://www.csis.org/media/csis/pubs/071106_csissmartpowerreport.pdf (accessed March 10, 2009).

10. Kurt M. Campbell and Robert J. Einhorn, "Concluding Observations," in *The Nuclear Tipping Point: Why States Reconsider Their Nuclear Choices,* ed. Kurt M. Campbell, Robert J. Einhorn, and Mitchell B. Reiss (Washington, DC: Brookings Institution Press, 2004), 318.

11. George P. Shultz, William Perry, Henry Kissinger, and Sam Nunn, "A World Free from Nuclear Weapons," *Wall Street Journal,* January 4, 2007, A15.

12. George P. Shultz, William Perry, Henry Kissinger, and Sam Nunn, "Toward a Nuclear-Free World," *Wall Street Journal,* January 15, 2008, A13.

13. Kurt M. Campbell and Robert J. Einhorn, "Concluding Observations," in *The Nuclear Tipping Point: Why States Reconsider Their Nuclear Choices,* ed. Kurt M. Campbell, Robert J. Einhorn, and Mitchell B. Reiss (Washington, DC: Brookings Institution Press, 2004), 320.

14. Thomas L. Friedman, "Allies Dressed in Green," *New York Times,* October 27, 2006.

15. Ibid.

16. Commission of the European Communities, "An Energy Policy for Europe," October 1, 2007, http://ec.europa.eu/energy/energy_policy/doc/01_energy_policy_for_europe_en.pdf (accessed March 10, 2009).

17. Sen. Richard Lugar, "Energy and NATO," keynote speech to the German Marshall Fund Conference (Riga, Latvia), November 27, 2006, http://lugar.senate.gov/energy/press/speech/riga.cfm (accessed March 10, 2009).

18. Marc Grossman, "An American Diplomacy for the 21st Century," speech given at Foreign Affairs Day (Washington, DC), September 10, 2001.

19. George L. Argyos, Marc Grossman, and Felix G. Rohatyn, *The Embassy of the Future Commission Report* (Washington, DC: Center for Strategic and

International Studies, 2007), http://www.csis.org/media/csis/pubs/embassy_of_the_future.pdf (accessed March 10, 2009).

20. David L. Phillips, *Unsilencing the Past: Track Two Diplomacy and the Turkish-Armenian Reconciliation* (New York and Oxford: Berghahn Books 2005) and Harold H. Saunders, *Politics Is about Relationship: A Blueprint for the Citizens' Century* (New York: Palgrave Macmillan, 2005).

21. Robert Gates, "Pre-Alfalfa Luncheon," speech given at the Center for Strategic and International Studies (Washington, DC), January 2008.

22. Ronald Neumann, Thomas R. Pickering, Ellen Laipson, and Thomas D. Boyatt, *A Foreign Affairs Budget for the Future: Fixing the Crisis in Diplomatic Readiness* (Washington, DC: American Academy of Diplomacy and the Henry L. Stimson Center, 2008).

23. Argyos, Grossman, and Rohatyn, *The Embassy of the Future Commission Report*, 5.

24. Ibid., 3.

Chapter 3

Reorganizing the U.S. Intelligence Community

Paul S. Oh*

On September 11, 2001, the United States became acutely aware that its attackers no longer fit into one of its preconceived threat categories. Basing its identity and action on ideology and structures borne in the pre-Westphalian era, al Qaeda does not abide by the rigid line modern nation-states draw between war and peace. This new threat sees no distinction between civilian and military affairs, and can easily operate across civilian and military domains. The same organization effectively used American civilian institutions to receive technical flight training to conduct a sophisticated military operation on America's symbols of strength. The United States, on the other hand, continues to operate with difficulty across these domains owing to the institutional cultures and decentralized nature of its governmental organizations. The very nature of the American democratic society produces gaps in its national security apparatus (see figure 3.1).

The lesson of 9/11 was that the United States needed increased cooperation and intelligence sharing within the Intelligence Community (IC) to effectively combat organizations like al Qaeda. The Intelligence Reforms of 2004 have encouraged this by promoting centralization and mandating organizational changes like the formation of the Office of Director of National Intelligence (DNI) and fusion centers like the National Counter-Terrorism Center (NCTC). But the strategic and institutional cultures of the American government make centralization of intelligence inherently difficult at the national level. Realizing these challenges, various agencies have fostered

*Paul S. Oh is Instructor of American Politics, Policy, and Strategy at the U.S. Military Academy at West Point and is the Course Director of the senior seminar, Intelligence and Policy. He has been an officer in U.S. Army intelligence for 12 years, including service in Iraq as a commander and intelligence staff officer.

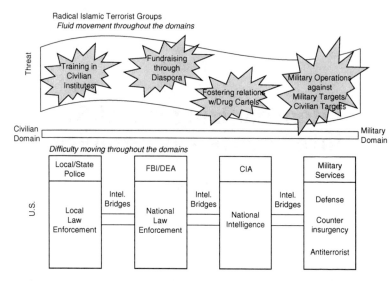

Figure 3.1   Threat Response Model

bottom-up efforts to actively conduct intelligence operations that span the military and civilian domains. What 9/11 has done is to accelerate these operational-level initiatives. The IC should continue to promote this trend and focus its efforts and resources on building these intelligence bridges. Senior leadership of the IC can encourage these initiatives by underwriting and rewarding the risks taken by intelligence professionals who venture outside of their bureaucratic walls.

Transdomain Entity versus Nation-State

Transdomain Entity

The 9/11 Commission Report noted that the terrorism fostered by bin Laden and al Qaeda was different from anything that the American government had seen before.[1] Al Qaeda remains an organization that is subnational, transnational, and also transdomain. Its ability to function in civilian society to execute a sophisticated operation against both military and civilian targets caught the American IC by surprise. The "holy warriors" of 9/11 trained in the camps of Afghanistan, learned to fly in civilian institutions like Air Fleet Training System in Teterboro, NJ,[2] and then coordinated a sophisticated military operation using four airplanes as flying missiles.

Al Qaeda's transnational and transdomain nature is due in part to the organization's worldview. Bin Laden inspires his followers with ideas rooted in a pre-Westphalian era. He and his associates have used selective interpretations of history to remind their followers of the golden age of Islam and to inflame the desire to recapture this glory. He has sought to form an identity among his followers that views war as a battle of civilizations to be waged not only by soldiers, but also by all true followers of Islam. Those who wage his "jihad"[3] know no wall between civilian and military affairs that westerners are so accustomed to. He is successful in part because he can trace his struggle right back to the roots and lineage of Islam while interpreting them to justify his actions.

Some view the Prophet Mohammed as a warrior-leader who led his followers in a fight for the survival of their faith.[4] The defense and expansion of Islam depended on "civilians" waging armed conflict for the ultimate formation of the caliphate. Caleb Carr notes that this necessary violence colored the tone of the Koran and the violent activities both within the Islamic world and between the Islamic and the outside world. This worldview influenced many extremist Islamic leaders, including the movement of the caliphate of al-Ma'mun. Al Ma'mun, in turn, became the spiritual inspiration for the Wahhabi sect in Saudi Arabia, which in turn influenced the ideology of bin Laden.[5] The terrorism of the 1970s and 1980s used violence to send political messages and not necessarily to cause mass loss of life. Bin Laden has linked his terrorism to actions of warrior leaders of a different era waging destructive war on peoples to achieve a higher religious objective.

This inspiration can plainly be seen in bin Laden's speeches. Bin Laden has called his followers to wage "jihad" not as soldiers, a term that connotes connection to a modern military apparatus, but as followers of the Prophet and the struggle he initiated. He reminds his young followers that "Muhammed's companions were young men. And the young men of today are the successor of the early ones."[6] Furthermore, bin Laden repeatedly connects today's actions with actions of long ago. In addressing the United States, he states that "All this [U.S. actions against Islam] causes us to revoke any treaty between us, as the Prophet...considered the al-Hudaybiyah peace null and void after Quraysh helped Bani Bakr against the Prophet's allies."[7] The implications are clear: today's call to all Muslims is the continuation of the "jihad" of long ago. Osama bin Laden and Ayman al-Zawahiri called for the murder of all Americans in the 1998 fatwa—that it is the "individual duty for every Muslim who can do it in any country in which it is possible to do it."[8]

This worldview in part facilitates al Qaeda's continued ability to move easily across military and civilian domains. Unlike nation-state threats of the past, al Qaeda's core organization is not bound by the demarcation between civilian and military affairs. Using the border area of Pakistan, al Qaeda still directs operations, stages attacks in support of the Taliban in Afghanistan, and trains new recruits.[9] They partner with criminal elements collaborating in activities such as money laundering, counterfeiting, bomb-making, smuggling, and trafficking.[10] And they continue to operate in western societies, raising and collecting money while enhancing their ability to strike the United States by improving "the identification, training, and positioning of operatives for an attack in the Homeland.[11]

American Strategic and Institutional Culture

American response, on the other hand, has been handicapped by the strategic culture of the country and the institutional cultures of its intelligence agencies. As the predominant democratic nation-state, the American worldview differs drastically from that of other countries. As Loch Johnson writes, "The American Constitution is grounded in a theory of governance that favors institutional diversity, a disaggregation of power to ensure liberty or ambition counteracting ambition, in Madison's conception."[12] The Constitution enshrined in the political institutions the strategic culture that fears centralization and accumulation of power. Subsequent events and legislation in American history before 9/11 have contributed to widening the gaps among the agencies, producing an Intelligence Community with components that focus almost exclusively on their respective domains of operations.

The anxiety over the national security apparatus can be seen as early as the debates over the need for a standing army. Great patriots like Patrick Henry resisted the idea of a standing army which, he predicted, "will execute execrable commands of tyranny."[13] Such sentiments, which reflected American suspicion of a strong military, would lead to distinct safeguards within the governmental framework. These sentiments and framework would help limit the role of the military and its intelligence arms in domestic settings and the extent to which it partners with domestic agencies throughout the republic's history.

Such need for decentralization also applied to the separation between civilian intelligence and law enforcement functions. President Truman, in the mid-1940s, reassured citizens that the American intelligence apparatus would not lead to a "Gestapo-like culture" in which "unchecked national security prerogatives and intrusive investigations in the name of state security would override due process of law."[14] These fears, at times inflamed by the diverse institutional actors, influenced the formation of the modern national security and intelligence structures created by the National Security Act (NSA) of 1947. Among other actions, this act formed the American Central Intelligence Agency, with responsibility for "national intelligence," or "intelligence relating to the national security."[15] It did not, however, create an "integrator of U.S. intelligence" that many policymakers hoped it would be.[16]

The NSA of 1947 allowed power of intelligence agencies to continue to accumulate in a decentralized fashion. Different intelligence arms continued to operate in their respective domains, guarded and supported jealously by their parent departments. National law enforcement agencies protected their preeminent role in domestic intelligence and counterintelligence. The Office of Naval Intelligence and the Army's G2 section both guarded their roles in intelligence operations against rival militaries. The State Department focused on its traditional intelligence gathering through diplomatic channels. As one scholar notes, "In an unusual coalition, sailors, soldiers, G-men, and diplomats came together and lobbied for a decentralized, confederal intelligence system."[17] Though various directors of Central Intelligence (DCIs) and presidents have sought greater centralization for increased effectiveness, the atmosphere of institutional inertia proved too stifling for any attempt at great reform.

As the nation matured in its role as a global power, the separation of duties and responsibilities among the Intelligence Community was for the most part found satisfactory by the American leaders and people. In fact, intelligence abuses exposed in the 1970s further ensured that intelligence agencies would not easily span across domains as the legal hurdles to interagency cooperation grew higher.[18] These agencies have over the years continued to focus on their traditional areas of expertise and "largely eschewed unity in favor of functional diversity."[19] While this system was arguably satisfactory to combat the Soviet Union, it proved incapable of preventing the catastrophic attacks of 9/11.

The United States, with its decentralized Intelligence Community, has had trouble dealing with al Qaeda's worldview. Debates of identity and classification of al Qaeda operatives sprouted with no easy answers to the way in which to view this non-Westphalian enemy. As the 9/11 Commission Report points out: "The existing mechanisms for handling terrorist acts had been trial and punishment for acts committed by individuals; sanction, reprisal, deterrence, or war for acts by hostile governments. The actions of al Qaeda fit neither category. Its crimes were on a scale approaching acts of war, but they were committed by a loose, far-flung, nebulous conspiracy with no territories or citizens or assets that could be readily threatened, overwhelmed, or destroyed."[20] Are al Qaeda operatives prisoners of war or supercriminals? Are they agents of evil or warriors of a bygone era? The questions of their legal status and how they should be punished still remain inadequately answered.

The Lesson of 9/11

The New Threat Rises

The 1990s were a tumultuous time for the intelligence community. With the demise of the Soviet Union, policy makers were debating the utility of a large and diverse IC. Many were eager to cash in on the peace dividend to reallocate funds to other pressing national priorities. At the same time, the crumbling of the bipolar system meant the once frozen struggles around the world would thaw into violent actions. U.S. intelligence agencies found themselves being asked questions about multiple countries acting outside the influence of major hegemons,[21] while they were struggling with budget cuts and unclear priorities for collection.

Concurrently, various commissions realized that the intelligence structure built to fight the Soviet Union needed reform and issued harsh critiques about the effectiveness of the IC in facing the threats of the post–cold war era. Amy Zegart notes that "between the fall of the Soviet Union and the September 11 attacks, six blue-ribbon commissions, three major unclassified governmental initiatives, and three think tank task forces examined the U.S. intelligence community, the FBI, and U.S. counterterrorism efforts."[22] These commissions found surprising agreement on four major problems: "the intelligence community's lack of "corporateness," insufficient human intelligence, personnel systems that failed to align intelligence needs with personnel skills or encourage information sharing, and weaknesses in setting intelligence priorities."[23] Although these commissions called for reform, most of the proposed changes failed to get implemented.[24]

The American bureaucracy proved highly resistant to refocusing on a looming terrorist threat. In truth, parts of the U.S. government had known for a long time their need to better share intelligence to fight terrorism. The Counter-Terrorism Center (CTC), for example, was formed as early as 1986 with representation from agencies across the U.S. government. The CIA experimented with "virtual stations" in 1996, creating experimental stateside units that would operate as if they were overseas.[25] The most famous of these, later known as the Alec Station, would be charged with finding Osama bin Laden.[26] Government as a whole, however, arguably did not give terrorism the priority it deserved; nor did it dedicate the resources to ensure success in eliminating it. Neither the Clinton nor the Bush administrations seemed to grasp the urgency of the threat.[27] Bureaucratic culture and institutional inertia, in the absence of political will from the agencies' masters, prevented a formation of a fluid system of intelligence sharing across the domains.

The Profound but Not Novel Lesson

Hence, the lesson of 9/11 was indeed profound but not very novel: information was not being shared across government agencies. The decentralized American national security apparatus had failed to connect the dots. Amy Zegart recounts the case of Khalid al-Mihdar, one of the hijackers of American Airlines Flight 77, who entered the United States even though the CIA was watching this operative and had a photograph, full name, passport number, and the knowledge that al-Mihdar held a multiple-entry visa to the United States. Unbelievably, al-Mihdar was not placed on the State Department's watch list and was allowed to enter the country.[28]

Post-9/11 investigations and debates advanced the view that a joint effort by the externally focused Intelligence Community and the internally focused law enforcement community would have offered the best chance of preventing the attacks.[29] The military's response in reacting to possible hostile aircrafts was also found wanting.[30] The 9/11 attacks brought renewed calls for increased centralization of the IC. In an answer to these calls, Congress passed the National Intelligence Security Reform Act of 2004, touted as the biggest change in the American Intelligence Community since the National Security Act of 1947.

The changes were mostly organizational in nature. The act, for example, created the position of Director of National Intelligence (DNI) who replaced the Director of Central Intelligence as the head of the IC. A critique of the 9/11 Commission Report was that the DCI had too many jobs that included running the CIA, managing the IC, and being analyst in chief for the government.[31] The DNI would be free of the weight of running an agency and would concentrate on running the community. To remedy the problem of information sharing, the DNI would be given access to all intelligence and be responsible for proper dissemination across the IC.[32] The DNI would oversee all the nation's intelligence agencies as well as the new National Counterterrorism Center, new National Counterproliferation Center, the National Intelligence Council (NIC), and the National Counterintelligence Executive.[33] As some intelligence officers and observers have noted, however, it is unclear whether another level of bureaucracy would increase the IC's centralization and effectiveness in the fight against terrorism.[34] As one scholar noted, successful reform must be more than organizational; it must also target routines and cultures.[35]

Intelligence Operations across Domains

If history is any guide, the quest for centralization within the American political system will prove as difficult as it was in 1947. Again, this is not surprising, given the American political culture of decentralization of power. The DNI still has only limited power over the intelligence budget, the secretary of defense still controls the majority of intelligence collection assets, and Congress is still not organized to provide effective financial guidance or oversight. Hence the notion that the recent intelligence legislation will produce a more centralized and effective IC may be hope misplaced. Efforts to remold the national intelligence structure will produce improvements, but only marginally.

What 9/11 did do, however, is to accelerate the efforts of various agencies to build intelligence bridges at the operational level. The 9/11 Commission Report noted how lead agencies with responsibility for certain problems have been constructing their own interagency entities and task forces.[36] These

Intergovernmental Task Forces are examples of bridges built to deal with specific problems to overcome the "community-wide fragmentation."[37] What has been clear to intelligence professionals since the 9/11 experience is that they need to become more comfortable operating across domains with partner agencies to keep up with the ever-fluid enemy.

There has been a renewed emphasis, for example, on a network of "FBI-local police" Joint Terrorism Task Forces since 2002–2003.[38] The military also has been experimenting with similar concepts even at the division level. The 101st Division in 2003 to 2004 experimented with AO North (Iraq) Joint Interagency Task Force (JIATF). AO North JIATF's mission was to "gather intelligence, coordinate and synchronize intelligence operations, and coordinate conventional, Special Forces, OGA [Other Government Agencies], and multinational operations in order to identify and neutralize hostile individuals and groups." Among others, AO North JIATF had representation from NSA, CIA, DIA, DHS, and FBI.[39] The IC should continue to encourage these initiatives and cultivate a culture in which the norm is intelligence professionals striving to build bridges with partner agencies at these lower levels. Agency leaders, then, need to supply the resources and afford freedom to intelligence professionals to work together to find "out-of-the-box," bottom-up solutions to the terrorism problem.

This cooperation may take many forms and produce striking results. Russell Howard offers one example of cross-domain operations. Howard contends that criminals—particularly dealing in drugs and arms, and human traffic—could be a valuable source of information and possibly even actionable intelligence against al Qaeda and affiliated groups. Though criminal actors are unsavory and they possess questionable human rights records, they are a valuable source of intelligence because they collaborate with terrorists in areas such as drugs, human trafficking, arms sales, counterfeiting, and corruption.[40]

Howard notes that though the crimes committed by these two groups are similar in substance, they do differ in motive. While crimes of terrorists are a means to support larger political and ideological objectives, crimes of criminals are businesses in themselves. And because criminals do not possess a terrorists' fanatic ideology, intelligence and law enforcement officials may more easily exploit a criminal's self-serving interests for the benefit of intelligence and counterterrorism operations.[41] Howard recommends that criminals who have special knowledge of transnational terrorist and criminal organizations be leveraged to fight terrorism.[42] For such operations to take place, intelligence professionals from multiple agencies will need to build bridges at the operational level to span the gaps produced by the governmental framework and institutional cultures.

Indeed, it seems that analysts and operatives on the ground have a growing realization of how interconnected their operations can be. One Drug Enforcement Administration (DEA) analyst reveals how the DEA's Bangkok Country Office (BCO) over the course of tracking narcotics realized how the terrorists also use international or underground financial systems, including Chinese Underground Banking Systems (CUBS) or Hawalas. Other techniques of money transfer common to both groups involved debit and credit cards and the use of Western Union. Drug and terror networks are using the same professional providers for false identity papers, money laundering, and courier services.[43]

The analyst noted how the DEA field office intelligence tradecraft contrasted sharply with the intelligence model that the IC had been using to track traditional threats. Among other things, this analyst suggests that the IC should find a way to harvest whatever substantive details and insights organizations like the BCO discover in the course of their counterdrug work that might assist with terrorism.[44] She clearly saw the need to integrate tradecraft and share lessons learned in tracking the financial modus operandi of terrorist networks.[45]

As cooperation at the operational level is still in its nascent stage, the IC must continue to foster bridge-building entities that span domains, allowing civilian and military intelligence and law enforcement officials to work together. These task forces are not without problems, however.[46] They do not readily solve issues such as streamlining of procedures, IT interface, and differences in intelligence analysis techniques and reporting procedures. But they do force professionals from across agencies to work together, no matter what the difficulties and initial inefficiencies are. These professionals can then push proposed solutions and lessons learned up their agency chains of command to foster innovative and adaptive solutions to complex problems.

The American system of government and its bureaucratic politics do make interagency efforts difficult. The United States has a 50-year history showing how agencies have failed to centralize for greater effectiveness.[47] In the unique bureaucratic structure of the American IC, then, the next best thing may be for the political masters and agency leaders to foster the bottom-up bridge-building culture at the operational level. This goes against the culture of many agencies and involves the risk of giving up control to younger leaders closer to the action and to outside actors. Buy-in from headquarters may be the hardest step in this process. Given the threat, however, agency leaders need to underwrite and reward the risks taken by professionals who venture outside of their bureaucratic walls. With proper guidelines, the IC can foster an environment in which networks of these cross-domain entities are defended at the operational levels. These entities can communicate across distances and domains, thus capitalizing on the American decentralized structure.

Conclusion

The preeminent threat to America remains the substate, transnational, and transdomain terrorist groups. Even if al Qaeda has suffered setbacks, Nielsen and Gunaratna's chapter makes it abundantly clear that the group is reconstituting in Pakistan's Federally Administered Tribal Areas and still has the capability to plan and strike the American homeland. The DNI's assessment of al Qaeda also depicts an organization that "continue[s] to pose significant threats to the United States at home and abroad."[48] The variables that fuel Islamic extremists will remain for years to come. The National Intelligence Council believes that the factors that gave rise to al Qaeda will not abate in the next 15 years.[49]

As the 9/11 attacks showed, the American Intelligence Community needs to become more effective in sharing information and operating across domains to meet this threat. The realities of American politics are, however, that the strategic culture and the institutional inertia will continue to make increased centralization difficult. Given these difficulties, partnerships must be promoted at the operational levels where multiple agencies work together across multiple domains. The political masters and agency leaders need to resource and foster a culture that rewards initiatives of intelligence professionals on the ground to think and operate outside the bureaucratic box with governmental partners to leverage the strengths of the American decentralized intelligence system. Intelligence operations that span the domains are inherently difficult, but necessary to fight nimble and adaptive adversaries.

Notes

1. *The 9/11 Commission Report: Final Report of the National Commission on Terrorist Attacks Upon the United States* (New York: W.W. Norton, 2004), 348.
2. Ibid., 242.
3. Bin Laden's use of the term "jihad" is not the common use of jihad in the Muslim religion. In appreciation of this, I have placed the term in quotes when referring to bin Laden's misuse.
4. Caleb Carr, *The Lessons of Terror* (New York: Random House Trade Paperbacks, 2003), 49.
5. Ibid., 54.
6. Osama bin Laden, *Declaration of Jihad on Americans*, transmitted through Al-Islah, 2 September, 1996.
7. Ibid.
8. From *The 9/11 Commission Report*, 47.
9. DNI J. Michael McConnell, *Annual Threat Assessment of the Intelligence Community for the Senate Armed Services Committee*, February 27, 2008, 4–5.
10. Russell D. Howard, *Intelligence in Denied Areas: New Concepts for a Changing Security Environment*, JSOU Report December 07–10, 2007, 9.
11. McConnell, *Annual Threat Assessment*, 5.
12. Loch Johnson, "The DCI and the Eight-Hundred-Pound Gorilla," in *Intelligence and the National Security Strategist*, ed. Roger George and Robert Kline (New York: Rowman & Littlefield, 2006), 476.

13. Patrick Henry, *Speech of Patrick Henry Before the Virginia Ratifying Convention*, June 5, 1788.

14. See discussion on American Strategic Culture by Jennifer E. Sims, "Understanding Ourselves," in *Transforming U.S. Intelligence*, ed. Jennifer E. Sims and Burton Gerber (Washington DC: Georgetown University Press, 2005).

15. Michael Warner, "Central Intelligence: Origin and Evolution," in *Intelligence and the National Security Strategist*, ed. Roger George and Robert Kline (New York: Rowman & Littlefield, 2006), 46.

16. Warner, "Central Intelligence," 46.

17. Amy Zegart, *Flawed by Design: The Evolution of the CIA, JCS, and NSC* (Stanford: Stanford University Press, 1999), 167.

18. Five Devin Rollis, "The Wall between National Security and Law Enforcement," in *Improving the Law Enforcement-Intelligence Community Relationship* (Washington DC: National Defense Intelligence College, 2007), 143.

19. Johnson, "The DCI," 476.

20. *The 9/11 Commission Report*, 348.

21. Ernest R. May, "The Twenty-First Century Challenge for U.S. Intelligence," in *Transforming U.S. Intelligence*, ed. Jennifer E. Sims and Burton Gerber (Washington DC: Georgetown University Press, 2005), 4–5.

22. Amy B. Zegart, "September 11 and the Adaptation Failure of U.S. Intelligence Agencies," *International Security* 29: 4 (Spring 2005): 85–86.

23. Ibid., 88.

24. See Zegart. Zegart attributes the adaptation failure to the "nature of bureaucratic organizations, which makes internal reform exceedingly difficult; the self-interest of presidents, legislators, and government bureaucrats, which works against executive branch reform; and the fragmented structure of the federal government, which erects high barriers to legislative reform."

25. George Tenet, *At the Center of the Storm* (New York: HarperCollins, 2007), 99.

26. Ibid., 100.

27. *The 9/11 Commission Report*, 343.

28. Zegart, "September 11," 78.

29. Robert B. Murphy, "Problems and Progress in Information Sharing," in *Improving the Law Enforcement-Intelligence Community Relationship* (Washington DC: National Defense Intelligence College, 2007), 166.

30. *The 9/11 Commission Report*, 44–46.

31. Ibid., 409.

32. Mark M. Lowenthal, *Intelligence: From Secrets to Policy* (Washington, DC: CQ Press, 2003), 30.

33. Ibid., 30–31.

34. Ibid., 279.

35. Zegart, "September 11," 110.

36. *The 9/11 Commission Report*, 402.

37. Johnson, "The DCI," 468.

38. Harvey Rishikof, "The Role of the Federal Bureau of Investigation in National Security," in *Intelligence and the National Security Strategist*, ed. Roger George and Robert Kline (New York: Rowman & Littlefield, 2006), 126.

39. Isaiah Wilson and others, "Joint Interagency Task Force: A Case Study of Interagency/Intergovernmental Coordination."

40. Howard, "Intelligence in Denied Areas," 8.
41. Ibid., 10.
42. Ibid., 13.
43. Gloria Freund, "Unmasking Networks: Drug Enforcement Administration Tradecraft for the Intelligence Community," in *Improving the Law Enforcement-Intelligence Community Relationship* (Washington DC: National Defense Intelligence College, 2007), 24.
44. Ibid., 38.
45. Ibid.
46. See Lowenthal, *Intelligence*, 282.
47. See Warner, "Central Intelligence."
48. J. Michael McConnell, *Annual Threat Assessment*, 4.
49. National Intelligence Council, *Mapping the Global World* (Government Printing Office, 2004), 94.

Chapter 4

Building and Maintaining a Post-9/11 All-Volunteer Military Force

Karin K. De Angelis and David R. Segal*

The force structure of the American military has changed during and after every major war. After World War II and the Korean War, the United States maintained its first long-standing force not engaged in major combat operations, and did so on the basis of conscription. During the Vietnam War, the United States deployed a large number of conscripts without participation of the Reserve Component. After Vietnam, the American government replaced conscription with an All-Volunteer Force. The military campaigns initiated after September 11, 2001, similarly have seen changes in the way the United States raises forces for war, including the recruitment and retention of an increasingly diverse force as well as growing reliance on the Reserves and civilians.

The United States military is in a historically unique position regarding its current manpower resources and policy and the operational demands necessitated by the post-9/11 mission. Whereas past wars of long duration utilized a conscripted force, the current missions in Afghanistan and Iraq rely predominantly upon volunteers, a change that highlights the importance of recruiting and retaining a skilled force. Policy analysis in the 1990s focused on the substitution of technology for manpower; however, the personnel demands required for Operation Enduring Freedom (OEF), and the subsequent Operation Iraqi Freedom (OIF), have placed personnel needs at

*Karin K. De Angelis is a doctoral student in military sociology at the University of Maryland. David R. Segal is Professor of Sociology and Director of the Center for Research on Military Organization at the University of Maryland and the author of several books including *The Postmodern Military* and *Recruiting for Uncle Sam*.

the forefront. Owing to the unexpected duration of the conflict and the All-Volunteer recruitment policy of the United States Armed Forces, the military has experienced unprecedented changes in the composition of its Total Force.

This chapter summarizes the demographic changes of today's All-Volunteer military with an emphasis on how these changes impact the manpower demands of a wartime force. First, we examine the broadening of recruitment eligibility guidelines. We also focus on the military's increased reliance on ethnic and racial minorities, particularly noncitizens, as well as women. We then review the Total Force composition of the armed forces, with an emphasis on the role of the Reserve Component and private military contractors. The Reserve Component, although a key force in most past operations, has become absolutely critical to mission success. Contractors are also playing a larger role in the war effort; however, this increased involvement brings greater scrutiny of their wartime role and behavior. By analyzing the manpower policies shaping each component of the Total Force, we demonstrate the consequences, both intended and unintended, of engaging in a long war without conscripts.

Recruiting Trends and Standards

Unlike the predictable deployment demands of the cold war and the short, although troop-intensive Gulf War, the demands necessitated by the long wars in Afghanistan and Iraq test the viability and effectiveness of today's All-Volunteer Force in a manner never seen before. Whereas conscription allowed military planners to select personnel directly, today's military must compete with commercial and educational opportunities for recruits.[1] Although the navy and the air force are downsizing, the army and Marine Corps are expanding during the ongoing War on Terror. The army alone wants to add tens of thousands of soldiers by the year 2011.[2] These recruitment challenges are further exacerbated by public opinion that has fluctuated on the current Global War on Terror, particularly regarding the OIF mission.[3] The combination of increased manpower needs and adverse public opinion has made recruiting and retaining a skilled force a challenge, leading to changes in certain accession standards and perhaps overall force quality.

Recruitment goals for each service include not just numbers, but also personnel quality, which is measured by educational attainment and Armed Forces Qualification Test (AFQT) scores.[4] Military recruits with AFQT scores in the top 50 percent who are high school graduates are considered high quality. Past studies on the AFQT provide evidence that personnel with higher scores tend to have greater productivity, higher performance, and less training requirements than those scoring in the categories below the median. There is also evidence that high-scoring personnel tend to perform better on military-related tasks, such as communications and tank gunner systems, aircraft maintenance, and air defense systems.[5] Further, high school graduates have lower attrition rates.[6] Because the military competes for these top personnel, the Office of the Secretary of Defense established a baseline of recruit quality, which each service may restrict further, that allows the recruitment of lower quality enlistees, and still requires 60 percent of new recruits to score within the top 50 percent of the AFQT and 90 percent of recruits to have a high school diploma.[7]

The army, in particular, has struggled with recruiting and retaining the quality force needed for the ongoing campaigns in Afghanistan and Iraq. In FY (Fiscal Year) 2005, the army was the lone Active Component that did not exceed the Department of Defense's quality requirements.[8] Whereas the other services had little change in quality metrics from FY2004 to FY2005, the army reported a significant change in recruit quality. The proportion of high school graduates dropped from 92 percent in FY2004 to 87 percent in FY2005, which is below the DOD (Department of Defense) baseline of 90 percent.[9] The army also reported a decline in high-scoring recruits, from 72 percent in FY2004 to 67 percent in FY2005, while also accepting more recruits in the lowest acceptable aptitude category.[10] This downward trend has continued through FY2006, reflecting the growing strain of recruiting an All-Volunteer force during war.

In addition to increased accessions of low quality personnel, waivers for recruits with criminal records, which range from minor traffic citations to felony convictions, also have increased, although mainly in the army and the Marine Corps. The army waived 8,219 recruits in FY2006; this number grew to 10,258 recruits in FY2007. The number of recruits with felony convictions for serious crimes such as theft and assault increased from 249 to 511. Likewise, the Marine Corps also waived more recruits as the number of conduct waivers increased from 16,969 in FY2006 to 17,413 in FY2007.[11] The number of recruits with felony convictions also increased from 208 to 350.[12]

Although these recruits make up less than 1 percent of total accessions for both the army and the Marine Corps, the military has been on the defensive regarding the moral quality of its recruits.[13] There are mixed results regarding the attrition rates of recruits with legal waivers during basic training; personnel with misdemeanors have higher attrition rates while those with felonies have lower attrition rates than those without moral waivers. In addition, there is evidence that waived recruits are more likely to be separated from the military for misconduct within their first term of service than those without waivers.[14] Consequently, the recruitment of personnel with criminal convictions may ease overall accession numbers, but may not support the military's retention goals. The granting of legal waivers may not be a cost-effective solution to the military's manpower needs.

The military's increased use of waivers also extends into the corporeal realm, with more recruits entering the service despite physical limitations.

Serious cases of asthma and obesity, for example, are causes for disqualification; however, personnel with these conditions may obtain medical waivers if they can demonstrate that these conditions are manageable.[15] Both asthma and obesity are health hazard trends that have grown within the general population; therefore, the military's steady increase over the past 10 years is somewhat reflexive. However, medical waivers have become even more prevalent, particularly in the army and the Marine Corps, since OEF and OIF.

In an effort to expand the recruiting pool, the army not only permits more medically restricted personnel into the force, but also has raised the maximum enlistment age for first-time recruits. In FY2006, Congress gave the services permission to increase the maximum age for recruits from 35 to 42 years; only the army acted upon this broadening of requirements.[16] The returns on this policy change are minimal, with the army only gaining a few hundred accessions per year, with the additional drawback that older recruits tend to attrite from basic training at almost twice the rate of younger ones.[17] Overall, the military remains a much younger workforce than the civilian sector with 87 percent of its recruits between the ages of 18 and 24.[18] The military continues to favor characteristics frequently associated with youth such as strength, stamina, and physical well-being, yet the expansion of the army's enlistment age suggests the difficulties of recruiting quality personnel during long, and at times unpopular, wars.

Racial and Ethnic Minorities

The downward trend in overall troop quality, particularly in the army, may be a symptom of the military's increasingly difficult task of recruiting and retaining a skilled force. However, concerns regarding troop composition, and whether low-status groups disproportionately shoulder the burden of wartime service, have been an ongoing topic of analysis for government and military leaders since the 1973 transition to the All-Volunteer Force. By transforming military service from a conscription-based calling to an economically motivated job, the military emerges as an appealing employer, particularly for populations that have experienced discrimination within the civilian sector, creating the possibility that poor communities and racial minorities would be overrepresented in the military.[19]

Despite the serious demands of military service, particularly during wartime, employment with the armed forces often is framed as a well-paid opportunity that may potentially clear a path for social mobility. Indeed, during the first few years of the All-Volunteer Force, more than 25 percent of new recruits were black; this was more than double the percentage of black recruits in 1970. Black enlistment levels peaked at 28 percent in 1979; their representation declined slightly after that, but remained around 20 percent until 2000.[20] Moreover, black service members were also more likely to reenlist than their white counterparts, further fueling the overrepresentation of blacks within the American military. The decision to join and remain within the military was, and continues to be, rational market behavior. Youths, and particularly blacks, faced significant unemployment after the Vietnam War. The military was perceived as a logical employment choice not only for the pay and benefits, but also because of the perception that the armed forces had less tolerance for racial discrimination than civilian employers.[21]

Despite the historical overrepresentation of black personnel in the American military, there have been significant changes in their enlistment behaviors. Beginning in the 1980s, the percentage of black enlistees began to decline, particularly in the army and the Marine Corps, with the most precipitous drop occurring between 1990 and 1991. This downward trend has continued through the ongoing wars in Afghanistan and Iraq, from 20 percent in 2000 to 13 percent in 2006, making black accessions proportionate to their military-aged population.[22] The decrease in black recruits, and in their enlistment propensity overall, suggests that military leaders may need to resituate their recruiting efforts, particularly since black service members historically have been relied upon to fulfill military manpower needs.[23]

The changes in the armed forces' racial composition, however, are not only linked to decreased enlistment propensity, but also represent a shift in the demographics of the American population generally. Whereas blacks were once overrepresented in the military, Latinos, who are the country's largest minority population, have been underrepresented in the American military. For example, in 2006, they were 18 percent of the civilian labor force, yet they were only 13 percent of enlisted accessions.[24] This trend is beginning to change, with Latinos entering the service in greater numbers, and as a consequence, potentially offsetting in part the negative impact of decreased enlistment propensity among blacks. However, when considered against the backdrop of military qualifications such as high school graduation, Latinos actually are overrepresented among enlisted service members.[25]

The racial and ethnic composition of American youth will change substantially within the next few decades with Latinos, especially Mexican Americans, having the largest increase while Anglos continue to decrease.[26] In response to these demographic changes, recruitment targets and tactics must change. Latinos, in particular, continue to demonstrate positive views toward military enlistment.[27] In addition, Latino youth serving in the Marine Corps currently demonstrate higher completion rates than recruits of other races or ethnicities for both basic training and the first term of service.[28] The Marine Corps has already demonstrated success in recruiting Latino men and women, a strength that it is building on by revamping its recruiting campaign, along with the army, to include more Spanish language material.[29]

Another recruiting tactic has involved expediting naturalization requests for noncitizen service members, a group that includes multiple nationalities, but claims a sizeable proportion of Latino immigrants.[30] Despite being noncitizens, legal permanent residents are eligible to serve in the American military, although they are not permitted in occupational specialties that require a security clearance; however, they cannot be commissioned.[31] It is estimated that 35,000 noncitizens currently serve in the Active Component of the military, and that 8,000 noncitizen recruits join the force every year.[32] In addition to racial and ethnic differences, noncitizen service members add linguistic and cultural diversity, a particularly valuable characteristic for the post-9/11 mission. Many noncitizens also demonstrate increased loyalty and military aptitude; black, Asian, Pacific Islander, and Latino noncitizens, for example, have lower attrition rates than white Americans, both at 3-months and 36-months time in service.[33]

The increased presence of immigrants within the United States military reflects a demographic shift in the American youth population, which will continue to expand with noncitizen residents as well as youth raised by immigrant parents. Approximately 4.1 percent of the eligible youth population consists of legal permanent residents; this equates to 1.5 million potential recruits.[34] In recognition of the service of noncitizens, as well as the potential to motivate an important recruitment pool, in 2002 President George W. Bush issued an executive order shortening the service requirement for expedited naturalization from three years of service to one day of service during wartime hostilities. Since the implementation of this provision, the United States Citizenship and Immigration Services has naturalized more than 39,835 service members and has granted posthumous citizenship to 116 members.[35] As the United States military continues to match manpower resources to mission requirements, policy changes such as expediting the citizenship process for noncitizen service members are logical steps toward building and maintaining a nationally representative volunteer force.

Increased Reliance on Women

In addition to the changing racial and ethnic demographics of the military, the armed forces have also experienced a substantial restructuring of their gender composition. Although women have participated in every major American conflict, their service has been limited by legal exclusion, gender quotas, and occupational restrictions. Women did not achieve permanent military status until the passing of the 1948 Women's Armed Services Integration Act, which, in addition to formalizing their military standing, established quotas for their participation and limited their occupational opportunities.[36] The 1973 transition to the All-Volunteer Force coupled with women's increased labor market presence, however, made women legitimate, and needed, recruiting targets.[37]

Recruiting efforts were also supported by the shifting of women into more combat-oriented jobs, rather than limiting them to administrative and medical positions.[38] In 1988, the Department of Defense clarified its Risk Rule, thereby opening 30,000 additional positions to women. Further, in response to the deployed service of over 40,000 women during the 1990–1991 Persian Gulf War, Congress repealed the laws prohibiting women from serving on combatant ships or as combat aviators.[39] In addition, in 1994 the then secretary of defense Les Aspin rescinded the 1988 Risk Rule and, through a new definition of ground combat, established the ground combat rules that presently restrict women from serving in offensive ground combat positions at the brigade or lower level.[40] Since this change, over 92 percent of the military occupational specialties have been opened to women.[41]

Building on the personnel policies of the past, women's military presence has grown, although they still remain a significant minority. Currently women constitute 14 percent of the active duty enlisted force and 16 percent of the active duty officer corps.[42] There are significant differences among the service branches with women constituting up to 20.1 percent of active duty air force enlisted personnel and 6.2 percent of active duty Marine Corps enlisted personnel.[43] Similar to the enlisted composition, the air force has the highest proportion of women officers at 18.2 percent and the Marine Corps has the lowest proportion at 5.8 percent.[44] The military reached its highest proportion of military women, at 15 percent, in fiscal years 2002 and 2003. Going by the overall percentages of women during the post-9/11 time frame, we can see that there have been no significant differences regarding proportions of female accessions or overall proportions of women service members.

Despite this stagnation, these numbers may increase if the services focus their recruiting efforts on nontraditional populations such as women.[45] High school women, for example, tend to have a lower propensity than their male peers to serve in the military. However, they also report a higher desire to serve despite their lower expectation that they will actually do so.[46] Women, then, remain an untapped labor pool for the American military.

Although women are a minority population with the military, their professional role garners significant attention from manpower analysts, the media, political leaders, and everyday citizens.[47] As demonstrated by the evolving personnel policies surrounding their participation, the integration of women into the military has been through incremental changes, largely in response to personnel needs.[48] The current debate about women's wartime service involves the direct ground combat exclusion rule that assumes conventional battlefields and does not apply well to the counterinsurgency environments of OEF and OIF. Women currently make up approximately 10 percent of personnel deployed in support of these operations and have suffered wartime injuries and death because of their participation.[49] They have also earned silver stars, the third highest combat award within the armed forces, in both OEF and OIF.[50]

The controversy surrounding women's wartime service does not stem from their performance, but from incompatibility between the army assignment policy, which predates the Department of Defense's policy, and the nonlinear battleground experienced in counterinsurgency operations.[51] Unlike past conventional wars, the post-9/11 battle terrain does not have a clear marking of forward and well forward positions; there is no obvious frontline.[52] The army's assignment policy, however, uses these terms to determine which positions are open to female soldiers.

Changes in combat operations coupled with the army's restructuring into modular brigades prompted several congressional leaders to review the Department of Defense's compliance with its assignment policy for women.[53] Recent research suggests that the army is in violation of its own policy, although it is still within the regulations set by the Department of Defense. Feedback from deployed soldiers, however, suggests that female soldiers, in addition to their professional skills, bring unique capabilities, such as their culturally sanctioned ability to interact with local women, to the battlefield. Owing to these strengths, the assignment policy for female soldiers, and for military women more broadly, will continue as a contested policy topic, particularly as the OIF and OEF missions demonstrate the need for diverse military personnel.

The Reserve Component

The United States military does not go to war with the Active Component alone. Across the full spectrum of conflict, and particularly missions centered on homeland defense and stabilization, contemporary military operations would not be possible without the participation of the Reserve Component of the armed forces.[54] Like the active duty forces, the Reserve Component also has experienced recruiting challenges and demographic changes within the past decade.[55] These manpower issues are further complicated by the important balancing act that military reservists, whose civilian capacities and roles make them a unique military resource, must negotiate with the high operations tempo necessitated by the post-9/11 military mission. The American military has not always funded or trained the Reserves as a full operational partner. However, the current wars in Afghanistan and Iraq, as well as ongoing internal threats, have demonstrated the centrality of these forces to mission success.

Although past debates frame the twentieth-century Reserve Component as a "strategic force," the Reserves, particularly the National Guard, have been the major source of military personnel from the American Revolution to today's ongoing wars.[56] Before World War II, the United States did not have a large standing army; state militias, for example, were mobilized to provide the overwhelming majority of manpower for both sides of the Civil War. Likewise, approximately 400,000 Guardsmen served in World War I and almost 300,000 Guardsmen served in World War II. The establishment of a standing military after World War II led to the subsequent development of the Reserve Component as an expansion base for cold war era conflicts. During the Korean War, reservists filled over one-third of manpower billets during the initial wartime mobilization.

Although the Reserves have played a significant role in all major American conflicts of the twentieth century, they were not mobilized in large numbers for overseas combat duty during the Vietnam War. This was the first time in modern American history that political leaders opted not to mobilize a substantial proportion of reservists.[57] For those reservists who did serve, a mere 36 units from the National Guard, they comprised less than 1 percent of the overall military force deployed during the Vietnam War. They also played a minimal role in ongoing deterrence efforts in Europe.

By not using the Reserves, political leaders reassured the American public of their limited military engagement in Vietnam. Military leaders, in contrast, viewed the misuse of reservists as a disastrous policy maneuver that led to increased reliance on conscripts to the detriment of already tenuous civil-military relations. To prevent a similar misuse of forces in future conflicts, military leaders, led by the then secretary of defense Melvin Laird and former chief of staff of the army, General Creighton Abrams, passed what is now known as the Abrams Doctrine. This doctrine restructured military manpower so that military missions, across the spectrum of military conflict, would require the mobilization of the Reserve Component.[58] By relying on a Total Force, the military would avoid overuse of active duty forces, would necessitate public support for even minor military operations, and would resituate the Reserves as an equal partner meriting on-par training, responsibility, and support.

The Abrams Doctrine was put into action in the 1990s, as active duty forces had been reduced by 30 percent.[59] Reserve units were activated for Operation Desert Storm, although no combat brigades actually participated in the conflict because of its short duration. In the mid-1990s, the military deployed Reserve personnel overseas as part of the American contingent to the Multinational Force and Observers in the Sinai Desert in support of the Camp David Accords.[60] Reserve success in that operation led to increased use of Reserve personnel for contingency operations such as Bosnia. These involved small proportions of overall personnel deployed and were generally limited to six months.[61]

Although the Reserves have always been a key operational force, their role has changed substantially during OEF and OIF owing to the intense operations tempo and the accompanying long, and sometimes, unpredictable deployments of these operations. In mid-2008, Reserve forces constituted 40–50 percent of American military personnel serving in the area of responsibility for counterterrorism operations.[62] They are at the core of many essential functions, such as transportation, medical service and civil affairs, in which they provide 80 percent, 75 percent and 98 percent, respectively, of military personnel.[63] Within the army, 53 percent of combat forces, 38 percent of combat support, and 34 percent of combat service support units are from the National Guard. Similarly, the Army Reserve adds 26 percent of combat support units and 34 percent of combat service support units.[64]

The military now stresses continued reliance on the Reserve Component and the importance of incorporating it as a full operational partner. The army, for example, states that full integration of Reserve units with their active duty counterparts is critical for mission success. The army has institutionalized this paradigm shift by recasting the Reserve Component as an equal-partner operational force through its Army Force Generation Model (ARFORGEN), which guides preparation and deployment of both active and Reserve brigade combat teams for global missions. To accomplish this, army and civilian leadership must structure, equip, train, man, and resource Reserve units at full and equal levels.[65] This involves reciprocal relationships of active duty and Reserve personnel where skill sets are promoted and exchanged equally.

Despite the goal of returning the Reserve Component to its pre-Vietnam capacity as full operational partners, the increased use of the Reserves for OEF and OIF has led to new problems.[66] The ongoing deployment demands required in the post-9/11 military landscape has strained all components of the military and has exposed the need to increase military manpower. The active duty army and Marine Corps already have secured increased end-strength; the Reserve Component also will grow by 9,200 additional troops within the next few years.[67]

The continuous deployment schedule also highlights the need for implementing a realistic mobilization schedule for reservists, their families, and their civilian employers. To prepare for the counterinsurgency and stabilization missions of OEF and OIF, reservists often require more preparation time than their active duty counterparts for mobilization, training, deployment, redeployment, and demobilization. This process adds 6 months to tours that are already 12 to 15 months in duration, a time requirement that is particularly burdensome for citizen-soldiers. The strain on both personnel and equipment prompted Lt. Gen Ron Helmly, the then chief of the Army Reserve, to inform other army leaders that the Reserve force "is rapidly degenerating into a broken force."[68] A year after, the DOD issued a "planning metric" directing the army to mobilize the National Guard once every five years and the Army Reserves once every four years; it also finalized the transformation of the Reserves' brigade structure and the modernization of its inventory with more light brigades.[69]

The centrality of the Reserve Component to the success of the post-9/11 missions demonstrates the importance of equipping, manning, and training Reserve forces at equal and interchangeable levels with their active duty counterparts. The Reserves already have seen their role rebound to their pre-Vietnam operational role. It remains to be seen how their involvement shapes public opinion, military action, and political decision making, as outlined in the Abrams Doctrine.

Private Military Contractors

In addition to the manpower changes experienced by uniformed service members, Department of Defense civilians, and particularly private military contractors (PMCs), have experienced significant developments regarding their role within post-9/11 missions. These changes are guided by the Department of Defense's Total Force concept that approaches manpower as a cohesive whole built from the Active and Reserve Components and Department civilians; each subset brings a unique capability to the mission. Although many military and political leaders consider private military contractors as "force multipliers" within OEF and OIF, the wartime presence of PMCs is controversial due to their significant representation within the Area of Responsibility (AOR) and the military's increased dependence on them for mission fulfillment.[70] Their use also challenges past conceptions of public service and state-sanctioned violence, particularly as they fill a void created by years of manpower reductions of uniformed service members.

The rise of PMCs coincides with the military's post–cold war downsizing and the transition from deterrence to peace operations. The United States' dependence on PMCs matured during the Balkan Wars of the 1990s, as the power vacuum created by the Soviet Union's collapse erupted in Europe's backyard and the downsizing of American military forces led to a surplus of personnel qualified for private security work.[71] The American public did not support major military operations in the former Yugoslavia, making Reserve mobilization, as outlined in the Abrams Doctrine, politically challenging.[72] Rather than call up 9,000 reservists, the American military transferred military manpower needs to private military contractors, setting precedent for the current use of private contractors in OEF and particularly OIF.

Whereas in the past, contractors fulfilled mainly support and consulting services, they now provide essentially military services, despite the unstable environment of the AOR and the fragility of counterinsurgency operations.[73] Further, the ratio of American troops to private contracts has changed significantly within the past decade: what was once a 51 to 1 ratio during Operation Desert Storm has developed into a 10 to 1 ratio in OIF.[74] The overall number of contractor personnel within Iraq is estimated to be approximately 196,000 with 127,00 employed under Department of Defense contracts and the remainder contracted through the Department of State (including the former Coalition Provisional Authority), and United States Agency for International Development (USAID).[75]

The decision to arm private contractors for ostensibly defensive purposes, such as convoy and personnel protection, places them in potentially explosive situations in which they may act, regardless of situational necessity, in ways that hinder military strategy and without the legal cover of combatant status.[76] Although it is argued that a significant percentage of contractors are prior military personnel familiar with military doctrine and strategy, there have been several major incidents within Iraq that demonstrate how contractors, particularly as they operate outside the command and control of uniformed commanders, may undermine military counterinsurgency operations.[77] There may be an increased tendency, known as the "loose cannon effect," for contractors to act without considering how individual actions affect the operational necessity of winning local "hearts and minds." This lack of transparency and accountability regarding contractor actions is further crippled by the government's inability to punish contractor infraction through current legal systems.[78]

There are also concerns that PMCs may shortchange equipment and personnel requirements to increase profitability. The exchange of mission safety and efficacy for private prerogatives potentially fueled incidents such as the 2004 ambush, shooting, and desecration of four Blackwater personnel in Fallujah.[79] There is also the potential to design sprawling military bases that, rather than support counterinsurgency operations, detract from them by separating troops from the local population.[80]

Despite concerns about their usage in counterinsurgency environments, private military contractors bring unique capabilities to the mission, further carving out their role as a Total Force component. Within Iraq, the majority of private contractors are natives or third-country nationals who, in addition to their underpaid service, provide cultural and linguistic assistance.[81] The use of for-hire bodies also minimizes military casualties; this is a consequence that is particularly beneficial when faced with low public support. Finally, government leaders claim that increased privatization of the Total Force creates cost savings that are returned to the tax-paying citizen; however, this point is unsubstantiated and its counter, increased spending, may be more common.[82]

Perhaps the most controversial benefit of using PMCs is the ability to engage in operations without explicit support from Congress or the public.[83] The Abrams Doctrine led to the restructuring of the military so that war could only be waged with the support of Reserve forces. Controversial wars using an All-volunteer Force would be tempered by the call-up of reservists, creating an internal check for the continuation of long, unpopular wars. Despite the operational presence of the Reserve Component in post-9/11 missions, political leaders and policy planners have blocked the overall significance of national mobilization through the use of contractors. Policy makers have been able to meet the demands of the wartime force without repeatedly mobilizing reserve units or most importantly, reinstating conscription.[84]

Conclusion

The military's current manpower policies and resources, which have been shaped by historical processes, are in an unprecedented position. The United States has entered into OEF and OIF with an All-Volunteer Force reliant upon the Reserve Component and civilian contractors for mission fulfillment. As demonstrated by our analysis, there are consequences, both intended and unintended, to engaging in a long war without conscripts.

First, whereas conscription allowed military planners to select personnel directly, today's military competes with other attractive occupational and educational paths for its recruits. The army and Marine Corps, in particular, must substantially increase their ranks within the next few years; this is a challenge that has led them to pursue decreased accession standards. Concerns regarding troop demographics also carry over into the changing racial and ethnic composition of the force. The percentage of black personnel has declined; however, the percentage of Latinos joining the service is increasing, thus offsetting the decreased enlistment propensity among blacks. Noncitizens are also joining the military in greater numbers, with many using it as a pathway to citizenship. Women remain a significant minority within all the service branches, despite the opening of most occupational specialties to them. Their presence and performance continue to garner significant attention from political and military leaders, particularly as the insurgency battleground does not allow for clear distinctions between offensive combat positions, from which women are prohibited, and combat support. The Reserve Component also has seen its role change substantially with the post-9/11 military mission. The military now stresses continued reliance on the Reserves and, in accordance with the Abrams Doctrine, views the Reserves as a full operational partner that must be mobilized during war. The presence of private military contractors, however, challenges the necessity of calling upon citizen-soldiers, and by extension courting public opinion, by allowing political leaders to circumvent unpopular mobilizations with for-hire bodies. The military's current manpower policies and resources, as demonstrated by the shifting boundaries between active duty, Reserve Component, and civilian forces, once again are experiencing unprecedented change. With conscription politically untenable, the question is how will political and military leaders maintain force quality, a demographically representative force, and perhaps most importantly, a uniformed force when faced with long, and at times unpopular, wars.

Notes

The writing of this chapter was supported by the U.S. Army Research Institute for the Behavioral and Social Sciences under Contract W74V8H-05-K-0007. The views expressed in this chapter are those of the authors and not necessarily of the Army Research Institute, the Department of the Army, or the Department of Defense.

1. See Meredith A. Kleykamp, "College, Jobs, or the Military? Enlistment during a Time of War," *Social Science Quarterly* 87, no.2 (June 2006): 272–290. Also, in July 2008 a new GI Bill was passed, partly to facilitate recruitment and retention. This bill, known as the Post-9/11 Veterans Education Assistance Act, covers a four-year degree at a public university. See U.S. Department of Veterans Affairs, *Fact Sheet: The Post-9/11 Veterans Education Assistance Act of 2008* (Washington, DC: Veterans Benefits Administration, 2008).

2. Ann Scott Tyson, "Military Waivers for Ex-Convicts Increase," *Washington Post,* April 22, 2008; Lawrence Kapp, *Recruiting and Retention: An Overview of FY2005 and FY2006 for Active and Reserve Component Enlisted Personnel* (Washington, DC: Congressional Research Service, 2006), 3.

3. *Baker-Hamilton Report Evokes Modest Public Interest* (Washington, DC: The Pew Research Center for the People & the Press, 2006); *Public Attitudes toward the War in Iraq: 2003–2008* (Washington, DC: The Pew Research Center for the People & the Press, 2008).

4. Beth J. Asch, John A. Romley, and Mark E. Totten, *The Quality of Personnel in the Enlisted Ranks* (Santa Monica, CA: RAND, 2005), 9.

5. Barry L. Scribner et al., "Are Smart Tankers Better? AFQT and Military Productivity," *Armed Forces & Society* 12, no. 2 (1986):193–206; M. S. Teachout and M. W. Pellum, *Air Force Research to Link Standards for Enlistment to On-the-Job Performance* (Brooks Air Force Base, TX: Air Force Human Resources Laboratory, Training Systems Division, 1991); Bruce R. Orvis, Michael T. Childress, and J. Michael Polich, *Effect of Personnel Quality on the Performance of Patriot Air Defense System Operators* (Santa Monica, CA: RAND, 1992).

6. Bruce R. Orvis and Beth J. Asch, *Military Recruiting: Trends, Outlook, and Implications* (Santa Monica, CA: RAND, 2000), 42.

7. Asch, Romley, and Totten, *The Quality of Personnel*, 1.

8. Kapp, *Recruiting and Retention*, 4.

9. Ibid.

10. Ibid. Beginning in the mid-1980s, the DOD limited recruits with lower mental aptitude to 2 percent of annual accessions; however, this benchmark was expanded to 4 percent of annual accessions for each service branch in 2005.

11. Tyson, "Military Waivers."

12. Ibid. The navy saw a decrease in felony waivers from 48 in FY2006 to 42 in FY2007. The air force did not have any felony waivers for either year.

13. U.S. Army, "Army Readiness Detailed," Army Public Affairs, http://www4.army.mil/ocpa/read.php?story_id_key=9568 (accessed July 8, 2008).

14. Leonard L. Etcho, "The Effect of Moral Waivers on First-Term, Unsuitability Attrition in the Marine Corps" (master's thesis, Naval Postgraduate School, 1996).

15. Paul Sackett and Anne Mavor, eds., *Attitudes, Aptitudes, and Aspirations of American Youth: Implications for Military Recruitment* (Washington, DC: The National Academies Press, 2003), 93–94.

16. U.S. Congress, *National Defense Authorization Act of Fiscal Year 2006,* 109th Congress, 2006, Public Law 109–163.

17. Lisa Burgess, "Army Raises Maximum Enlistment Age," *Stars and Stripes,* June 23, 2006; Tom Vanden Brook, "Older Recruits Are Finding Less Success in Army," *USA Today,* February 19, 2007.

18. U.S. Department of Defense, Office of the Under Secretary of Defense, Personnel, and Readiness, *2006 Population Representation in the Military Services,* 2.

19. Charles C. Moskos, "From Institution to Occupation: Trends in Military Organization," *Armed Forces & Society* 4, no. 1 (1977): 41–50; Harry A. Marmion, *The Case against a Volunteer Army* (Chicago: Quadrangle Books, 1971); Morris Janowitz and Charles C. Moskos, "Racial Composition in the All-Volunteer Force," *Armed Forces & Society* 1, no. 1 (1974): 109–123.

20. David R. Segal and Mady Wechsler Segal, *Army Recruitment Goals Endangered as Percent of African American Enlistees Declines* (Washington, DC: Population Reference Bureau, 2005).

21. David R. Segal, *Recruiting for Uncle Sam* (Lawrence, KS: University Press of Kansas, 1989), 112.

22. Ibid. *2006 Population Representation in the Military Services,* 2.

23. Michael Wilson et al., *Youth Attitude Tracking Study 1992: Propensity and Advertising Report* (Alexandria, VA: U.S. Army Research Institute for the Behavioral and Social Sciences, 1993); Segal and Segal, *Army Recruitment.*

24. *2006 Population Representation in the Military Services,* 3.

25. Mady Wechsler Segal and David R. Segal, *Latinos Claim Larger Share of U.S. Military Personnel* (Washington, DC: Population Reference Bureau, 2007).

26. Sackett and Mavor, *Attitudes, Aptitudes and Aspirations,* 255.

27. David L. Leal, "American Public Opinions toward the Military: Differences by Race, Gender, and Class?" *Armed Forces & Society* 32, no. 1 (2005), 131.

28. Anita U. Hattiangadi, Gary Lee, and Aline O. Quester, *Recruiting Hispanics: The Marine Corps Experience, Final Report* (Alexandria, VA: Center for Naval Analyses, 2004), 1.

29. Ibid.

30. The largest proportion of noncitizen soldiers is from the Philippines, followed by Mexico. The complete distribution of countries of citizenship for noncitizen service members is in Margaret Mikyung Lee and Ruth Ellen Wasem, *Expedited Citizenship through Military Service: Policy and Issues* (Washington, DC: Congressional Research Service, 2003), 7.

31. Hattiangadi et al., *Non-Citizens in Today's Military: Final Report* (Alexandria, VA: Center for Naval Analyses, 2005), 32.

32. Ibid., 1.

33. Ibid.

34. Ibid., 6.

35. U.S. Citizenship and Immigration Services, Office of Communications. "Fact Sheet: Naturalization through Military Service," http://www.uscis.gov/files/pressrelease/milnatz_280108.pdf (accessed July 10, 2008).

36. Martin Binkin and Shirley J. Bach, *Women and the Military* (Washington, DC: Brookings Institution, 1977), 4; This legislation ruled that women could constitute no more than 2 percent of the total force and that women officers could only constitute up to 10 percent of that 2 percent. This legislation was later modified by Public Law 90–130 that lifted the 2 percent quota. The Women's Armed Services Integration Act also forbade women from serving on navy vessels (except for

medical transport ships) and in combat aircraft. See Lory Manning, *Women in the Military: Where they Stand*, 5th ed. (Washington, DC: Women's Research and Education Institute, 2005).

37. U.S. Department of Labor and U.S. Bureau of Labor Statistics, *Women in the Labor Force: A Handbook* (Washington, DC: Government Printing Office, 2007).

38. Martin Binkin, *Who Will Fight the Next War? The Changing Face of the American Military* (Washington, DC: Brookings Institution, 1993), 18.

39. Ibid., 22–24.

40. Les Aspin, Secretary of Defense, "Direct Ground Combat Definition and Assignment Rule," memorandum, January 13, 1994.

41. U.S. Department of Defense, Office of the Under Secretary of Defense, Personnel, and Readiness, *2005 Population Representation in the Military Services*, 3.

42. U.S. Department of Defense, *2006 Population Representation in the Armed Forces*.

43. Ibid., table D-13.

44. Ibid., table D-19.

45. Douglas Quenqua, "Sending in the Marines (to Recruit Women)," *New York Times*, April 21, 2008.

46. David R. Segal et al., "Propensity to Serve in the U.S. Military: Temporal Trends and Subgroup Differences," *Armed Forces & Society* 25, no. 3 (1999): 416.

47. Binkin, *Who Will Fight the Next War? The Changing Face of the American Military*.

48. For additional information on how cultural values shape women's military roles, see Mady Wechsler Segal, "Women's Military Roles Cross-Nationally: Past, Present, and Future," *Gender & Society* 9, no. 6 (December 1995): 757–775.

49. From the beginning of OEF until May 1, 2008, 590 women have been injured and 107 women have been killed in action. See Headquarters, U.S. Department of the Army, Army Regulation 600–13, Army *Policy for the Assignment of Female Soldiers*, March 27, 1992; Margaret C. Harrell et al., *Assessing the Assignment Policy for Army Women*, (Arlington, VA: RAND, 2007); Ann Scott Tyson, "Women in the Line of Fire," *Washington Post*, May 1, 2008.

50. The Silver Star recipient for OEF is Army PFC (Private First Class) Monica Brown, a medic. Within a week of her heroic actions, PFC Brown was removed from her squad because, as a woman, she was not allowed to serve in a combat unit. See Ann Scott Tyson, "Woman Gains Silver Star—And Removal from Combat," *Washington Post*, May 1, 2008; The Silver Star recipient for OIF is Sgt. Leigh Ann Hester, a Guardsman from Kentucky. See Ann Scott Tyson, "Soldier Earns Her Star for Her Role in Defeating Ambush," *Washington Post*, June 17, 2005.

51. Headquarters, U.S. Department of the Army, *Army Policy for the Assignment of Female Soldiers*; Harrell, et al., *Assessing the Assignment Policy for Army Women*.

52. Harrell et al., *Assessing the Assignment Policy*, 16.

53. U.S. Congress, *National Defense Authorization Act of Fiscal Year 2006*.

54. The Reserve Component includes the Army and Air National Guard, the Army Reserve, the Air Force Reserve, the Navy Reserve, the Marine Corps Reserve, and the Coast Guard Reserve. See Christine E. Wormuth et al., *The Future of the National Guard and Reserves: The Beyond Goldwater-Nichols Phase III Report* (Washington, DC: Center for Strategic and International Studies, 2006).

55. Kapp, *Recruiting and Retention*.

56. For more information on the ongoing discussion framing Reserve forces as strategic versus operational forces, see Ralph Wipfli and Dallas D. Owens, *Colloquium Brief: State of the U.S. Military Reserve Components* (Carlisle Barracks, PA: U.S. Army War College and 21st Century Defense Initiative of the Brookings Institution, 2008).

57. David R. Segal and Mady Wechsler Segal, *U.S. Military's Reliance on the Reserves* (Washington, DC: Population Reference Bureau, 2005).

58. Timothy I. Sullivan, *The Abrams Doctrine: Is It Viable and Enduring in the 21stCentury?* (Carlisle Barracks, PA: Strategic Studies Institute of the U.S. Army War College, 2005).

59. Ibid.

60. Ruth H. Phelps and Beatrice J. Farr, eds. *Reserve Component Soldiers as Peacekeepers* (Alexandria, VA: U.S. Army Research Institute for the Behavioral and Social Sciences, 1996).

61. David R. Segal, "Military Sociology," in *21st Century Sociology: A Reference Handbook,* ed. Clifton D. Bryant and Dennis L. Peck (Thousand Oaks, CA: Sage, 2006).

62. Ibid.

63. Wipfli and Owens, *Colloquium Brief.*

64. Sullivan, *The Abrams Doctrine,* 7.

65. Joseph. E. Whitlock, *How to Make Army Force Generation Work for the Army's Reserve Components* (Carlisle Barracks, PA: Strategic Studies Institute of the Army War College, 2006).

66. Lynn E. Davis et al., *Stretched Thin: Army Forces for Sustained Operations* (Santa Monica, CA: RAND, 2005), 3.

67. Wipfli and Owens, *Colloquium Brief,* 2.

68. Bradley Graham, "General Says Army Reserve Is Becoming a Broken Force," *Washington Post,* January 6, 2005.

69. Davis et al., *Stretched Thin,* 36.

70. Jennifer K. Elsea and Nina M. Serafino, *Private Security Contractors in Iraq: Background, Legal Status, and Other Issues* (Washington, DC: Congressional Research Service, 2007), 24.

71. P. W. Singer, *Corporate Warriors* (Ithaca, NY: Cornell University Press, 2003); Allison Stanger and Mark Eric Williams, "Private Military Corporations: Benefits and Costs of Outsourcing Security," *Yale Journal of International Affairs* 2, no.1 (Fall/Winter 2006): 5.

72. Singer, *Corporate Warriors,* 6.

73. Ibid. Elsea and Serafino, *Private Security Contractors,* 1.

74. Stanger and Williams, "Private Military Corporations," 4.

75. Elsea and Serafino, *Private Security Contractors,* 3; William M. Solis (statement), *Military Operations: Implementation of Existing Guidance and Other Actions Needed to Improve DOD's Oversight and Management of Contractors in Future Operations* (Washington, DC: U.S. Government Accountability Office, 2008), 1.

76. Elsea and Serafino, *Private Security Contractors.*

77. Singer, *Corporate Warriors.* The most prominent examples are Najaf, the Nisoor Square shootings in Baghdad, and Fallujah. All these incidents involved Blackwater employees. The Department of Justice indicted five Blackwater employees involved in the Nisoor Square shootings in December 2008. The trial is

tentatively scheduled for February 2010. See Del Quentin Wilber, "Judge Refuses to Dismiss Charges against Blackwater Guards," *Washington Post,* February 19, 2009.

78. For further discussion on the legal questions surrounding contractors working in the Area of Responsibility, see Elsea and Serafino, *Private Security Contractors.* The United States has agreed, in concurrence with Iraqi request, to drop immunity from security contractors operating in Iraq. See Karen DeYoung and Sudarsan Raghavan, "U.S. Iraqi Negotiators Agree on 2011 Withdrawal," *Washington Post,* August 22, 2008.

79. In this situation, there is evidence that Blackwater management sent out a four-man convoy team without armor-plated vehicles and with two less personnel than required. See United States House of Representatives, Committee on Oversight and Government Reform, *Private Military Contractors in Iraq: An Examination of Blackwater's Actions in Fallujah,* 2007.

80. P. W. Singer, *Can't Win with 'Em, Can't Win without 'Em: Private Military Contractors and Counterinsurgency* (Washington, DC: Brookings Institution, 2007). Also see, Rajiv Chandrasekaran, *Imperial Life in the Emerald City* (New York: Vintage Books, 2006).

81. Elsea and Serafino, *Private Security Contractors,* 4.

82. Ibid.

83. Stanger and Williams, "Private Military Corporations," 8.

84. Elsea and Serafino, *Private Security Contractors,* 24.

Chapter 5

FEMA in Shambles: 9/11 and the Nation's Capacity to Deal with Catastrophic Disasters

William L. Waugh, Jr.*

The attacks on 9/11 had profound effect upon the nation's system for dealing with catastrophic disasters. In the decade before the attacks, the Federal Emergency Management Agency (FEMA) and its state and local counterparts had developed a common approach to natural and unnatural (man-made) hazards and collaborative processes for managing major disasters. The response to the 9/11 attacks was not without flaw, but the system did work. FEMA supported local and state emergency management efforts in New York and local agencies in Virginia came to the aid of Pentagon officials. In some measure, the responses to 9/11 demonstrated the importance of local emergency management capacities in large-scale disasters. Local and state capabilities have expanded since 9/11, but federal capabilities have been seriously damaged since 2001. This chapter begins with an assessment of the impact of 9/11 on federal capabilities, largely in terms of the impact upon FEMA, and concludes with an assessment of the impact upon state and local capabilities to deal with catastrophic disaster.

Introduction

The 9/11 attacks focused the nation's attention on the threat of terrorism and away from the threats from natural and technological disasters that had been

---
*William L. Waugh, Jr., is Professor of Public Administration and Urban Studies at Georgia State University. He is the author of seven books including *Living with Hazards, Dealing with Disasters*, and *International Terrorism*.

the very reason why FEMA was created in 1979. Decision processes were centralized; the FEMA director lost direct contact with the president; and the agency was stripped of critical resources and some part of its mission. Before FEMA's integration into the Department of Homeland Security in 2003, much of the agency's work was conducted through its 10 regional offices. The regional offices were closely linked to state and local emergency management offices that facilitated support before, during, and after major disasters. While the links were not without friction, they were vast improvements on the relationships that existed during the 1980s and, especially, during the early 1990s when Congress threatened to disassemble the agency and return its constituent parts to the departments from whence they had originally come. The regional offices lost their autonomy, and their relationships with state and local agencies deteriorated quickly as new mandates were issued. FEMA had been much more proactive in responding to major disasters and had become a leader in developing the profession of emergency management at all levels. Under DHS, however, the agency became reactive. When tested by Katrina's landfall on the Louisiana and Mississippi coasts in 2005, it proved no longer able to deal with a catastrophic disaster.

By most measures, the responses to Hurricanes Katrina and Rita were a disaster. News coverage of the victims in the New Orleans Superdome was an embarrassment to local, state, and federal officials from the mayor's office in New Orleans to the White House in Washington. The political costs of failure were felt most acutely in Baton Rouge, where widespread criticism encouraged Governor Blanco not to run for reelection (and a new Republican governor took office), and in Washington where President Bush's approval ratings dropped precipitously.[1] Public confidence in national leadership was seriously damaged, as was the United States' image around the world. While the disaster response included extraordinary, indeed heroic, actions, the failures were revealed dramatically in the national and international media. What happened?

The after-action reports concluded that there were leadership, communications, logistics, and command-and-control problems. Critical state resources, that is, National Guard units, were unavailable because they had been deployed to Iraq and Afghanistan. State and local agencies were ill-prepared to deal with a major hurricane even though an exercise to deal with a hypothetical hurricane, "Hurricane Pam," had been conducted in Baton Rouge only a little over a year earlier. In many respects, the weaknesses were known but not addressed. Moreover, what happened in New Orleans and other coastal communities was not a surprise. FEMA was at the center of the controversy as the director's e-mail messages revealed a lack of connection with the events unfolding in New Orleans' Superdome; the Homeland Security secretary's and the president's public statements similarly revealed a lack of understanding of the scope of the catastrophe and the need for quick action. Federal assets were deployed slowly and officials struggled to address the critical needs of the coastal communities and the evacuated populations.[2] Years after Katrina dissipated in the north Atlantic, FEMA is still trying to find permanent housing for victims living in trailers and to discourage rebuilding in floodplains that may be inundated by the next major hurricane. The recovery process has been intensely political as communities wrestle with land-use issues.

What happened to FEMA between its "golden age" during the Clinton administration and its failures during the Katrina disaster? The short answer is 9/11 and the absorption of FEMA into the Department of Homeland Security (DHS). A more complex answer is the shortsightedness of disaster policy makers, the disruptions caused by an almost constant state of reorganization, incompatibilities in organizational culture within DHS, slow implementation of plans and procedures for dealing with catastrophic disasters, a political milieu characterized by severe budget constraints, reliance upon third parties for the delivery of public services, and a changing definition of the government's role in addressing risks to people, property, and the environment. Conflicts over governmental authority in the federal system and a demographic shift in public employment further compounded the problems.

The Fixation on Terrorism

Craig Fugate, the head of the Florida emergency management agency, has complained about "terrorism hysteria" because too many officials are fixated on the threat of terrorism when there are many other threats, some more certain and some more lethal.[3] For officials in Florida, hurricanes are *the* major risk. For officials in California, earthquakes are *the* major risk. To divert attention and resources away from the most likely threats is not responsible. That does not mean that terrorism is not an important issue, but it does mean that the threat of terrorism is a less compelling issue and resources may be better used on the primary risk.

A truism in disaster policy is that new government programs tend to address what happened during the last disaster and not what is likely to occur in the next. The focus of DHS has largely remained on the threat of terrorism and budget allocations for the protection of civil aviation and the nation's borders have grown, but there is considerably more interest and investment in catastrophic planning. The major disasters in the U.S. before Katrina were the four hurricanes that crossed central Florida in 2004. Governor Jeb Bush was the "incident commander" and he made sure that state officials guided the responses. The federal government was clearly in a supporting role despite DHS's evident interest in taking more of a lead. The same year, the great tsunami in the Indian Ocean devastated the coastlines of Indonesia, Thailand, Sri Lanka, and other literal nations as it crossed the Pacific to Africa. Budget and personnel cuts in the U.S. tsunami program were restored and ultimately the United States aided in the development of a tsunami warning system in the Indian Ocean, in addition to extending its own program into the Atlantic. The growing interest in catastrophic planning is probably due to these recent disasters.

Emergency management in the United States has been built around the all-hazards perspective. Having an emergency plan for every conceivable or even most likely circumstance is not practical or cost efficient. All-hazards plans focus on the similarities among disasters and typically outline the common evacuation, shelter-in-place, mass feeding and sheltering, and other needs with supplementary annexes outlining needs specific to particular kinds of disasters, if necessary. While there are obvious differences between a terrorist attack and an earthquake, there are more similarities than differences in how emergency management organizations might respond. The collapse of the World Trade Center towers was very much like a high-rise fire, a structural collapse, and a hazardous materials accident—albeit on a much larger scale. Fifteen planning scenarios, twelve terrorist-related disasters and three natural disasters (a hurricane, an earthquake, and a pandemic), have guided Homeland Security planning and decision making. The focus on terrorist-related disasters has alienated state and local emergency management officials who have to be concerned with the most likely kind of events in their jurisdictions.

Reorganization Problems within DHS

Coordination of the agencies and programs within the Department of Homeland Security is a continuing problem. Reorganizations are disruptive. The reorganization of the Department of Defense in 1946 is still causing ripples and branches of the military compete for resources and missions. When the Department of Homeland Security was created in 2003, FEMA was a very small part of a very large bureaucracy. The FEMA director had enjoyed cabinet-level status during the Clinton administration and decisions regarding presidential disaster declarations and lesser declarations could be worked out directly with the president. The proximity to the Oval Office also afforded the director greater authority in coordinating federal disaster assistance. Twenty-two agencies and programs were drawn into the new department. FEMA's manpower numbered a little over 5,000 in a department with over 170,000 employees, not counting the 25,000 to 30,000 passenger screeners hired soon thereafter. The major components of the new department were the U.S. Coast Guard, the Transportation Security Administration, the Border Patrol, the Immigration and Naturalization Service, the Animal and Plant Health Inspection Service, and the Secret Service—all with law enforcement functions—and FEMA. Dealing with natural and technological disasters simply was not a priority for DHS.

A Government Accountability Office report in 2007 concluded that FEMA "experienced near constant organizational change from fiscal years 2001 through 2005 that caused considerable flux in FEMA's resources." The report went on to note that "a significant number of programs and their associated funding moved into and out of FEMA" and that "the movement was disruptive to operations and created uncertainty about the availability of resources."[4]

Diversion of Resources from FEMA to DHS

The 9/11 attacks focused the nation's attention on the threat of terrorism and emergency managers became soldiers in the War on Terror. FEMA was subsumed into the Department of Homeland Security in 2003. The agency was tasked with supporting counterterrorism programs, personnel were transferred to law enforcement and security programs, and the director's direct link to the president during disasters was eliminated. FEMA's role in dealing with hazards and disasters was proscribed by the department's priorities. Along with resource and mission constraints, the culture of collaboration that FEMA had developed in the 1990s conflicted with the culture of Homeland Security. As a result, morale suffered and FEMA lost experienced personnel through early retirements and transfers.

In the Senate hearing on the Katrina response, Mr. Michael Brown described the problems that plagued FEMA during the period before and during the disaster. He stated that "[FEMA's] mission had been marginalized. Its response capability had been diminished. There's the whole clash of cultures between DHS mission to prevent terrorism and FEMA's mission to respond to and to prepare for responding to disasters of whatever nature." A study had been commissioned from the Mitre Corporation early in 2005 and its March report indicated that the agency had "unclear lines of responsibility" that caused accountability problems and a lack of administrative support with operational experience. The agency's senior officials were political appointees with little or no emergency management experience. In essence, officials lacked experienced advisors. The top of the agency hierarchy was layers of political appointees without emergency management expertise. In 2004, a group of "senior FEMA operational professionals, the federal coordinating officers cadre," warned that teams were unprepared with "zero funding" for training and equipment. The group recommended recreating the response and recovery directorate that was disassembled by DHS.[5]

The agency was also entrusted with the task of providing start-up funding for DHS; however, the funds allocated were disproportionate to the needs of the larger agencies in the department. Poor planning within FEMA exacerbated the funding problems. "Even FEMA staff's strong sense of mission is no substitute for a plan and strategies for action," according to the report.[6]

Cultural Incompatibilities between FEMA and DHS

Because DHS's leadership has been drawn from law enforcement and national security agencies, including the U.S. Coast Guard, its culture has been strongly influenced by those disciplines. FEMA has historically had national security functions, including responsibilities for dealing with the threat of terrorism, but the dominance of the old civil preparedness programs had waned as the focus changed to natural and technological disasters. The focus also changed from emergency response to disaster mitigation. From the 1980s onward, emergency management agencies at all levels were increasingly built around the four phases or functions of mitigation, preparedness, response, and recovery. The emphasis was on mitigation programs to prevent or lessen the effects of disaster rather than on disaster response. Project Impact, the "disaster resistant" communities program, represented the leading edge in risk reduction and the mantra became "one dollar spent on mitigation saved four dollars in recovery."[7] To make those programs work, FEMA became more open and collaborative. Strong working relationships with the agency's state and local counterparts were essential, particularly when the agency lacked authority to force compliance with national goals.

Those changes in culture were reflected in the profession and practice of emergency management. Emergency managers defined their profession and identified the requisite skills and competencies for professionals in the field. The Certified Emergency Manager (CEM) program requires at least three years of broad emergency management experience, one hundred hours of education and training in emergency management, and one hundred more in general management, and continuing involvement in the profession as reflected in activities ranging from leadership positions to making public presentations. The CEM examination questions are drawn from the major reports, books, and other publications recognized as essential to professionals in the field. A common body of knowledge has been defined. The CEM program is administered by the International Association of Emergency Management, the major professional organization for local emergency managers, but FEMA helped initiate the program and it continues to provide support.[8] The CEM designation is recognized as the basic credential for professionals in the field and is adapting somewhat to address Homeland Security functions. But, emergency managers are distinguishing their role and functions clearly from those of Homeland Security officials. The Homeland Security approach is seen simply as inappropriate and ineffective in the practice of emergency management.

Cultural interoperability is critical for effective disaster operations. "FEMAites" refer to the "gun toters" of DHS and joke about how the agency would fare better in the competition for budget allocations if its personnel also wore guns. More seriously, emergency managers had spent decades trying to overcome the stereotype image of the officious Civil Defense warden barking orders.[9] Much of the national emergency management system is nongovernmental and effective relationships are based upon collaboration and open communication.[10]

Bad Times for Government Programs

It may be an understatement to characterize the current political and economic milieu as "bad times" for government programs, but the times are not conducive to investments even in necessary programs and the compelling issues are energy, the war in Iraq, and climate change. Even the concern about terrorism is waning as 9/11 fades from the public memory. Outside of NYC and Washington, DC, many communities do not respond to elevations in the Homeland Security Advisory System because they do not feel as threatened, they do not have the money to pay for increased security precautions, and the system itself offers too little information for most communities to feel affected. FEMA, like other public organizations, has been greatly affected by the notion of a reduced government role, human resources problems caused by the retirement of the "baby boom" generation, and decades of budget constraints. FEMA has never been funded at levels that would permit the agency to address many of the nation's major hazards. In fact, the agency has historically used appropriations for major disasters to build capacity and to implement mitigation programs to reduce the likelihood and/or impact of future disasters. Currently, the Emergency Management Performance Grant (EMPG) program is the barometer of federal support for local capacity building and it has taken a strong lobbying campaign by professional emergency managers, principally through the International Association of Emergency Managers, to maintain funding.

Rebuilding the National Emergency Management System from the Bottom Up

The focus up to this point has been on the impact of 9/11 on FEMA. However, emergency management systems are built from the bottom up rather than from the top down. Local emergency responders and emergency managers most often have to deal with catastrophic disasters until help arrives. The theory is that state agencies provide assistance when local capabilities are overwhelmed and federal agencies provide assistance when state and local capacities are overwhelmed. The reality is that the capabilities are interdependent. Assistance need not be withheld until it is clear that it is needed. In fact, it may be too late if officials wait for requests for assistance on proper forms or via proper channels with documentation of need. Lives may be lost and property destroyed. That was the lesson from Hurricane Hugo in 1989 and Hurricane Andrew in 1992. Material and personnel need to be prepositioned. While federal officials may not respond without a request from the governor, they can facilitate that request and be ready to respond immediately—not 72 or 96 hours after the disaster begins. Nonetheless, local officials may be on their own for days, even weeks, before help arrives. Some communities in Louisiana and Mississippi did not receive help for over a week after Katrina passed through. The scale of the disaster, debris on the roads, damaged bridges and roads, and other impediments, including loss of the telephone systems, left many to fend for themselves. As a result, there is growing sentiment that residents and communities should lower their expectations concerning government assistance and should be prepared to survive on their own for days or even weeks. How much water, food, and other supplies individuals and families should keep is debatable. The old wisdom was that all should have 72-hour kits so that they can survive for at least three days without assistance. After Katrina, some experts suggested kits that would last five to ten days or even longer. The threat of pandemic would suggest that families should have supplies for a much longer time, months, so that they can maintain social distance.

Communities are also developing mechanisms to share resources, including people and equipment, without state or federal assistance. Communities frequently have mutual assistance agreements with neighboring communities for fire and police services (and increasingly other kinds of services, such as information technology). Mississippi generally faired better than Louisiana in the Katrina disaster, because it had a statewide mutual assistance law that facilitated the sharing of resources among communities. Mississippi officials also had good relationships with officials in Florida that facilitated resource sharing.[11] The Emergency Management Assistance Compact deployed almost 66,000 personnel during the Katrina and Rita disasters. Such state-to-state assistance further reduces reliance upon federal resources.[12]

Finding Emergency Management

What was apparent during the Katrina response was that many officials at all levels, as well as the news media and the public, did not understand the role of emergency managers. Many of the decisions made during the response reflected a lack of understanding of emergency management principles and practice. The assumption that "mandatory evacuation" orders would ensure that few residents would remain behind in coastal communities, including New Orleans, was not one that a professional emergency manager would make, for example. Mandatory evacuation is not mandatory in a practical or often even in a legal sense. There is over a half century of social science research on mass evacuation, risk communication, warning systems, and other essential functions. The common wisdom has been tested again and again and professional emergency managers are expected to be knowledge-able and experienced. Nonetheless, the Katrina response made it all too clear that elected officials at all levels evidently did not understand what it is that emergency managers do. Emergency managers were lumped together with firefighters, police officers, search-and-rescue team members, emergency medical services personnel, and others responsible for emergency response. Their role as coordinators and facilitators of emergency response was too often usurped by first responders, military personnel, and public officials without emergency management expertise.

As a result, an initiative was begun in late 2006 by Michael Selves, the then president of the International Association of Emergency Managers, to better define the profession of emergency management and its guiding "principles." What was clear was that emergency managers felt uncomfort-able in the top-down world of Homeland Security. Indeed, many felt that they could not be effective if they followed the guidance being issued by the Department of Homeland Security. While, as Professor Kettl indicated, the structures were not an impediment, the organizational culture was a serious impediment to the development of effective working relationships among federal, state, and local emergency management officials, the media, and the public. The Principles of Emergency Management were identified by a group representing state and local government emergency managers, private sector emergency managers, the Emergency Management Accreditation Program (EMAP) Commission, the National Fire Protection Association (NFPA) 1600 Committee, and the academic community. There was remark-able agreement on the eight principles that underlie the profession and practice of emergency management and the list has been endorsed by the professional organizations represented by the group. A process for review and amendment of the principles has been put in place to ensure that the list will be a living document.

- Comprehensive—including all stakeholders, all phases/functions, all impacts, and all-hazards.
- Progressive—focusing on developing community resilience to prepare for future disasters.
- Collaboration—working closely with public, private, and nonprofit organizations and volunteers toward common goals.
- Integration—meshing governmental and nongovernmental resources.
- Coordination—ensuring common purpose and effective use of resources.
- Flexible—adapting plans to circumstances, innovating, and improvisa-tion when necessary.
- Risk-driven—focusing on real, measured risk.
- Professional—relying upon proven professional standards, scientific knowledge, and the lessons drawn from past disaster experience.[13]

The command-and-control model followed by the Department of Homeland Security was based upon assumptions about the relationships among the participants that were erroneous and about the role of the federal government in natural and unnatural (man-made) disasters that were at least questionable. Increasingly government agencies work in an environment characterized by shared authority among levels of government and among agencies, dispersed resources among governmental and nongovernmental organizations, and expectations of transparency and open communication. The emergency management paradigm has changed from a cavalry approach with agencies rushing in to save the day to a capacity building, supportive approach with government agencies help communities prepare and respond to disasters[14] and, increasingly, encouraging and helping communities manage hazards effectively to prevent or minimize losses. A closed command structure simply does not work and other stakeholders will operate outside of the structure if they have to. In fact, many volunteers and nongovernmental organizations are uncomfortable in a bureaucratic environment and may choose to work outside of the system even if officials try to integrate them into it.[15]

Also, there are now standards and benchmarks for public emergency management programs including mechanisms for collaboration that are increasingly driving disaster operations. The Emergency Management Accreditation Program is recognized as an American National Standards Institute (ANSI)-recognized standard-setting body and it has accredited over half of the state emergency management programs and increasing numbers of local programs.[16] Fundamental to the EMAP standards is the idea that "programs" include the public, private, and nongovernmental organizations that a state or community relies upon in a disaster and formal mechanisms for effective collaboration have to be in place. Agencies are not accredited—programs are. Also fundamental are the ideas that administrative capacity and financial support are critical to the effectiveness of the program.

Conclusions

The 9/11 attacks have had a profound impact upon the nation's system for managing catastrophic disasters—some bad and some good. While FEMA has suffered under the current regime and lost capacity, its state and local counterparts may be stronger, particularly if resources are made available to address weaknesses such as the need for interoperable communications. Some of FEMA's problems predate 9/11 and continue to plague the agency. The Nunn-Lugar-Dominici Act (Defense Against Weapons of Mass Destruction Act) of 1996 distinguished between "crisis management" and "consequence management." The act assumes a clear distinction between the two and relegates emergency management agencies to a secondary and reactive role in the War on Terror dealing with the consequences of disaster rather than a proactive role in preventing and reducing losses. The term "consequence management" is frequently used to suggest that only FEMA should have a role in the aftermath of attacks.

Similarly, the "all-hazards" approach that has been used by emergency management programs for over 30 years is not well understood by many public officials, including many DHS officials. The National Response Framework (NRF) issued in late 2007 uses the term frequently but without evident acknowledging what it implies. The NRF still cites the 15 Homeland Security planning scenarios as the basis for emergency planning. The NRF also provides for a principal federal official (PFO) on the ground during disasters to represent the Homeland Security secretary although authority for the response presumably resides in the federal coordinating official (FCO). While FCOs normally have emergency management experience, it is uncertain whether the PFOs will have any related experience. The PFO role overlaps with the FCO role and having a more senior official on the ground during a disaster is certain to create authority issues. These issues were raised during hearings on the draft NRF by the Subcommittee on Economic Development, Public Buildings, and Emergency Management of the U.S. House of Representatives Committee on Transportation and Infrastructure in September 2007.[17] The PFO position remained in the NRF, however.

Government Accountability Office (GAO) reports following Katrina had found that "DHS needs to more effectively coordinate disaster preparedness, response, and recovery efforts."[18] Leadership was a problem. Disaster management capabilities needed attention. Also, accountability systems to support quick, flexible responses while preventing waste, fraud, and abuse were needed. Authority needed to be defined better to facilitate decision making. To improve disaster capabilities, according to GAO, DHS needs to focus on "(1) situational assessment and awareness; (2) emergency communications; (3) evacuations; (4) search and rescue; (5) logistics; and (6) mass care and sheltering." The comptroller general also recommended that there be a "strategic and integrated approach to prepared for, respond to, recover, and rebuild from catastrophic events." He suggested that Congress evaluate progress with the National Preparedness System, assess state and local capacities and what the federal government can do to improve them, look at regional planning, evaluate preparedness exercises, and examine DHS's policies regarding oversight. In short, the recommendations were to pull together the functions that FEMA had before the creation of DHS and improve its capabilities.

One problem area that GAO has also identified is succession planning.[19] Human resource issues are certainly affecting the functioning of FEMA. Senior FEMA managers warned that many senior officials left when the agency was brought into the new department in 2003. Institutional memory was lost.[20] A change of administration is likely to lead to more retirements and transfers. Because FEMA, as well as DHS itself, has so many political appointees who will depart when President Bush leaves office, there is danger of a leadership vacuum during the transition. This is particularly problematic in agencies with several layers of political appointees—like FEMA. The retirement of "baby boomers," too, having impact on the agency's human resource capacity. The FBI, the FAA, and other agencies have warned of serious "brain drains" caused by retirements. The public service has been more politicized in the past several decades and career civil servants, in many cases, are far removed from the top ranks. There has been little investment in leadership development and succession. FEMA has had so many vacancies that senior managers have often had to take on the responsibilities of more than one position. When Katrina made landfall, FEMA was roughly three-quarters of full strength and Congress has pressed the agency to fill positions in recent years. However, morale problems make recruitment and retention particularly difficult.

The Post-Katrina Emergency Management Reform Act of 2006 did address some of the problems within FEMA and between FEMA and DHS, but DHS has been slow to implement the "New FEMA." Restoring the preparedness function to FEMA was critical. Separating preparedness from response—training and planning from responding—was a major weakness in the national programs. It is likely that the next administration will have to reexamine the implementation of the Post-Katrina Reform Act. Whether the cultural issues can be resolved is uncertain, although there is growing dissatisfaction with the Homeland Security culture and, as 9/11 fades from memory, there is less tolerance of the department's approach.

Can the nation's capacity to deal with catastrophic disaster be repaired? A very positive sign can be found in the proposal to let FEMA focus more of its training activities on emergency management practice and to provide training for its own employees, as well as for state and local emergency managers and officials. Restoring human resource capacity is essential. This would also be an opportunity to build curricula and training programs around the values expressed in *The Principles of Emergency Management.* The development of greater local emergency management capacity is the most positive sign. Collaboration will increase surge capacity. Growing vulnerabilities owing to climate change, as well as terrorism, should make emergency management capacity building a national priority. Emergency managers work in a networked world and the ability to collaborate effectively is an essential skill.[21]

Notes

1. See William L. Waugh, Jr., "The Political Costs of Failure in the Responses to Hurricanes Katrina and Rita," *Annals of the Academy of Political and Social Science* 604 (March 2006): 10–25.
2. Ibid.

3. Craig Fugate, "The State of Federal Emergency Management" (Plenary), 31st Annual Natural Hazards Research and Applications Workshop, Boulder, CO, July 9–12, 2006.

4. Government Accountability Office. *Budget Issues: FEMA Needs Adequate Data, Plans, and Systems to Effectively Manage Resources for Day-to-Day Operations* (Washington, DC: GAO, January 19, 2007).

5. U.S. Senate, Committee on Homeland Security and Government Affairs, Hearing on Government's Response to Hurricane Katrina, February 10, 2006.

6. Government Accountability Office. *Homeland Security: Preparing for and Responding to Disasters* GAO-07-395T (Washington, DC: GAO, March 9, 2007).

7. William L. Waugh, Jr., "Local Emergency Management in the Post-9/11 World," in *Emergency Management: Principles and Practice for Local Government*, 2nd ed., ed. William L. Waugh, Jr., and Kathleen Tierney (Washington, DC: ICMA Press, 2007), 2–23.

8. The CEM program is described on the homepage of the International Association of Emergency Managers, www.iaem.com (accessed on August 2, 2008).

9. Waugh, William L., Jr., "Organizational Culture, Communication, and Decision-Making: Making Multi-Organizational, Inter-Sector and Intergovernmental Operations Work," 2002 National Conference on Catastrophic Care for the Nation, National Disaster Medical System, Atlanta, GA, April 13–17, 2002; William L. Waugh, Jr., "Building a Seamless Homeland Security: The Cultural Interoperability Problem," National Conference of the American Society for Public Administration, Portland, OR, March 28–30, 2004.

10. William L Waugh., Jr., and Richard T. Sylves, "Organizing the War on Terrorism," *Public Administration Review* (September 2002): 145–153; William L. Waugh, Jr., "Terrorism, Homeland Security and the National Emergency Management Network," *Public Organization Review* 3 (2003): 373–385; William L. Waugh, Jr., and Greg Streib, "Collaboration and Leadership for Effective Emergency Management," *Public Administration Review*, Special Issue on Collaborative Management 66 (December 2006): 131–140.

11. William L.Waugh, Jr., "EMAC, Katrina, and the Governors of Louisiana and Mississippi," *Public Administration Review*, Special Supplementary Issue on "Administrative Failure in the Wake of Katrina" 67 (December 2007): 107–113.

12. William L Waugh., Jr., "Mechanisms for Collaboration: EMAC and Katrina," *The Public Manager* 35/4 (Winter 2006–2007): 12–15.

13. Michael Selves et al., *The Principles of Emergency Management* (Emmitsburg, MD: Emergency Management Institute, Federal Emergency Management Agency, 2007).

14. William L. Waugh, Jr., and Kathleen Tierney, "Future Directions in Local Emergency Management," in *Emergency Management: Principles and Practice for Local Government*, 2nd ed., ed. William L. Waugh, Jr. and Kathleen Tierney (Washington, DC: ICMA Press, 2007): 317–333.

15. William L. Waugh, Jr., "Mechanisms for Collaboration in Emergency Management: ICS, NIMS, and the Problem of Command and Control," in *The Collaborative Manager*, ed. Rosemary O'Leary (Georgetown University Press, 2008).

16. Emergency Management Accreditation Program, www.emaponline.org (accessed on August 11, 2008).

17. U.S. House of Representatives, Committee on Transportation and Infrastructure, Subcommittee on Economic Development, Public Buildings, and Emergency Management, Hearings on "Readiness in the Post-Katrina and Post-9/11 World: An Evaluation of the New National Response Framework," September 11, 2007.
18. Government Accountability Office, *Homeland Security.*
19. Government Accountability Office. *Human Capital: Succession Planning and Management Is Critical Driver of Organizational Transformation* (Washington, DC: GAO, GAO-04-127T, October 1, 2003).
20. Government Accountability Office, *Homeland Security.*
21. Waugh and Streib, "Collaboration and Leadership"; and Waugh and Tierney, "Future Directions."

Chapter 6

Urban Planning in
New York City after 9/11

*Peter Marcuse**

The attack on the World Trade Center on 9/11 changed urban planning in New York City, with repercussions elsewhere, but in ways that continued a direction in which it was evolving even before that date. This chapter outlines the process and enumerates the directions of change.

The Structure of Planning in New York City

New York City has a well-established tradition of urban planning, fought for over many years of charter reforms, elections, and political controversy. The city has 59 Community Boards, originally Community Planning Boards, appointed by elected representatives of those communities in the City Council and borough president's office. Local developments that involve any type of public discretion must go through a Uniform Land Use Review procedure (ULURP), in which information is provided to the Community Boards; they hold hearings and vote; their votes are reported to the City Planning Commission, and thence to the elected City Council. A City Planning Commission was established in the 1930s for the city, as part of the wave of democratic reform associated with the New Deal; its members are appointed by the elected mayor and elected borough presidents, and are required by charter to act on all land-use decisions after full public hearings. Their purpose is to serve as an independent but democratically responsive buffer against the pressures of day-to-day politics. A separate Environmental Impact Statement is required to be prepared and made publicly available on

---

* Peter Marcuse is Professor Emeritus of Urban Planning at Columbia University and author of several books.

any project with a significant environmental impact; even its scope is subject to public input. Their decisions then are transmitted to the City Council, elected by the people of the city every two years. The mayor in turn has a veto right over decisions of the council, which may override his veto by a 2–3 vote. This is the normal way in which planning is done in the city.

The reality does not match the expectations that this process might awaken. Community Board votes have no binding effect in law; City Planning Commission members are in fact directly responsive to the politicians who appointed them. Elected officials are, in the opinion of many, more responsive to real estate interests and property developers on major development issues than to residents. Environmental Impact Statements are generally prepared by proponents of a proposed development, and framed to support the proposal. Nevertheless, there is at least pro forma extensive opportunity for public participation, and major issues are ultimately subject to the processes of representative democracy. At least the formal right to participate in planning exists in New York City.

After the World Trade Center was destroyed on September 11, the city of New York and its residents reacted in a number of ways, some inconsistent with others, in deciding what should be done with the site of the destruction and what should be done to repair the collateral damage caused there. The basic reactions bypassed the established institutionalized procedures, in part in ways that expanded the scope of participation in the public debates and the flow of information about the issues, in part in ways that contracted participation in the actual decision making on the key questions. But these reactions cannot be understood without a look at the long-term market forces shaping the directions of city development.

The Key Market-Driven Forces Shaping Development

Priority to the Financial Services Industry

The overriding priority in economic development in the city of New York has been for some time the prosperity and growth of its globally oriented financial sector, including banks, stock brokerages, real estate, and global trading firms, concentrated in lower Manhattan, although in some tension with the concentration of related activities, also globally oriented, including media firms, advertising, and producer services such as accounting and legal firms. In this policy, Manhattan is the driving force in New York City's economy, and lower Manhattan and midtown are where its motor lies. This was true of the Giuliani administration, and even more obvious in the Bloomberg administration, under a mayor whose own business was headily involved in global financial services. The latest major planning document to be issued by the city, PlanNYC2030, is heavily oriented to preserving New York's place—and with it the place of New York's two central business districts—in the global business hierarchy, seeing New York as preeminently a "global city" with the financial sector as its heart.[1]

Before 9/11, in the competition between midtown and lower Manhattan for the location of the major players in this sector, midtown was winning. The 9/11 attacks, which destroyed the single largest office cluster in this sector in lower Manhattan, the World Trade Center, with over 10,000,000 square feet of office space, of course dealt a major further below to the area, in which office buildings had already been converted to residential uses in a declining market. The 9/11 attacks paradoxically served to bolster lower Manhattan's fortunes. Not only was the restoration of the space lost in 9/11 heavily subsidized and promoted by the city, but transportation planning, a key ingredient in determining business and residential locations was also oriented in its direction. Thus, the long-discussed "one-seat ride" from JFK airport to Manhattan, which might have logically ended in midtown, where the major node in the city's transportation lines already existed, was instead replanned for termination in lower Manhattan.[2]

Concentrated Decentralization

Concentrated decentralization is an appropriate term for the regional spatial market-driven pattern of development taking place in the New York area. Planning policies in New York City, and specifically in the absence of any structure for regional planning or effort to do such planning by intergovernmental agreement, facilitate this pattern of development process. Within the boundaries of the city, the development of scattered megaprojects, discussed below, represents the same trend. The fear of a terrorist attack after 9/11 has undergirded the pattern.

Employment patterns have for some time been toward decentralization of almost all types of jobs, with only a very narrow band of activities remaining concentrated in the central business districts of major cities, and most activities focusing on less central areas of the city, the suburbs, edge cities, with a noticeable movement from primary cites to secondary and even tertiary (economically defined) cities. A number of factors came together to shape this trend: the availability of technology to make both transportation and communication easier across greater distances; the pressure on central real estate prices in a market dominated by private land ownership; the costs of congestion and environmental degradation; and, last but hardly least, the social tensions and insecurities that result from increasing polarization of the population and continuing racial division tied, both in fact and even more in perception, to life in big cities. To these negative aspects of concentration the advantages of agglomeration have offered a counterpoise: the efficiencies of shared services, the importance of face-to-face meetings, in some cases the reduced friction of transportation, and the desirability of a creative, diverse, lively, urbane milieu.

In this balance, the fear of terrorism now added a significant weight to the side of decentralization. Overagglomeration is equated with danger. In the more "global" cities, this balance has hitherto been more on the side of concentration than it has been in other cities; that balance has now changed. The centers of global cities will no longer be exempt, even to the extent that they ever were.

The pattern is already visible in New York City. The New York Stock Exchange will not build its long-planned new trading floor and 900-foot tower across the street from its current headquarters, but may build a secondary trading site outside lower Manhattan.[3] Many say it should move to trading on an electronic network. More shares are traded on the NASDAQ stock exchange, which exists only on computer systems and the screens of its dealers, than on the Big Board. "With faster computers and data transmission, traders no longer have to meet in person to buy and sell shares," says the chief executive of the Cincinnati Stock Exchange.

"Outside the United States, floors are disappearing really quickly, and automated auctions are the wave of the future," Mr. Madhavan said. "The U.S.A. is the lone holdout, and it's the holdout because it has a strong group of dealers who are politically connected." He's head of ITG, which operates a computer trading system that competes with the Big Board.[4]

So one trend is for certain business activities to leave the concentrated center(s) of the city. Which activities? Those that are largely self-contained, that have internalized a large part of their externalities; and those that do not, with the use of modern communications and transportation technologies, need to be in the same physical location as the headquarters they serve. So the headquarters of major industrial firms and those directly marketing services to consumers may move out, and back offices will move out. Nothing new here. Yet the trends will accentuate, and the definition of back offices will expand. As Saskia Sassen has pointed out,[5] the destruction in the financial district has permitted some firms that had previously massively concentrated their activities there to do what they had already begun to do, but now much more quickly: disaggregate their activities into those that really needed to stay agglomerated in a concentrated downtown, and those that could (increasingly as technology advances) be deconcentrated.

But those moving out of the concentrated center are not moving to just anywhere; they remain concentrated in specific locations away from the center, most but not all remaining within the metropolitan area.

In the first place—and this is perhaps unique to New York City—there are two "downtowns," and there is a continuing competition within the real estate industry between them: midtown and the "downtown" financial district. That competition[6] has been going on for some time; estimates are that in 1950 downtown had more workers than midtown, but today midtown has three times as many as downtown has.[7] Even after the loss of space in the lower Manhattan financial district, the office vacancy rate has doubled between September and January, "leaving some analysts to wondering which companies will move into the empty space, let alone any new towers that might be built."[8]

The hyperconcentrations of jobs in service-center-oriented office buildings in the CBDs (Central Business Districts) of the more globalized large cities (and both the high- and the low-paying jobs associated with them) is shrinking, as multinational businesses change their spatial strategies in the search for security in more outlying areas. The focus will initially be within the same metropolitan regions (e.g., American Express renting—on long-term leases—spaces in Jersey City, Stamford, etc.). The estimated impact on the downtown economy included the flight of 64,909 jobs to Midtown, New Jersey, and elsewhere.[9] Many major firms already had large satellite offices in fringe locations to which they quickly moved on September 11; in some cases decisions to move more operations out of New York City to those locations were simply accelerated by the attack. The Bank of New York had 3,000 employees in its headquarters building at 1 Wall Street; they are all back at work there now. But it had 4,000 employees at 101 Barclay Street at one of its data centers; they have been moved. "[We are] just too concentrated in Manhattan."[10] Long Island City in Queens is touted, not only by self-interested developers but also by Senator Charles Schumer of New York, as "an ideal location for creating a new central business district."[11] Empire Blue Cross took temporary quarters in Melville, Long Island. It had 460,000 square feet in the World Trade Center. It has leased 322,220 square feet at Metrotech in downtown Brooklyn, and less than 100,000 square feet at 11, West 42nd Street, Times Square, where the chief executive and other top executives will be located.[12] Deutsche Bank began building a backup operation in Jersey City. Marsh & McLennan, a major tenant at the World Trade Center, took some space in midtown, and planned to move 2,000 employees across the river to Hoboken, in New Jersey.[13] Goldman Sachs decided to move its entire equity trading department to Jersey City, across the Hudson River, to a $1 billion complex it is building there (with, incidentally, a 42-story skyscraper, the highest skyscraper in New Jersey). According to a major real estate firm, "Goldman's decision is a significant setback because it affects the downtown core of financial services. It's not so much the number of jobs that's significant, but the kind of jobs. Equity trading is the heart and soul of any investment bank."[14]

Five months after September 11, a business newspaper headlined on its front page: "Empire State Emptying Out as Tenants Flee. Anxiety Lingers; Vacant Space Triples."[15] The Empire State Building, the tallest building in New York after the fall of the World Trade Center, had a vacancy rate of 1.7 percent in 2000, before 9/11; in 2006 vacancies stood at 18.2 percent.[16]

Thus the movement out of the center will be primarily to the immediately adjacent but somewhat less dense and less expensive fringes, the outer boroughs in New York City and across the Hudson. But there will also be a smaller move to the suburbs, and beyond them to the edge cities (not just in Joel Garreau's narrow sense): Stamford, White Plains. The tendency toward centralization, the pressure of agglomeration economies, all those factors that are now widely accepted as concomitant of the globalization, and the increasing importance of the financial sector that is one of its present-day hallmarks, make themselves felt at the same time. The result of these conflicting forces—deconcentration out of fear of terrorism and concentration to centralize control functions and the services they require[17]—leads to the development of megaproject forms in large cities as well as the concentrated decentralization outside them described above.

Megaproject Development in lieu of Comprehensive Planning[18]

Megaprojects are nothing new in urban planning,[19] and they are hardly confined to New York City.[20] Rockefeller Center was built in the 1930s within blocks of downtown Manhattan, but it was a pioneering development. Urban renewal or other forms of public direct support was fiercely resisted in the immediate postwar years, although Robert Moses was, nevertheless, able to push through several projects like, for example, Lincoln Center. Even the construction of the World Trade Center was fiercely resisted at the time, and Battery Park City, a classic megaproject, could only be developed because it was built on new and publicly owned land. And the trend is global: look at how the project architect of Steven Holl's Beijing office describes his new mammoth development there: "[E]ight squarish towers and one round one…Holl placed the towers in a ring around property, connecting them with glass-enclosed bridges at various heights—a kind of public, or semi-public, street in the sky…. Each bridge contains some facility that the tenants share—a gym, a café, a bookstore…a swimming pool, which feels as if it were floating in the air, seventeen stories above Beijing. We wanted to create all city functions inside the project."[21]

New York is however, a prime site for such projects, because it has such a heavy concentration of the financial and business services industries that prefer such projects, and has access to the global financing that the scale of most of such projects requires. What is new in New York City after 9/11 are three things: the extent of megaproject construction and planning; the extent of city governmental planning and economic development policy support for them; and the extent to which they are scattered in the city, rather than concentrated in its central business district. Queens West, Atlantic Yards, Jamaica Center, are all examples. Community Boards have been opposed to many of the major rezonings that such projects require, but their negative views were overridden by a strong executive whose economic development policies have largely replaced the more cumbersome formal planning processes still technically in effect.[22]

Decision-Making Authority Preempted by the Executive Branch, at the Expense of the City's Planning Infrastructure

The City Planning Commission and the City Planning Department, of which the commission's president is also the director, have been quietly but methodically shunted aside in the city's planning since 9/11. The way this has happened is described below, in recounting the defeat of the upsurge in citizen participation that followed the destruction of 9/11. Since then, the focus 9/11 permitted on economic development, and particularly the development of lower Manhattan as the city's financial motor, has allowed the mayor to channel all major planning decisions to his deputy mayor for Economic Development, rather than through the Planning Department. The pattern of approval of megaprojects has virtually ignored the institutional planning process, and/or overridden it where it was legally unavoidable.

The most recent example of this trend has been the development of what New York City calls PlanNYC2030, a broad infrastructure plan presented in a large glossy brochure under the banner of guiding the city's inevitable growth over the next 20 years. Leaving aside its questionable content,[23] what is noteworthy about it is that it has been prepared by a new Office for Sustainable Development within the office of the Deputy Mayor for Economic Development, not by the City Planning Department or Commission, and has not been submitted to the City Council for approval, as the normal planning process would have required.

And within the executive branch, after 9/11, the role of the police department has become decisive wherever it intervenes, overriding and at the expense of all other planning considerations. The most striking instances come directly in the area immediately affected by 9/11: Ground Zero, the site of the World Trade Center towers and its immediate surroundings. The so-called Freedom Tower, advertised as rising to 1,776 feet to symbolize in some unobservable way the idea of freedom, will have a very "unfree" base: 20 stories of concrete with no windows at its base, as a requirement imposed by the police department in the name of protection against terrorism. The developer and the architect did not seriously question the decision; instead, the 20-story base will be clothed in prismatic mirrors to conceal the bomb-proof bunker-like base beneath them.

Elsewhere police measures are similarly being imposed. An account of steps undertaken by the police to "enhance security after 9/11" are described in a recent the *New York Times* story as follows:

> [The Chairwoman of CB1 is quoted as saying:] Security can't be set up like the checkpoint at the New York Stock Exchange, which is inhospitable to anyone living or working the area. Seven small business there closed within a year of the N.Y.P.D setting up its checkpoint...

[At the World Trade Center site itself]…many people favored the reopening of [two streets through the superblock,] They sought to animate the streets by including shops and a performing arts center. That vision was incorporated into the master plan…and adopted by the city, the state, and the Port Authority. "Nobody contemplated that you wouldn't have free entrance to the site," said Alex Garvin [the two desired streets, though running through the site, will have check-points at each end].[24]

Tendencies toward More Participatory Planning

There was however a countertendency to the post-9/11 weakening of the participatory planning process in favor of executive decisions: the impact of the upsurge in citizen participation following 9/11. Its ultimate impact is ambiguous.

The planning for Ground Zero is a classic example.[25] Formal planning and decision making for Ground Zero bypassed the existing formal structures of planning and relied on ad hoc institutions and processes created to undertake that work, dominated by the executive branches of the city and state governments. The upsurge in citizen participation that immediately followed 9/11 has not lasted.

A special corporation, the lower Manhattan Development Corporation, was created, with eight members appointed by the governor and eight by the then and the former mayors. The majority had vested financial interests in the outcome of the process, and/or close connections to those that had. The corporation was given the power of eminent domain by a grant from the state government, and authority over the expenditure of billions of dollars allocated by the federal government to compensate for the damages of September 11. The World Trade Center itself was owned by the Port Authority of New York and New Jersey, a bistate public agency with members appointed by the governors of the two states. These two entities have the authority to make all planning decisions (and largely to implement them) affecting the impacted area of lower Manhattan public hearings, but the extent to which they were listened to is much contested.

Citizen groups nevertheless have had some impact on the direction of planning after 9/11, but only in a very limited sense, and primarily to critique specific proposals for the development of the site of the World Trade Center and its surroundings, and even there not to become formally involved in the planning process. In the meantime, the City Planning Commission, the body legally entrusted with planning for the welfare of the city, has barely been audible in the deliberations.

As for information and discussion, a number of civic groups began to involve themselves actively. Rebuild New York, under the sponsorship of the New York Partnership and the New York Real Estate Board, produced massive documentation on the exact economic impact of September 11. Although the partnership represented a clearly defined and limited range of interests (the "voice of New York City's business community," it describes itself), the information it provided contributed to the official planning process. Its spin-off, New York New Visions, consisting of approximately 20 professional organizations in planning and architecture, assembled a wide range of further materials and provided some strong suggestions as to what might be done. Somewhat narrowly focused on lower Manhattan, R-DOT—Rebuild Downtown Our Town—was an active group based in lower Manhattan (broadly conceived) that advocated vigorous public participation in the process. The Civic Alliance, pulled together by the Regional Plan Association, was perhaps the broadest of the civic groups, including now approximately hundred of such groups in its coalition. Other grassroots, community, and labor groups were also active. The Community Labor Advocacy Network was, for instance, what its name implies, and sought influence on what happens. The process needs discussion and critique, and these groups are all doing what they can to forward public debate.

At the high point of the participatory process, a public meeting of over 4,000 persons convened by the Civic Alliance at New York's Convention Center was shown proposals put forward for the World Trade Center site and allowed to vote on them; a majority of the voters was severely critical. It had some impact on the resulting decisions, but more on their architectural form than their planning content: the program for the site, including a commitment to construction of millions of square feet of office space, was not put in doubt.

Today, more than seven years after 9/11, the citizens' groups so actively involved in planning then have largely become quiescent, and the bypassing of the regular planning process put underway then is no longer being challenged.

Conclusion

Thus the shift in planning's role has been two-sided. On the one hand, it has strengthened the role of the mayor's office, and on the other, the city government's economic development structure in spheres normally within the orbit of planning, has been expanded. The issue of security has been used to expand substantially the police role in making decisions on urban structure and management. In parallel fashion, the city's role in shaping infrastructure development to enhance the role of the financial sector, that which was attacked on 9/11 and is accepted as an inviolable major focus for city protection and support, has been enhanced; the investment in lower Manhattan, and in megaprojects throughout the city, is part of that process. The kind of opposition that historically urban renewal projects have encountered has been much less visible in the planning for the megaprojects that are the new urban renewal. The popular participation in the planning process, after a brief upsurge, has diminished, and the formal structures for democratic participation have been largely bypassed or overridden.[26] In both cases, the tendency has been to strengthen market forces, in ways substantially accelerated, both directly and indirectly, by the reactions to 9/11, with an aggregation of power in the direction of the executive, rather than the legislative branch of government, paralleling developments at the national level to date.

What remains of the post-9/11 experience that may ultimately strengthen the planning process in New York City is the acceptance of the critical role of the city government itself in the shaping of the future of the city, and the image of how involved an aroused citizenry is willing to be when the circumstances permit.

Notes

This paper draws on several prior publications of the author, which may be consulted for sources not contained in the text. "What Kind of Planning after September 11? The Market, the Stakeholders, Consensus—or…?" in *After the World Trade Center: Rethinking New York City,* ed. Michael Sorkin and Sharon Zukin (New York: Routledge, 2002), 153–162; "After the World Trade Center: Deconcentration and Deplanning," *Quaderns d'arquitectura i urbanisme* 232 (January 2002): 38–45; "Planning after September 11: The Issues in New York," *Planners Network* 150 (Winter 2002): 36–39; "The Architectural Competition for the World Trade Center Site," *City* 7, no. 1 (April 2003): 113–116; Review of *Wounded City: The Social Impact of 9/11* by Nancy Foner (Ed.), *Journal of Urban Affairs* 29, no. 5 (2007): 546–548; Review Essay, "New York after 9/11," reviewing Howard Chernick, ed., *Resilient City: The Economic Impact of 9/11,* Nancy Foner, ed., *Wounded City: The Social Impact of 9/11,* and John Mollenkopf, ed., *Contentious City: The Politics of Recovery in New York City,* in *Contemporary Sociology* 36, no. 6 (November 2007): 525–528; "Letter to the Editor: A Critical Response to plaNYC2030," *Metro Planner* (January–February 2007), 10.

1. Tom Angotti, "Daniel Doctoroff's Legacy," *Gotham Gazette,* December 11, 2007.
2. Although the attempt to gain major federal financing for the project on the theory that it was needed because of the damage from 9/11 did not fly in Washington, and its ultimate outcome is still uncertain.
3. Edward Wyatt, "Stock Exchange Abandons Plans for a New Headquarters Building across the Street," *New York Times,* August 2, 2002.
4. *New York Times,* October 12, 2002, C4.
5. "Correspondence with Saskia Sassen," *Quaderns d'arguitectura I urbanisme* 232 (January 2002): 24.
6. Midtown for this purpose is defined as between 34th and 59th Street, 8th Avenue to the East River, and downtown as Manhattan south of Canal Street—not the definition used by the Lower Manhattan Redevelopment Corporation, which takes in all of the area below Houston Street.

7. CoStar Group reports, September 21 and October 16, 2001, quoted in Edward L. Glaeser and Jesse M. Shapiro, "Cities and Warfare: The Impact of Terrorism on Urban Form," Harvard Institute of Economic Research, December 2001, 20.

8. Charles V. Bagli, "Seeking Safety, Downtown Firms Are Scattering," *New York Times*, January 29, 2002. See also M. Heschmeyer, "Attack Magnified Existing New York City Office Trends," The CoStar Group, October 16, 2001, www. costargroup.com.

9. TenantWise, WTC Overview: April 2, 2003, accessed at http://www.tenantwise. com/reports/04022003wtc.asp on April 22, 2009.

10. *New York Times*, October 6, 2002, C1.

11. *Grid Magazine*, October 24, 2001. In fact, since his speech, a $700,000,000 contract has been awarded by the City's Economic Development Corporation for the construction of a major mixed-use development there, expected to bring 7,000 jobs to this location in Queens. Globest.com, October 26, 2001, "City Picks Developer for $700 Mil. Queens Project."

12. See Empire Blue Cross Blue Shield Press Release, "New Corporate Headquarters to Be Located at 9 Metrotech Center in Brooklyn," November 20, 2001.

13. Charles V. Bagli, *New York Times*, January 29, 2002, B2.

14. Quoted in Bagli, *New York Times*, January 29, 2002, B2. In the event, a significant number of employees refused to move, and the firm also constructed a similarly tall skyscraper just north of the World Trade Center site, and employees shuttle back and forth across the Hudson between the two locations by ferry.

15. Lore Croghan, "Empire State Emptying Out as Tenants Flee; Anxiety Lingers; Vacant Space Triples," *Crain's New York Business*, February 4, 2002, 1. The story goes on to say: "Concerns about terrorism plague other trophy towers, as well. Some businesses have refused to consider sublets in the Chrysler Building since September 11...Many companies seeking space are issuing a new mandate to their brokers—'find us anonymous buildings'—in a blanket disapproval of all well-known properties."

16. Julie Satow, "Empire State Falls Short as Midtown Gains," *Crain's New York Business*, March 2006.

17. See Saskia Sassen, *Global Cities*, 2nd ed. (Princeton, NJ: Princeton University Press, 2001).

18. See Susann Fainstein, "The Return of Urban Renewal: Dan Doctoroff's Great Plans for New York City," *Harvard Design Magazine* 22 (Spring/Summer 2005): 1–5, and my criticism of PlanNYC2030, in *Gotham Gazette*, forthcoming.

19. Bent Flyvbjerg, Nils Bruzelius, and Werner Rothengatter, *Megaprojects and Risk: An Anatomy of Ambition* (Cambridge: Cambridge University Press, 2003).

20. See, for instance, on Asian projects, Kris Olds, *Globalization and Urban Change: Capital, Culture and Pacific Rim Mega-Projects* (Oxford: Oxford University Press, 2001).

21. Pau Goldberger, "Forbidden Cities," *New Yorker*, June 30, 2008, 78.

22. Courtney Gross, "Reshaping the City: Who's Being Heard—and Why?" *Gotham Gazette*, August 25, 2008.

23. Tom Angotti, "The Past and Future of Sustainability," *Gotham Gazette*, June 29, 2008.

24. Charles V. Bagli, "Police Want Tight Security Zone at Ground Zero," *New York Times*, August 12, 2008, B4.

25. Excellent, if now somewhat dated, descriptions are given in the Sage series edited by Nancy Foner, *Wounded City: The Social Impact of 9/11* (New York: Russell. Sage Foundation, 2005).

26. But see comments of Thomas Angotti in the Land Use section of *Gotham Gazette*, cited above, and intermittent discussion within the Metro Chapter of the American Planning Association in New York.

Chapter 7

What Has al Qaeda Been Doing Lately? The Tribal Areas of Pakistan and Beyond

*Rohan Gunaratna and Anders Nielson**

After the US-led coalition's intervention in October 2001, both practitioners and scholars have debated on the shape, size, structure, location, and leadership of Jama'at al Qaeda al-Jihad.[1] Has al Qaeda been able to reconstitute itself as a group or is it a diffused network of groups and cells bound by a common ideology? After al Qaeda was dislodged from Afghanistan in late 2001, we argue that al Qaeda has been able to reconstitute itself in the Federally Administered Tribal Areas (FATA), on the 1520-mile long border between Afghanistan and Pakistan.

After the locus of al Qaeda leadership shifted to FATA, it has used its tribal affiliations as well as nurtured and built a clerical support base. As it did when functioning in Afghanistan, al Qaeda has rebuilt a well-structured hierarchical leadership organization. Today, al Qaeda is both an operational group and an ideological movement.

Operating out of FATA, al Qaeda has unleashed a dispersed and a vibrant threat by spreading its ideology globally. Al Qaeda has galvanized and mobilized many disparate Islamist groups in the global south creating an al Qaeda movement. With representation from more than two

*Rohan Gunaratna is Head of the International Center for Political Violence and Terrorism Research, Nanyang Technological University, Singapore and author of 12 books, including *Countering Terrorism* and the *New York Times* best seller *Inside Al Qaeda*. Anders Nielson is a Research Associate at the International Center for Political Violence and Terrorism Research, Nanyang Technological University, Singapore.

dozen groups, FATA has become the de facto headquarters of the global jihad movement. Furthermore, al Qaeda has penetrated Muslim territorial communities in the South as well as diaspora and migrant communities in the West. Directly and through its associated groups, al Qaeda is offering research-intensive training to homegrown and other terrorists to conduct spectacular attacks especially against the United States , its allies, and its friends. Despite being the most hunted terrorist leadership, al Qaeda is directing, facilitating, supporting, and approving key operations against its enemies from FATA.

The Context

Three profound developments characterize the post-9/11 global threat landscape. First, after the U.S.-led intervention in Afghanistan, the ground zero of terrorism has moved from Afghanistan to Pakistan's FATA. Second, after the U.S. invasion and occupation of Iraq, al Qaeda in FATA has gained a foothold in the Middle East establishing a forward operational base 2290 km (1420 miles) closer to the West.

At the very heart of these developments is the leadership of Jama'at al Qaeda al-Jihad led by Osama bin Laden, the leader of the 9/11 attack. Increasingly his deputy Dr. Ayman al-Zawahiri, also the principal architect of the global jihad movement, has assumed control of al Qaeda's operations. Although Jama'at al Qaeda al-Jihad's strength has depleted from 3,000–4,000 members at 9/11 to a few hundred members today, al Qaeda is still resilient. Furthermore, al Qaeda is accepting new like-minded groups seeking to name themselves after al Qaeda to adopt its ideology of global jihad and operational tactics of suicide.

To respond to the challenges posed by radicalization, extremism, and their operational manifestations—terrorism—we must take a closer look at how al Qaeda's presence in FATA has enabled it to survive and evolve. With field research,[2] interviews, and review of government and other documents as the basis, we examine why al Qaeda has been forced to establish its headquarters in this region; we also examine its support and operational activities.

The Leadership

The key strength of al Qaeda has been the ability of its leadership to survive and fight back. After the Northern Alliance supported by Coalition Forces moved into southern Afghanistan, the main structures of al Qaeda relocated from Afghanistan to two neighboring countries—Pakistan and Iran. The location of the leadership remains in dispute between various security and intelligence agencies. However, all evidence points out that the core leadership of al Qaeda, al-Zawahiri, and possibly bin Laden fled to the area between

Nuristan, Konar Province in Afghanistan to the area around Chitral and FATA in Pakistan.[3]

According to Pakistani President General Pervez Musharraf's book, *In The Line of Fire*,

> Khalid Sheikh Muhammad, the third-ranking member of al Qaeda... denied having met Osama after 9/11, but told us that Osama was alive and well and that they had been in touch. He said that the last letter he had received from Osama came through courier. He also said that Osama had been helped before Operation Anaconda to move out of Tora Bora to Waziristan by Jalal ul Din Haqqani; two Afghans, Muhammad Rahim and Amin ul Haq and the Iranian Baloch, Ahmed al-Kuwaiti. On March 4th 2003, KSM speculated that Osama was in Konar in Afghanistan.[4]

After moving to Waziristan and staying there during a part of 2002, Ayman al-Zawahiri eventually moved to Bajaur Agency. He married a woman from the Mahmund tribe in Bajaur Agency after the death of his wife and two children during U.S. attacks in Afghanistan. This enabled the deputy leader of al Qaeda to develop strong tribal links to the leadership of the militant Deobandi movement of Tehrik Nifaz Shariat Muhammadi (TNSM) in Bajaur Agency. While in the Bajaur Agency, al-Zawahiri strengthened his relationship with Maulana Faqir Muhammad (who is also from the Mahmund tribe), who leads TNSM in Bajaur Agency, and Liaquat Hussein who, ran the Ziaul Uloom Taleemul Koran seminary in Chingai in Bajaur until his death in October 2006.[5]

Through these contacts al-Zawahiri was able to avoid arrest and reconstitute a scattered al Qaeda in disarray. Al-Zawahiri reestablished contact with al Qaeda cells in Pakistan and overseas. He also built alliances with groups in the Arabian Peninsula, the Horn of Africa, Southeast Asia, and Iran.

To enhance security within the group, bin Laden decided to divide al Qaeda's operational structure into External and Internal Operations. The head of External Operations was tasked with conducting attacks outside the Pakistan-Afghanistan arena, which became the domain of the head of Internal Operations. Khalid Sheikh Muhammad alias Mukht (The Brain) alias KSM was chosen to lead al Qaeda's External Operations, while Mustafa al-Uzayti alias Abu Faraj al-Libi assumed leadership of Internal Operations.[6]

The Inter-Services Intelligence Directorate (ISID) located, tracked, and detained KSM in Rawalpindi in Pakistan in March 2003. It was 9/11 that made al Qaeda an internationally notorious group, and KSM was the architect of this iconic attack. To compensate for this colossal loss, al Qaeda underwent immediate restructuring. Abu Faraj al-Libi became more involved in External Operations, which the Egyptian Hamza Rabia came to lead. According to the Office of the Director of National Intelligence in the United States,

> Abu Faraj was a communications conduit for al-Qa'ida managers to Bin Ladin from August 2003 until his capture. He was the recipient of

couriered messages and public statements from Bin Ladin and passed messages to Bin Ladin from both senior lieutenants and rank-and-file members. Some of his work almost certainly required personal meetings with bin Ladin or Zawahiri, a privilege reserved since 2002 for select members of the group.[7]

The letter written by al Qaeda's second-in-command, al-Zawahiri, on July 9, 2005, indicates how close the contacts were between al Qaeda's leadership and Abu Faraj. The letter alludes to the trepidation, which existed among al Qaeda's leadership, when Abu Faraj was arrested in Pakistan in May 2005. Al-Zawahiri states that

> [t]he enemy struck a blow against us with the arrest of Abu al-Faraj, may God break his bonds. However, no Arab brother was arrested because of him. The brothers tried and were successful to a great degree to contain the fall of Abu al-Faraj as much as they could.[8]

From his base in Bajaur Agency of FATA, Abu Faraj had managed to stay in close contact with the al Qaeda leadership. Furthermore, he also managed to order and oversee an assassination attempt against the Musharraf. This double suicide attack against Musharraf's motorcade, on December 25, 2003, was ordered by Abu Faraj, but planned and executed by members from the Pakistani groups. The select members of Jamiat ul-Furqan, Harakat ul-Jihad ul-Islami, and Jamiat ul-Ansar functioned under the leadership of the Abu Faraj's Pakistani lieutenant, Amjad Faruqi. The attack was a declaration of war against the Pakistani state and it showed al Qaeda's capacity to strike directly at the political leadership in Pakistan.

After al Qaeda targeted the Pakistani leadership, Arab militants including al Qaeda faced mounting pressure within Pakistan. Al Qaeda became vulnerable when operating within and communicating between al Qaeda's various elements at home and overseas. Quite early on, al-Zawahiri understood that the greatest strength of the U.S. military was its ability to follow the electron. When a bodyguard used his Thuraya phone, Mohammad Atef a.k.a. Abu Hafs al-Masri, al Qaeda's military commander, was killed by a U.S. missile attack in Kandahar, Afghanistan, in November 2001. Although al Qaeda lacked the discipline initially, it prohibited the use of Thuraya and Inmarsat satellite phones within the group. As a learning organization, the core leadership refrained from using easily detectable communication. This ensured al Qaeda's survival. After moving to FATA, the leadership of al Qaeda communicates through a complex system of couriers. According to Musharraf's book *In the Line of Fire*, al Qaeda's courier system is four-tiered: "with distinct layers for administration, operations, media support, and the top hierarchy."[9] In more detail Musharraf explains that the courier network for al Qaeda's top leadership in Pakistan was separated from couriers dealing with other activities. These couriers

> [t]ry not to pass messages in writing, except where that is unavoidable, as with letters from KSM and Libbi. Normally, the leaders make their best, most trusted die-hard couriers memorize messages to al Qaeda's operational hierarchy, and then convey them verbatim.[10]

At least a part of al Qaeda leadership around al-Zawahiri seems to have stayed together in Bajaur Agency, and from there dispensed their strategic guidance. Al Qaeda's operational structure was split into two groups—Iran and Pakistan. The first part of al Qaeda's main operational structure was sent into Iran. This group was led by the head of al Qaeda's Security Committee, Sayf al-Adl and the head of al Qaeda's Training Subsection, Ahmad Abdallah Ahmad alias Abu Muhammad al-Masri. The group also came to include bin Laden's two sons, Muhammad and Saad bin Laden.

From Iran, Sayf al-Adl helped relay orders from Ayman al-Zawahiri to Tanzim Qaedat fi al-Jazeeratul Arab (the al Qaeda organization on the Arabian Peninsula), telling al Qaeda's branch on the Arabian Peninsula to start attacks in Saudi Arabia.[11] From Iran, Sayf al-Adl was also involved in mediating a dispute between the head of al Qaeda on the Arabian Peninsula, Yusuf Salih Fahd al-Ayiri alias Abu Qutaybah al-Makki and his military chief, Ali Abd al-Rahman al-Faqasi alias Abu Bakr al-Azdi, concerning the strength needed to engage Saudi Arabian security forces.[12] However after some hesitation, on behalf of the Iranian Intelligence Service (MOIS); the Iranian part of al Qaeda was arrested in 2003 and we believe that, at the time of writing, these high-ranking al Qaeda members are still under house arrest in Iran.[13]

KSM's structures in Sindh and Baluchistan composed the second group. KSM, who headed Jama'at al Qaeda al-Jihad's Media Committee since 2000, was also the head of al Qaeda's special operations group. He planned the Ghazwah Manhattan (Manhattan Raid), which al Qaeda carried out on September 11, 2001. He became the head al Qaeda's External Operations, after the death of Muhammad Atef alias Abu Hafs al-Masri, the head of al Qaeda's Military Committee in November 2001.[14] After the fall of the Taliban in Afghanistan, KSM's group fled to Karachi in Pakistan, which had been KSM's main base since he returned to Pakistan from the Philippines via South America and Qatar in the mid-1990s. Karachi had also been central to KSM's planning and training of the 19 hijackers who executed the attacks in New York and Washington on September 11, 2001.[15]

From his base in Karachi, KSM relayed orders from Osama bin Laden to the wider al Qaeda structure outside Pakistan. Together with other members of his al-Arish family and Yemenis surrounding his lieutenant, Walid bin Attash a.k.a. Tawfiq bin Attash a.k.a. Silver, he financed or coordinated or planned a whole range of attacks worldwide. This includes the killing of Daniel Pearl in Pakistan in February 2002, the attack in Djerba in Tunisia in April 2002, and, the bombings in Bali in October 2002. He was also involved in the attacks in Mombassa in November 2002 and the May 2003 attacks in Riyadh, Saudi Arabia. From Karachi and Baluchistan, KSM's structure was also deeply involved in conducting attacks against aviation. Despite billions of dollars spent—by Western governments—on target hardening, KSM was determined to use his creative genius to identify gaps and loopholes and penetrate the aviation domain. The foiled attacks included an attack on a civilian passenger plane by Richard Reid alias "Shoe-Bomber" in December 2001; the second-wave attacks involving the use of civilian airliners or sports planes on the Library Tower (renamed the Bank of America building) in Los Angeles in February 2002; the attack on the Heathrow Airport and the Canary Wharf tower in London in 2003–2004; and the attack on the U.S. Consulate in Karachi with a sports plane carrying 300 pounds of explosives in April 2003.[16]

However, in March 2003, KSM's structure suffered heavily from the arrest of its leader, KSM, and his Saudi Arabian accountant, Mustafa Ahmed Hawsawi in Rawalpindi. The latter functioned as the international accountant of al Qaeda, managing the finances including the wire transfers for the 9/11 attack. In April 2003, KSM's lieutenant Walid bin Attash a.k.a. Silver and KSM's relative and confidant Ali Abd al-Aziz Ali a.k.a. Ammar al-Baluchi were arrested in Karachi. Subsequent to these arrests, al Qaeda was forced to remove its Arab structure from Pakistan's urban areas. Instead, al Qaeda started to operate in Pakistan's cities mainly through like-minded Pakistani groups such as Jamiat ul-Furqan (also known as Jaish Muhammad, Abdul Jabbar Faction) and Jamiat ul-Ansar (also known as Harakt ul-Mujahedin ul-Alami). Under severe pressure from the authorities and their own leaders, members, and supporters, these groups either merged or split. For instance, Jamiat ul-Ansar and Jamiat ul-Furqan merged in March 2007. Another Pakistani group that works closely with al Qaeda is Harakat ul-Jihad ul-Islami as well as members from sectarian groups like Laskhar e-Jhangvi. In Baluchistan (both Iranian and Pakistani), al Qaeda was forced to rely almost entirely on the remaining members of KSM's al-Arish family. KSM's 41-year-old nephew, Musaad Aruchi a.k.a. Abu Musab al-Baluchi assisted al Qaeda specifically. Dhiren Barot alias Abu Issa al-Hindi alias Abu Issa al-Brittani and Muhammad Naim Nur Khan alias Abu Talha al-Pakistani were both British citizens. Abu Talha planned to strike targets in the United Kingdom, while Abu Issa was targeting a range of sites in the United States during 2004 (more details on these plots are presented later in the chapter).[17]

Aside from supporting Abu Talha al-Pakistani and Abu Issa al-Brittani, Abu Musab al-Baluchi also formed the group Jundallah (Soldiers of God), which carried out the attack on the Pakistani army Karachi Corps commander, Lieutenant General Ahsan Saleem Hayat, on June 10, 2004.[18]

Abu Musab al-Baluchi was finally detained by Pakistan's ISID on June 12, 2004 in Karachi and the importance of the al-Arish family—within al Qaeda—has since diminished.[19]

Return to FATA

After the capture of KSM in Rawalpindi and Tawfiq bin Attash in Karachi, in early 2003, al Qaeda's center of operations moved to FATA especially to South Waziristan. With ISID gaining intelligence dominance in the big cities of Pakistan, al Qaeda lost several hundred of its operatives. More than 25 percent of the detainees in Guantanamo Bay, Cuba, were arrested in Pakistan.[20] Having suffered severely in Pakistani cities of Karachi, Lahore, and Rawalpindi, al Qaeda retreated to FATA. Although its communication and contact to the outside world was limited, hampered, and disrupted, al Qaeda focused on building and strengthening their networks in FATA. Here they received the protection and support from local clerics and tribal members from the Mehsud and Wazir tribes, many of whom had been serving with the Taliban in Afghanistan since 1990s.[21] The Ahmadzai-Wazir tribe and specifically local Taliban members of the clans living in the Shakai valley were the main hosts of the Arabs while the Yargulkhel subclan of the Zalikhel clan (Ahmadzai-Wazir tribe) became the main host of the Uzbeks on the Wana plains of South Waziristan.[22] The Ahmadzai-Wazir's are mostly situated in the western and southern areas of South Waziristan, while the Mehsud's dominate the northern and central part of South Waziristan.

Al Qaeda's presence in South Waziristan was not curbed until the Pakistani army mounted a major incursion into South Waziristan during the spring of 2004. The operations continued into the fall of 2004, finally ending when the Pakistani authorities signed an agreement with the Ahmadzai-Wazir tribe in November 2004 and the Mehsud tribe in February 2005. Unlike some Uzbeks, Tajiks, Uighurs, and the Chechens who stayed and fought alongside the local Taliban in South Waziristan,[23] members of al Qaeda chose to flee South Waziristan and abandon their training infrastructure in the Shakai valley.[24] Al Qaeda has been strategic in orientation—instead of defending the land they had established a sanctuary, al Qaeda moved to preserve its depleted strength. In keeping with its long-held practice of preserving its strength to fight the real enemy—the United States and its Western allies—al Qaeda avoided confrontation with the Pakistani military.

In March–April 2007, Uzbek, Tajik, Uighur, and Chechen fighters were chased out from their main base on the Wana plains, near the towns of Azam Warsaq, by tribesmen from the Darikhel subclan of the Zalikhel clan and local Taliban loyal to Mullah Nazir from the small Kakakhel subclan of the Zalikhel clan. These local Taliban and tribal militants fought and defeated other local Taliban forces from the much larger Yargulkhel subclan of the

Zalikhel clan and Uzbeks, Tajiks, Uighurs, and Chechens loyal to the Islamic Movement of Uzbekistan (IMU) and its leader Tahir Yuldashev.[25] The forces loyal to the IMU had become increasingly unpopular among the Darikhel and Kakakhel subclans, as they participated in the killing of tribal leaders, in battles for power among the local Taliban within the Zalikhel clan, and built their own power base and structures in the form of landholdings and prisons.[26] It is still unknown exactly how much support the Pakistani government provided to the fighters from the Darikhel and Kakakhel subclans, but considering the relative weakness of these subclans compared to the powerful and well-respected Taliban leaders from the Yargulkhel subclan, the support must have been considerable for the Darikhel and Kakakhel commanders to prevail in this manner.[27] It remains to be seen where the IMU has moved, but we believe they have probably sought shelter either in the Mehsud territory or among members of the Uzbek, Islamic Jihad Union, in North Waziristan. Removing the Yargulkhel commanders from the Wana plains had become a priority for the Pakistani authorities after it had become clear that the suicide bombers, who struck Islamabad, Peshawar, Dera Ismail Khan, and North Waziristan in January 2007, were indoctrinated near Azam Warsaq by members of the IMU and various commanders from the Yargulkhel subclan of the Zalikhel clan.[28] These revelations came from interrogations of individuals captured in Karachi and near Tank.[29] During the interrogations of those detained in Karachi, it also became clear that aside from the IMU and local Taliban commanders, the mastermind behind the attack on the U.S. Consulate in Karachi in March 2006, Qari Zafar, had also been involved in launching this campaign of attacks.[30] (More details of the U.S. Consulate attack follow.)

Impact of the Jihadist Enclave in FATA

After the expulsion of al Qaeda from South Waziristan, the group moved its training infrastructure to North Waziristan. There it came under the leadership of the Egyptian, Muhsin Musa Matwali Atwa a.k.a. Abu Abd al-Rahman al-Muhajir. Al Qaeda's leader of External Operations, Hamza Rabia, also survived the move to North Waziristan Agency and remained in his position during most of 2005. Contrary to this, Abd al-Hadi al-Iraqi sought and was removed from his position as leader of al Qaeda operations in Afghanistan. Abd al-Hadi is a brilliant military commander, but we believe his personality is very rough. He was therefore often at odds with other senior commanders in al Qaeda. However, his very direct and candid nature also made him a natural choice, when al Qaeda had to negotiate with leaders of other militant groups, who had similar personalities. After the U.S. invasion of Iraq in March 2003, Abd al-Hadi acted as a conduit between Osama bin Laden and Ahmed Fadil Nazzal al-Khalayleh alias Abu Musab al-Zarqawi, the leader of

Jamiat Tawhid wal Jihad (which would later become Tanzim Qaedat fi Bilad al-Rafidayn or the al Qaeda organization in the Land of the Two Rivers/al Qaeda in Iraq).[31] Abd-al Hadi was an essential broker in bringing Osama bin Laden and al-Zarqawi into the agreement, which would serve as the basis for bringing Abu Musab's organization into al Qaeda.[32] We believe that during 2005, Abd-al Hadi al-Iraqi was intent on returning to his native country and serving with Abu Musab. However, knowing the great disenchantment among al Qaeda's leadership in Pakistan with his leadership in Iraq, Abu Musab feared that Hadi al-Iraqi was sent to replace him and refused to assist his entry into Iraq. In Abd al-Hadi's absence, Osama bin Laden appointed the Egyptian, Khalid Habib, as al-Iraqi's replacement. Khalid Habib is a very able commander and a close friend of both Hamza Rabia and al-Zawahiri, but we believe he is more of an introvert than Abd al-Hadi and a much less inspiring military commander. When Abd al-Hadi returned to North Waziristan, we assess that the leadership of al Qaeda decided that his military skills were too important to leave unused, and they therefore decided to reappoint him as the commander of al Qaeda operations in southwestern Afghanistan, while Khalid Habib remained in overall command of operations in Afghanistan and regionally in command of operations in southeastern Afghanistan.[33]

During the latter part of 2004 and early 2005, al Qaeda also recreated their training infrastructure in North Waziristan. This infrastructure was situated in the areas surrounding the towns of Mir Ali and between Miran Shah and Shawal Valley,[34] at Sedgi[35] and Data Khel.[36] This infrastructure was led by the Egyptian Muhsin Musa Matwali Atwa a.k.a. Abu Abd al-Rahman al-Muhajir. The main hosts of al Qaeda in North Waziristan were members of the Utmanzai-Wazir tribes, who inhabit southern and western areas of the Agency, while members of the Dawr tribe inhabit the towns of Mir Ali and parts of Miran Shah. During the increasing "Talibanization" in both North and South Waziristan, the tribal maliks (chiefs) had lost considerable power to the local clerics, who had mobilized the locals for jihad in Afghanistan and against the Pakistani army. Many maliks were killed and replaced with clerics, thus permanently altering the social fabric in some parts of FATA. Today we believe that the local clerics are the main supporters of foreign militants in the Waziristans.[37] We believe that the strengthened clerical elite in Waziristan have solidified the position of the foreign militants in the Agencies. Instead of being heavily dependent on a steady flow of money from Saudi Arabia to pay tribal maliks for sanctuary, members of al Qaeda and foreign militants, in general, have built strong ideological and personal links with the clerical elite and the local Taliban in the two Waziristan Agencies. Together with local Taliban, the foreign militants have also fought the Pakistani army, building blood bonds between the foreign and local militants. However, owing to the interference of foreign militants in local affairs, there does seem to be an increasing opposition to the presence of foreigners among tribal elders and some senior clerics in North Waziristan. A local tribal elder in North Waziristan said: "All the foreigners will have to leave but a few of them will probably remain in the region for future planning."[38] The September 2006 agreement between the Utmanzai-Wazir tribes, the local Taliban in North Waziristan, and the Pakistani government seems to have further worked toward this goal. The Dawr cleric Maulana Sadiq Noor has largely assumed command of the local Taliban in parts of the Dawr tribal areas of North Waziristan. He has been increasingly opposed to the presence and influence of certain Arab commanders in North Waziristan.[39] Some Arab militants have therefore had to reestablish close ties to the Mehsud tribal leaders, Abdullah and Baitullah Mehsud, so as to be able to use their tribal areas in the central and northern part of South Waziristan to rebuild their training and operational infrastructure. However in North Waziristan, al Qaeda leaders are still believed to be staying under the protection of the Dawr local Taliban in the region around Miran Shah and Mir Ali and al Qaeda's main training infrastructure is still believed to be in the Utmanzai-Wazir areas south of the Tochi River, specifically in the Razmak area, on the border between North and South Waziristan, the area between Razmak and Miran Shah and in the Shawal Valley.[40] The alliances with the various Pashtun tribes provide al Qaeda with much needed space in which to recreate their structure and train new cadre.[41]

We believe that al Qaeda has managed to rebuild their training infrastructure on the border between South and North Waziristan, replacing the ones they had abandoned in the Wazir areas of South Waziristan and those destroyed during the Pakistani army's major operations in North Waziristan from March until June–July 2006.[42] We believe this training infrastructure provides training to militants from Europe, the Gulf, and North Africa. International Crisis Group reported: "militant training centres still thrive in the Waziristans."[43] It is not known how many camps train al Qaeda fighters in Waziristan, but according to a report in February 2007,

> the training camps had yet to reach the size and level of sophistication of the Qaida camps established in Afghanistan under Taliban rule but groups of 10 to 20 men are being trained at the camps and the Qaida infrastructure in the region is gradually becoming more mature.[44]

The training sites are located in wooded and rugged terrain, making it difficult to obtain good overhead imagery. Only a few of the camps in Waziristan are run by al Qaeda for training militants to fight with the Taliban in Afghanistan and for operations outside the Pakistan/Afghanistan arena. In January 2007, the Pakistani military targeted one camp (however, most likely not an al Qaeda camp), located in the Mehsud tribal areas around Zamazola in South Waziristan on the border with North Waziristan. In mid-January the Pakistani military executed an early morning helicopter attack against three sites allegedly wounding a senior Arab commander and killing 20–30 other militants.[45] In May 2007 the Pakistani military executed a ground and air assault on a compound in Zargakhel, 25 kilometers south of Miran Shah in North Waziristan. The compound was reportedly serving as a training site for Uzbek trainees, four of whom were killed during the assault.[46] This attack was preceded by a missile strike in late April 2007, targeting a compound in Sedgi (situated between Shawal Valley and Miran Shah), killing four individuals. The missile attack was reportedly launched by a U.S. unmanned aerial vehicle (UAV) operating in the border area between Afghanistan and Pakistan.[47]

With the difficulty of training foreigners in Iraq, a very hostile environment, al Qaeda has realized the critical importance of training recruits elsewhere. The main problem for al Qaeda is to get the militants into FATA, train them, and send them back to their home or target countries, without arousing suspicion. It is very difficult for any nontribal individual to gain entry into FATA and especially into South and North Waziristan Agencies. To avoid the scrutiny of the Pakistani authorities, when entering Pakistan, many militants not of Pakistani origin choose to enter via Iran. Many Saudi Arabian militants travel to Tehran on legal documents and visas, but subsequently move to Iranian Baluchistan, which has a vibrant smuggling community, to cross the border into Pakistan. In September 2006, Pakistani border guards arrested four Saudi Arabian men, aged 18–25, and one Pakistani near the Iranian-Pakistani border town of Taftan. The four Saudi citizens had valid visas for Iran, but no visa for Pakistan. They were arrested for attempting to enter Pakistan without a visa.[48] During their interrogation the young Saudi males claimed that they were entering Pakistan to study at a madrassa (religious seminary), but their age, nationality, and travel pattern suggest they may also have intended to travel to FATA for training with al Qaeda. Some militants from Europe also enter Pakistan through Iranian Baluchistan. According to an article in the U.S. magazine *Newsweek*, most European militants "take a clandestine overland route across Turkey, Iran and Afghanistan, escorted by a network of professional smugglers."[49]

While Arabs and convert Muslims from the West are suspected, there is one high-risk category that has easier access to FATA. It is usually easier for militants of Pakistani origin and especially Pashtuns who live abroad, to enter FATA. They can do this under the pretext that they are visiting family or conducting business. Some militants also travel to Pakistan to attend the Jamiat Dawah wal Tabligh (The Society for Call and Preaching, which is a nonpolitical society) Ijtima (gathering) in the Pakistani city of Raiwind. This Tabligh gathering often attracts many hundred thousands of worshippers, many of whom come from abroad. Acquiring a Pakistani entry visa to attend the Raiwind Ijtima is therefore relatively easy and Ijtima attendees may even receive financial assistance from Jamiat Dawah wal Tabligh to help them travel to Pakistan.[50] Since the earthquake in October 2005, many militants have also traveled to Pakistan as part of Islamic nongovernmental organizations

(NGO);[51] however they still need contacts among the local tribes in FATA either to be smuggled in or to pass through checkpoints manned by Pakistani security forces surrounding North and South Waziristan.

Al Qaeda's Current Structure

Al Qaeda's current leadership structure is believed to be situated around al-Zawahiri in Bajaur Agency of FATA. With al Qaeda's newfound space in North Waziristan, al-Zawahiri may be considering a move to this Agency, but any move there will either take him through several Afghan provinces such as Kunar, Nangahar, Paktia, and Khost, where he could easily be captured by North Atlantic Treaty Organization (NATO) or Afghan forces. The alternative route goes through Mohmand, Khyber, Orakzai, and Kurram Agencies, which would be even more dangerous as the population in large parts of Khyber and especially Kurram Agency is unfriendly if not hostile to foreign militants.

Among other senior al Qaeda members, who are believed to be situated with Ayman al-Zawahiri in Bajaur is the head of al Qaeda's Media Committee, the Moroccan Muhammad Abaytah alias Abd al-Rahman al-Maghrebi.[52] Shortly after the U.S. air attack on a house in Damadola in Bajaur Agency on January 13, 2006, media reports speculated that Abd al-Rahman al-Maghrebi and three other high-ranking al Qaeda or al-Jihad members had died in the strike.[53] However no information has yet surfaced to support these speculations, and we therefore still believe that al-Maghrebi is alive and operating. Abd-al Rahman al-Maghrebi is the son-in-law of al-Zawahiri. After being born and raised in Morocco, Abd al-Rahman al-Maghrebi left to study in Germany in 1996. He settled and studied software programming in the German city of Cologne. In 1999, Abd al-Rahman left for Afghanistan, where he trained at the al-Faruq camp near Kandahar, but was pulled from his training because of a specific request,[54] most likely by KSM, the then head of al Qaeda's Media Committee. KSM also administered Bait al-Shuhadah (House of Martyrs), where Abd al-Rahman stayed during his training at al-Faruq.[55] According to the German magazine, *Der Spiegel*, Abd al-Rahman subsequently had a brilliant career inside al Qaeda. His software and computer skills made him a great asset within the group's Media Committee. After the fall of Afghanistan in 2001, Abd al-Rahman fled to Iran, but returned to Pakistan in 2003. We believe he lives close to his farther-in-law, most likely in the Mahmund Tehsil of Bajaur Agency, where he plays a key role in the technical aspects of designing al Qaeda's media products.

However, al Qaeda's main structure remains in North Waziristan where the head of its Internal and External Operations and Finance Committee are believed to be staying. Since 1995 the Egyptian Mustafa Ahmed Muhammad Uthman Abu Al-Yazid a.k.a. Abu Said al-Masri has headed al Qaeda's Finance

Committee.[56] He was born in Egypt on December 27, 1955 and was later schooled as an accountant. He joined the Egyptian Islamist group Gama'at al-Islamiyah, but later switched to al-Zawahiri's al-Jihad. He became head of Osama bin Laden's finances in 1995, when they were both based in Sudan.[57] He is known as being a very stringent administrator, who keeps tight control of al Qaeda's finances. On May 26, 2007 an interview with Abu Said al-Masri, conducted by al-Sahab (The Cloud), was posted on the Internet. In this interview Abu Said declares that he has assumed command of Tanzim al Qaeda al-Jihad fi al-Khorasan (al Qaeda and Jihad Organization in Afghanistan), which seems to have replaced al Qaeda's Internal Operations pillar. In the interview Abu Said focuses on the role of the Arab mujahedin in Afghanistan and their ability to buttress the Taliban. He praises the cooperation and coordination that al Qaeda has with the Taliban Emirate in Afghanistan, but suggests that Tanzim al Qaeda al-Jihad is in need of a cash infusion for the organization to offer its full potential to the jihad in Afghanistan.[58] It is unknown whether Abu Said has retained his position as head of al Qaeda's Financial Committee, but we believe that Abu Said's appointment as head of al Qaeda in Afghanistan is another sign of the preeminent position of Egyptians among the leaders in al Qaeda. As Tanzim al Qaeda al-Jihad fi al-Khorasan is one of the al Qaeda branches, which is most frequently involved in military operations, it would be natural to appoint one of the many skilled military commanders within this branch. But instead of appointing an extremely respected commander like Abu Layth al-Libi, al Qaeda chose to appoint its accountant to lead its military operations in Afghanistan. This could lead to some internal rumblings in al Qaeda, as some members of other nationalities may start doubting the meritocratic credentials of the organization.

The Egyptian Khalid Habib was, until recently, heading al Qaeda's Internal Operations, but may now have assumed leadership of al Qaeda's External Operations. According to an article in the Pakistani newspaper *Frontier Times*, he was in North Waziristan, during and immediately before September 2006, in an effort to influence the agreement between the Pakistani government and the Utmanzai-Wazir tribe. He was also preparing for what, the foreign militants believe, is the inevitable breach of this agreement by the Pakistani government. The foreign militants in North Waziristan believe that Western and particularly U.S. pressure on the Pakistani government for renewed military operations in North Waziristan, will grow to such an extent that Musharraf will eventually comply.[59]

From his base in North Waziristan, Abd-al Hadi al-Iraqi previously led al Qaeda's External Operations. In August 2006 Abd al-Hadi was described as al Qaeda's number three by the *New York Times* and we believe that he together with Abu Ubayda al-Masri planned the previously described "Liquid/Airline Plot," which was foiled in the United Kingdom in August 2006.[60] However, in April 2007, U.S. authorities announced that they had detained Abd al-Hadi and that he was being moved to the U.S. detention facility at Guantanamo

Bay in Cuba. Abd al-Hadi al-Iraqi was captured in late 2006, while traveling to Iraq, where he was to have served in al Qaeda's local branch.[61] Abd-al-Hadi was most probably replaced by one of the Egyptians, Abu Ubayda al-Masri, Khalid Habib, or the Gulf Arab Hamza al-Jawfi as head of al Qaeda's External Operations.

Abd al-Hadi al-Iraqi's capture, while traveling to Iraq, was the second time, Jama'at al Qaeda al-Jihad failed while trying to reinforce al Qaeda in Iraq. In September 2006, British forces killed the Kuwaiti-born Iraqi, Mehmud Ahmed Muhammad a.k.a. Umar al-Faruq in the southern Iraqi city of Basra. Before his arrest, in June 2002 in Indonesia, Umar al-Faruq had been a senior member of al Qaeda in Southeast Asia.[62] After his arrest, he was transferred to Bagram, but during the summer of 2005, he and three others managed to escape.[63] He subsequently appeared in several videos, taunting the U.S. government, detailing his escape and the harsh treatment he had been subjected to during his imprisonment.[64] However, during the summer of 2006, he was apparently ordered to travel to Iraq to support the current head of al Qaeda's local branch, Abd al-Munim Izzedine Ali-Ismail a.k.a. Abu Ayyub al-Masri a.k.a. Abu Hamza al-Muhajir.[65] Prior to his trip, Umar al-Faruq is believed to have been staying in either in North Waziristan Agency of FATA or immediately across the border, in Khost Province of Afghanistan. One of his fellow inmates, Muhammad Jafar Jamal al-Qathani a.k.a. Abu Nasir al-Qathani from Saudi Arabia, who escaped together with Umar al-Faruq, was also rearrested in southern Khost Province in November of 2006.[66]

The Extended al Qaeda

There are much larger and more resourceful groups worldwide than al Qaeda. Examples include the LTTE in Sri Lanka, the MILF in the Philippines, the LeT in Pakistan, and FARC in Columbia. However, by forging alliances and co-opting groups, al Qaeda has been able to grow ideologically and operationally at a global level. Its ability to replicate the ideological and operational virus is the key strength of al Qaeda. Two militant groups have merged with al Qaeda during 2006, and more are likely to merge in the coming years. The second merger was announced in al-Zawahiri's September 11, 2006 interview with al Qaeda's media arm, al-Sahab (The Cloud), when al-Zawahiri stated:

> Our Amir, mujahid Shaykh and lion of Islam Usama Bin Ladin, may God protect him, has instructed me to give the good news to Muslims in general, and my brothers the mujahedin everywhere that the Salafi Group for Call and Combat has joined Al-Qa'ida of Jihad Organization. So, praise is due to God, praise is due to God, and praise is due to God for this blessed alliance, which we ask God that it will be a bone in the throats of the Americans and French Crusaders and their allies that would bring on them distress, trepidation, and dejection in the hearts of the traitorous

apostate sons of France. We beseech Him Almighty to guide our brothers at the Salafi Group for Call and Combat to success in order to crush
the pillars of the Crusader alliance, especially their old immoral leader,
America.[67]

Since the accession of the Groupe Salafiste pour la Prédication et le
Combat (GSPC) into al Qaeda, the leadership of the GSPC has twice changed
the emblem of the group—initially from an oval-shaped symbol centered on
an open Koran, which appears to be standing on a grey brick wall as well as
a sword and an AK-assault rifle; to a black flag attached to a Kalashnikov
rifle. The Kalashnikov, which presumably reinforces that victory can only be
achieved through fighting, is placed on top of a globe, confirming the global
agenda, which the GSPC has supported since Hassan Hattab was ousted as
leader of the group in 2003.[68] In January 2007 GSPC rescinded its previous
name to become part of the Tanzim Qaeda bi-Bilad al-Maghreb al-Islami (the
al Qaeda Organization in the Islamic Maghreb), which has since conducted
two major attacks against international oil workers in Algeria and the first
suicide attacks in Algeria's history.[69] However, despite the new name and the
recent attacks against international targets,[70] we believe that GSPC's merger
with al Qaeda was merely the last step in a long series of steps taken by the
GSPC since 2003—the group has moved from being a mostly Algeria-focused
group toward the global agenda of al Qaeda. Since 2003 the GSPC has become
steadily more focused on conducting attacks outside Algeria, culminating in
the attack on the Mauritanian Army Base in Lemgheitty in June 2005.[71]

Before the accession of the GSPC into al Qaeda, another merger had already
occurred. This merger occurred in early August 2006, when al-Zawahiri
announced that "the unification of a great faction of the knights of the Gamaa
Islamiya...with the al-Qaida group."[72] According to al-Zawahiri, the faction
of Gama'at al-Islamiyah that joined al Qaeda was led by Muhammad Shawqi
Islambouli a.k.a. Abu Jafar al-Masri the brother of Khalid Islambouli, who
took part in the assassination of Egyptian President Anwar Sadat in 1981.[73]
However, we do not believe that Muhammad Shawqi Islambouli is anything
other than a figurehead for this faction. He has so far not delivered any video,
audio, or written statement. We believe this is because he is currently detained
in Iran, which makes it more difficult for him to communicate.[74] So far the
45-year old Gama'at al-Islamiyah member Muhammad Khalil Hakaymah
a.k.a. Abu Jihad al-Masri has been the main spokesperson for this faction of
Gama'at, which broke away from the main group after it declared a unilateral cease-fire with the Egyptian government in 1997. Abu Jihad al-Masri was
born in Aswan in Upper Egypt and has a master's degree in social sciences.[75]
He appeared in a separate clip of Ayman al-Zawahiri's video speech, which
was broadcast by the television station, Al-Jazeerah.[76] Abu Jihad's main role has
so far been a range of publications on his Web site, Al-Thabitun Ala-al-Ahd
(Steadfast on the Covenant), ranging from books called "Unmasking U.S.

Intelligence"[77] and "How to fight alone"[78] to political statements supporting the Islamic courts in Somalia.[79] He has also criticized the militant Palestinian movement Hamas for participating in a democratic process, which he sees as a ploy aimed at getting Muslims to live by rules and laws other than those of God.[80] In January 2007, he published a five-part version of his memoirs detailing his activities between 1979 and 2002.[81] According to Abu Jihad al-Masri, his Web site is "a free website that has been designed and supervised by one of the admirers of the Islamic brothers in Europe."[82]

However, in January 2007, a statement was posted to a jihadi Web site, suggesting that the administrator of Al-Thabitun Ala al-Ahd had been arrested and the site was closed.[83] According to the statement the site's administrator, the Gama'at al-Islamiyah member Walid Abd-al-Hamid al-Sharqawi al-Mihdar al-Idrisi al-Alawi a.k.a. Abu al-Harith al-Midhar, had been arrested in "a Western country on suspicion of having ties to terrorist groups."[84] This statement was followed by a statement posted on the Web site Midad al-Suyuf on January 26, 2007, where a newly released Abu Harith al-Midhar condemns the British antiterror police. According to Open Source Center, Al-Midhar specifically stated that he "had had enough of the injustice" and went on to describe his detention and questioning by the British antiterrorism force. Al-Mihdar said that he was expecting to be sent to Guantanamo Bay because he "was certain of the filthy nature" of the British government—"the dogs of America." He said that he "was eager to hear the charges" against him, and ready to admit his "love for Usama Bin Ladin."[85]

After the closure of Thabitun Ala al-Ahd, the site has reopened at a new URL. Shortly after the site was reopened, the Gama'at faction, which joined al Qaeda, was named Tanzim Qaedat al-Jihad fi-Ard al-Kinanah (the al Qaeda Organization for Jihad on the land of Kinanah (Egypt)). The creed of this organization was laid out by Abu Jihad al-Masri and posted on Thabitun, under the title, "Toward a New Strategy in Resisting the Occupier."[86] In this posting Hakaymah continues and mirrors the strategic vision presented in al-Zawahiri's letter of July 9, 2005 and from his speeches.[87] He legitimizes attacks against civilian citizens in countries that occupy Muslim lands. Considering the international security situation and the problems related to the establishment of hierarchical organizations, he suggests that such attacks may be carried out by individuals or small groups.[88] He also decries the transgressions that some mujahedin have committed in not taking sufficient precautions to avoid killing Muslims and being excessively cruel against the enemy.[89] Again mirroring Zawahiri, Hakaymah suggests that such transgressions could erode the most important base for mujahedin operations, namely popular support. To maintain public support, Hakaymah also urges the mujahedin to refrain from publishing their disputes with the Ulema (Sunni Clerical elite), warning that as

> the public considers the ulema to be the symbol and badge of Islam, disparaging them could lead to public disdain for religion and the clergy. It could

encourage atheists and secularists to belittle everything Islamic. This will cause more harm than the benefit to be gained by criticizing a scholar for an innovation that does not constitute unbelief or for a legal position.[90]

Reaching Out to Nationalist-Islamist Groups

Unlike during its days in Afghanistan, al Qaeda has limitations to expanding its size in FATA. Therefore, al Qaeda is reaching out to like-minded groups worldwide to augment its force. Operating out of FATA, the leadership of al Qaeda is co-opting other militant groups with local battle experience. By this process of co-option, al Qaeda's global organization has grown at an unprecedented rate. In the absence of major successful attacks on Western soil, the leadership of al Qaeda is trying to portray itself as the headquarters of the global jihad movement with fronts in North Africa, Iraq, the Gulf, Asia, and the Horn of Africa.[91]

However, FATA has also become a base from where al Qaeda has formulated and directed a new strategic approach. This is to move away from purely dealing with like-minded groups. The leadership of al Qaeda is instead advocating that their local branches reach out and co-opt nationalist campaigns and especially Islamist-Nationalist campaigns. The aim and necessity of this new strategy was initially formulated by al-Zawahiri in his July 2005 letter to Abu Musab, but most clearly stated in another letter to Abu Musab, written by the Libyan al Qaeda leader, Shekh Atiyah Abd al-Rahman in December 2005. In the letter Sheikh Atiyah advises Abu Musab al-Zarqawi to

> take caution against being zealous about the name "al-Qa'ida," or any name or organization. Although all mujahedin are our brothers, the Sunni are our brothers and our friends, as long as they are Muslims, even if they are disobedient, or insolent; whether they come into the organization with us or not, for they are our brothers, our friends, and our loved ones.[92]

Atiyah believes that this is necessary because

> all the mujahedin, are still weak. We are in the stage of weakness and a state of paucity. We have not yet reached a level of stability. We have no alternative but to not squander any element of the foundations of strength, or any helper or supporter. We are unceasing in our efforts to unite our nation's strength and resources.[93]

The aim being that

> when God opens the way, and we have the wherewithal, then we can behave differently in accordance with what is appropriate for that time.[94]

In other words; recognizing al Qaeda's current weakness, the leadership proposes that al Qaeda temporarily cooperate with any repenting secular or Sunni Islamist group. Even if those groups or individuals practice heresy or are disobedient, such groups fighting for a local cause can provide territory and protection for al Qaeda's structures and bases. Through this strategy al Qaeda is aiming to regain strength, allowing the groups to behave differently and if necessary to enforce what their ideology commands.

We believe this strategy is far more politically mature and inclusive than the very rigid and uncompromising approach undertaken by Abu Musab, the former al Qaeda leader in Iraq. Through this strategy, al Qaeda may become a much more calculating political actor, capable of making temporary broad political alliances with Sunni groups or factions. The overall political objectives may be different from those of al Qaeda, but al Qaeda will seek to cooperate with these groups as long as they can provide a safe haven for al Qaeda's organization and training opportunities. However, al Qaeda and especially the group's Iraqi branch, Tanzim Qaedat fi Bilad al-Rafidayn, will find it very difficult to shed the group's uncompromising reputation—built during the leadership of Abu Musab—and stop the confrontational relationship, which the group shares with most Nationalist and Islamist Resistance groups in Iraq. Even outside Iraq, the attraction of al Qaeda's outreach program to Islamist-Nationalist groups is likely to be limited, but in some cases, as was seen with the Islamic Courts in Somalia, al Qaeda may indeed be able to infiltrate and receive protection and safe haven from a local Islamist organization. This threat generally needs to be countered by diligent political means and patience, instead of military operations, which could otherwise bring al Qaeda's global Jihadi Salafists closer to the local national Islamists. If the diligent approach is taken, rifts will inevitably occur between the global Jihadi Salafists and the Islamist-Nationalists, usually ending in the sidelining of the former, owing to lack of popular support.

The Future

Once again, al Qaeda has successfully carved out a semi–safe haven in FATA. The Afghan-Pakistan border has emerged as the new headquarters of the global jihad movement. The subject of al Qaeda dominates the international media, but until five years after 9/11, its presence in FATA has not been a subject of intense international debate. In the meantime, al Qaeda, determined to attack the West, has recruited globally and struck its enemies through its inspired and instigated cells.

From FATA, and particularly North Waziristan, the group is resting, reorganizing and regenerating. Compared to the Afghan Taliban and the local Taliban in FATA, al Qaeda's presence and influence in Pakistan and across the border in Afghanistan is relatively weak.[95] The local Taliban has grown significantly in strength and in the coming years it will be a significant factor influencing both Afghanistan and Pakistan.

The error effect of al-Zawahiri's continued threats are slowly wearing off. Therefore, the al Qaeda's leadership must show that the group retains capabilities to strike against Western targets outside its normal areas of operation in Iraq and Afghanistan. While creating new structures and linking up with existing platforms globally, al Qaeda is using FATA to impart training and direction to a new generation of both traditional and homegrown cadre. As long as FATA is a sanctuary for the jihadists, there can be no genuine peace and stability in Afghanistan and beyond. Without dismantling of the al Qaeda and the associated jihadist enclave in FATA, the incessant guerrilla and periodic terrorist attacks will continue. Taking into consideration the increased infiltration from FATA into Afghanistan, the media has mostly dealt with the problems for NATO and Afghan security forces, but not the threat to the rest of the world. Very little has been documented on the threat from this jihadist enclave to the rest of Pakistan and to the West. From this sanctuary, al Qaeda is building skill and empowering a new, albeit small generation of Western recruits. In addition to imparting propaganda, translating into support for al Qaeda and its movement globally, al Qaeda is providing operational and improvised explosive device (IED) knowledge, which make young jihadis from the West able to plan and conduct attacks that are much more sophisticated than what is normally seen among homegrown groups.

As for Pakistan, the government has a clear interest in upholding the various agreements signed in South and North Waziristan and Bajaur Agencies of FATA. Any further major military operation will be very unpopular inside the country's own military establishment, as it would expand the Pakistani army's unpopular role in North and South Waziristan. As stated by a senior Pakistani military official, the "tribal areas are 1/20th of the size of Pakistan, but we have 85,000 Pakistani troops deployed in the tribal areas. It is double the troop deployment in Afghanistan."[96] After suffering the loss of over 400 soldiers in fighting, the Pakistani forces adopted a new approach of seeking to win hearts and minds. They built hospitals, road, water wells, and schools as well as provided the tribal youth access to the best schools in the rest of Pakistan. Unless the Pakistani military balances its military operations vis-à-vis its civil operations, it will not be able to regain support among the tribes. In addition to spreading instability into the settled areas of NWFP, any further large-scale military activities could face a backlash, which could strengthen the local Taliban.

However, for the rest of the world, and Europe and the United States in particular, the problem remains. As long as al Qaeda has a presence on the strategic border area between Afghanistan and Pakistan, they are at risk. The local Pakistani Taliban in North Waziristan are unlikely to expel al Qaeda anytime soon. With al Qaeda able to disseminate propaganda, recruit, run training camps, and direct operations, the question remains: can the West afford to wait? Similar to the period preceding the 9/11 attacks, when the West marked time hoping for a split to develop between al Qaeda and Taliban in Afghanistan, will the West this time also wait for a split to occur between local Taliban and al Qaeda?

The West, particularly the United States, has no option but to enhance its engagement with Pakistan. Pakistan under Musharraf once again became a frontline state in the fight against terrorism and extremism. But without the understanding of the West of the difficulties Pakistan faces, the progress of the Pakistani state will be limited. Instead of threatening to impose sanctions, the West must understand why all terror roads lead to Pakistan. The surviving core leadership of al Qaeda, which is actively leading the global jihad, lives and works in FATA. If the jihadist enclave in FATA is not dismantled, al Qaeda leadership will continue to harm not only the adjacent areas of Afghanistan and Pakistan but inflict grave damage to the rest of the world also. While understanding the geopolitical concerns of Pakistan, the West must step up the existing engagement with Pakistan on a number of fronts. Whatever investment made in Pakistan, whether it is to develop its economy, educate its youth, train Pakistani military, law enforcement and intelligence officers or to groom its next generation of leaders, will help, at this crucial juncture, to reduce the growing global threat of extremism and violence.

Notes

1. The official name of al Qaeda led by Osama bin Laden and his deputy Dr. Ayman al-Zawahiri is Jama'at al Qaeda al-Jihad (al Qaeda al-Jihad Group) or Tanzim Qaedat al-Jihad (al Qaeda and Jihad Organization).
2. While Nielsen was in Khyber, Mohamand, and Bajaur Agency of FATA in May 2007, Gunaratna was in Islamabad and Lahore in April 2007.
3. Ibid., 221.
4. Ibid., 220.
5. *The News* (Internet Version-WWW), November 18, 2006, "Pakistan: Villagers Start Rebuilding Seminary Destroyed in Bajaur Airstrike."
6. Office of the Director of National Intelligence September 2006, "Profile on Abu Faraj al-Libi" and "Khalid Sheikh Muhammad."
7. Office of the Director of National Intelligence September 2006, "Profile on Abu Faraj al-Libi."
8. Ayman al-Zawahiri's letter dated July 9, 2005.
9. Pervez Musharraf, *In the Line of Fire* (New York: Simon & Schuster, 2006), 221.
10. Ibid.
11. Ron Suskind, *The One Percent Doctrine* (New York: Simon & Schuster, 2006), 235.
12. Ibid.
13. *Dawn*, August 19, 2006, "'Son-in-law of Zawahiri Was Mastermind.'"
14. Office of the Director of National Intelligence September 2006, "Profile on Khalid Sheikh Muhammad."

15. http://www.gpoaccess.gov/911/pdf/sec7.pdf, 226.

16. Office of the Director of National Intelligence September 2006, "Profile on Khalid Sheikh Muhammad" and "Profile on Ali Abd-al Aziz Ali"; *New York Times* May 3, 2003, "Aftereffects: Al-Qaeda; U.S. Reports Plot to Fly a Plane into U.S. Consulate in Pakistan."

17. Suskind *One Percent Doctrine*, 317–318.

18. Musharraf, *In the Line of Fire*, 233.

19. Suskind, *One Percent Doctrine*, 317–318.

20. Interview, Inter-Services Intelligence, Islamabad, April 2007.

21. *New York Times,* December 11, 2006, "Taliban and Allies Tighten Grip in North of Pakistan" and Musharraf, 267–269.

22. BBC, April 5, 2007, "Pakistan's Tribal District of South Waziristan, on the Border with Afghanistan, Is in the Throes of Turmoil Once Again."

23. International Crisis Group Report, December 11, 2006, "Pakistan's Tribal Areas: Appeasing the Militants," 21.

24. Musharraf, *In the Line of Fire,* 265–270.

25. BBC, April 5, 2007, "Pakistan's Tribal District of South Waziristan, on the Border with Afghanistan, Is in the Throes of Turmoil Once Again."

26. Ibid. *The News,* March 29, 2007, "Tribal Militants Pledge to Evict Uzbeks from Wana" and *The News,* April 7, 2007, "Letter Explains Drive against Foreign Militants in Waziristan."

27. BBC, April 5, 2007, "Pakistan's Tribal District of South Waziristan, on the Border with Afghanistan, Is in the Throes of Turmoil Once Again."

28. Geo TV, February 16, 2007, "Pakistan: Arrested Suicide Bombers Said Trained by 'Foreign Terrorists' in Wana" and *Herald,* April 2007 issue "Training to Explode."

29. Geo TV, February 16, 2007, "Pakistan: Arrested Suicide Bombers."

30. Ibid.

31. *Newsweek,* April 11, 2006, "Terror Broker."

32. Ibid.

33. Hikmat Karzai, January 4, 2006, "Afghanistan and Globalisation of Terrorist Tactics," Institute for Defence and Strategic Studies, Nanyang Technological University.

34. International Crisis Group Report, December 11, 2006, "Pakistan's Tribal Areas: Appeasing the Militants," 21.

35. BBC, March 2, 2006, "Pakistan Raid Toll 'climbs to 45.'"

36. Associated Press, October 4, 2006, "Afghanistan Arrests 17 Would-Be Bombers."

37. International Crisis Group Report, December 11, 2006, "Pakistan's Tribal Areas: Appeasing the Militants," 22.

38. *The News,* August 1, 2006, "Local Taliban, Foreigners Part Ways in N. Waziristan."

39. *The Post* August 19, 2006, "Cracks Appear in Taliban over North Waziristan Leadership."

40. ABC News, February 5, 2007, "Spain Emerges as Base for AQ-Linked Terror Groups."

41. *New York Times,* December 11, 2006, "Taliban and Allies Tighten Grip in North of Pakistan."

42. *Newsweek,* December 25, 2006, "Al-Qaeda's Western Recruits" and *New York Daily News,* August 13, 2006 "Al-Qaeda Camps Surge: New Videos Tout Terror Training."

43. International Crisis Group Report, December 11, 2006," Pakistan's Tribal Areas: Appeasing the Militants," 21.
44. *New York Times,* February 19, 2007, "Terror Officials See Al-Qaeda Regaining Power."
45. *The News,* January 16, 2007, "Security Forces Kill over 20 Miscreants in S. Waziristan Operation."
46. AFP, May 22, 2007, "Pakistan Strikes Al-Qa'ida Training Center for Uzbeks, Source Says Four Dead."
47. *India-Defence* April 28, 2007, "American Drone Launches Missile Strike on Terrorist Training Camp in Pakistan," http://www.india-defence.com/reports/3095.
48. *Daily Times,* September 6, 2006, "4 Saudis Held for Alleged Illegal Entry from Iran."
49. *Newsweek,* December 25, 2006, "Al-Qaeda's Western Recruits."
50. ICPVTR Briefing, "Bojinka 2, What Can We Learn about Present-Day al-Qaeda?"
51. Ibid.
52. *Der Spiegel,* January 29, 2006.
53. AFP, January 19, 2006.
54. Al Qaeda's Mujahedin Data Form, recovered by the CIA, Global Pathfinder, ICPVTR Database.
55. *Der Spiegel,* January 29, 2006, and Office of the Director of National Intelligence September 2006 "Profile on Khalid Sheikh Muhammad."
56. *Daily Times,* December 18, 2004, "Interpol Alleges Senior Bin Laden Advisor Hiding in the Tribal Areas."
57. Ibid.
58. Jihadist Web sites, OSC Summary, May 30, 2007, "Afghan 'General Official' Says Al-Qa'ida's Goal Is 'Annihilation' of America."
59. *Frontier Times,* September 22, 2006, "Local and Foreign Taliban in Waziristan Have Started Preparations to Cope with the Situations as They Fear the Government May Breach the Peace Agreement" and *Fourth Rail,* September 23, 2006 "Taliban behind Waziristan Accord."
60. *New York Times,* August 13, 2006, "Accounts after 2005 London Bombing Point to al-Qaeda Role."
61. *Times,* April 28, 2007, "7/7 'Mastermind' Is Seized in Iraq."
62. *Times,* September 26, 2006, "Fugitive bin Laden Protégé Shot Dead by British Troops."
63. Ibid.
64. Site Institute, March 9, 2006, "A Video from al-Sahab Production of an Interview with Mujahid Farouq al-Iraqi, an Escapee from Bagram Prison in Afghanistan."
65. ICPVTR Personality Profile on Abu Hamza al-Muhajir.
66. *The News* (Internet Version-WWW), November 13, 2006, "Al-Qaeda Man Rearrested."
67. Jihadist Web sites, OSC Report September 12, 2006, "Al-Zawahiri Calls on Muslims to Wage 'War of Jihad', Reject UN Resolutions."
68. ICPVTR Group Profile on GSPC/ al Qaeda Organization of the Islamic Maghreb.
69. Reuters, February 13, 2007, "Algeria Hit by Bombings, Six Dead."

70. ICPVTR Analysis of April 11, 2007 attacks by Tanzim al Qaeda al-Jihad bi-Bilad al-Maghreb al-Islami in Algiers, available in ICPVTR Database.

71. Ibid.

72. AP, August 6, 2006, "Al-Qaida's No. 2 Welcomes Egyptian Group."

73. Ibid.

74. *Dawn*, August 19, 2006, "Son-in-law of Zawahiri Was Mastermind."

75. *Al-Sharq al-Awsat*, August 2, 2006, " UK Islamists Say IG Leader Al-Hakayimah Escaped from Iran, Is in Asian Country."

76. AP, August 6, 2006, "Al-Qaida's No. 2 Welcomes Egyptian Group."

77. Jihadist Web sites, OSC Report, August 11, 2006 "Book on 'Unmasking' US Intelligence."

78. Ibid., October 20, 2006, "Translation of Al-Hakaymah's Book 'How to Fight Alone.'"

79. Ibid., December 19, 2006, "Jihadist Websites Express Support for Somali Islamists, Brand Ethiopians as 'Crusaders.'"

80. Ibid., November 8, 2006, "Egyptian Jihadist Al-Hakaymah Writes 'Hamas and the Democratic Deception.'"

81. Ibid., January 3, 2007, "Egyptian Muhammad Al-Hakayimah Publishes Memoirs Detailing Jihadist Involvement, Travel."

82. Al-Sharq al-Awsat, November 27, 2006, "Al-Qa'ida Leader Al-Hakayimah Responds to Islamic Group: Do not Underestimate me…and Qa'idat al-Jihad Shelters me, Al-Islambuli and Others among the Leaders."

83. Jihadist Web sites, OSC Report, January 10, 2007, "Webmaster Arrested, Site Shut Down by Western Country."

84. Ibid.

85. Jihadist Web sites, OSC Report, February 1, 2007, "Former Moderator of Jihadist Website Describes Arrest, Mocks Algerian Claims."

86. http://www.althabeton.co.nr/ "Toward a New Strategy in Resisting the Occupier."

87. Al-Jazirah, New Al-Zawahiri Tape aired on August 4, 2005.

88. http://www.althabeton.co.nr/ "Toward a New Strategy in Resisting the Occupier."

89. Ibid.

90. Ibid.

91. Jihadist Web sites, OSC Report 30, 2006, "Website: Al-Zawahiri Congratulates Muslims on Id Al-Adha, 'Defeat' of Americans."

92. Combating Terrorism Center, United States Military Academy, September 25, 2006 , "Letter Exposes New Leader in Al-Qa'ida High Command."

93. Ibid.

94. Ibid.

95. European Parliament Web site, September 13, 2006 "Pakistani President Hopes for More Trade with the EU."

96. General Ehsan, Chief of Defence Staff, Pakistan, Interview, Singapore, June 1, 2007.

Chapter 8

Al Qaeda and
the Global Salafi Jihad

*Jerrold M. Post**

The al Qaeda suicidal skyjackers of 9/11 differed strikingly from the youthful Palestinian suicide bombers operating in Israel. Older, they were in their late 20s to early 30s; Mohammad Atta, the ringleader, was 33. A number of them had higher education; Atta and two of his colleagues were in graduate training at the Technological Institute in Hamburg. And, for the most part, they came from comfortable middle-class families in Saudi Arabia and Egypt (15 of the 19 were Saudis). As fully formed adults, they had internalized their values. They were "true believers" who had subordinated their individuality to the group. They had uncritically accepted the directions of the destructive charismatic leader of the organization, Osama bin Laden, and what he declared to be moral was moral and indeed was a sacred obligation.

Al Qaeda: Ideology and Philosophy

The ideological and philosophical underpinnings of al Qaeda can be found in several important documents. During my service as expert witness in the spring 2001 trial of al Qaeda terrorists convicted for the bombings of the U.S. embassies in Kenya and Tanzania, I was provided with a copy of the al Qaeda operations manual. This document, introduced into evidence by the U.S. Department of Justice, was seized in Manchester, England, in the home of Anas al-Liby, a fugitive charged in the al Qaeda terrorism conspiracy.

* Jerrold M. Post is Professor of Psychiatry, Political Psychology, and International Affairs at George Washington University. He is the author of ten books including *Political Paranoia* and *The Mind of the Terrorist: The Psychology of Terrorism from the IRA to al Qaeda*.

Ayman al-Zawahiri, Osama bin Laden's personal physician and designated successor, probably played a central role in developing the al Qaeda terrorism manual.

This is an altogether remarkable document. On the one hand, it resembles nothing more than a basic tradecraft training manual, concerned with how to operate in a hostile environment. There are detailed instructions on everything from ciphers to how to resist interrogation. It is also a manual of terror, with no less than three of the eighteen lessons (chapters) devoted to techniques for assassination.[1]

But it is not merely a list of instructions, for it is also written to inspire the undercover operator as he carries on his dangerous work; the language at times is quite eloquent. The document reflects a sophisticated approach on the part of al Qaeda operational officials, for there is a continuing emphasis on lessons learned. Many of the chapters cite previous mistakes, which provide the basis for the points emphasized in the lesson. And they do not learn lessons only from their past mistakes, but from adversaries as well. In one section, they cite the astute observational skill of an Israeli Mossad counterespionage agent who foiled a terrorist plot, and cite Soviet KGB sources in others. Thus the manual reflects the adaptive learning of the organization, and the care with which al Qaeda prepares its operatives. No detail is too small, as exemplified by the instruction in lesson eight, which is concerned with Member Safety: "Do not park in no parking zones."

Many of the instructions are accompanied by elaborate justification, citing suras (verses) from the Koran, scholars who have provided commentary on the Koran, or hadiths (words or deeds of Prophet Mohammed). These elaborate justifications are offered especially when the instructions recommended seem to contradict Islamic teaching. In this text, the suras are not numbered, and while some are fairly well known, others are more obscure. The authenticity of many of the suras and hadiths is questionable, and several of the suras are taken out of context. For the Islamic youth taught to respect without questioning religious scholars, these can provide apparently persuasive religious authority in justifying acts of violence. As Daniel Brumberg sagely notes, in evaluating the authenticity of the sources, sura 3, 78, which speaks to Christians and Muslims, seems most aptly to apply to the writers of this manual.

> There are among them (People of the Book)
> A section who distort
> The Book with their tongues
> (As they read the Book) you would think
> It is part of the Book
> But it is not part
> Of the Book: and they say
> "That is from Allah,"

But it is not from Allah:
It is they who tell
A lie against Allah
And (well) they know it.

As an example of an incorrectly cited authority, the assertion that the Prophet says, "Islam is supreme and there is nothing above it" cannot be found in the Koran. The singular in the statement is discordant with many suras in the Koran, which while advancing the truth of Islam, do not imply that Islam is superior, nor are they meant to suggest that previous religions were intrinsically untrue. Indeed there are many suras that speak of the people of the book.

The manual goes a long way toward explaining how the September 11 hijackers were able to maintain their cover in the United States, "the land of the enemies." Lesson Eight, "Measures that Should Be Taken by the Undercover Member," instructs the members to

1. have a general appearance that does not indicate Islamic orientation (beard, toothpick, book, (long) shirt, small Koran),
2. be careful not to mention the brothers' common expressions or show their behaviors (special praying appearance, "may Allah reward you," "peace be on you," while arriving and departing, and so on, and
3. avoid visiting famous Islamic places (mosques, libraries, Islamic fairs, etc.).

The explanation offered to "An Important Question: How can a Muslim spy live among enemies if he maintains his Islamic characteristics? How can he perform his duties to Allah and not want to appear Muslim?" in Lesson Eleven is compelling. Concerning the issue of clothing and appearance (of true religion), Ibn Taimia—may Allah have mercy on him—said, "If a Muslim is in a combat or godless area, he is not obligated to have a different appearance from (those around him). The (Muslim) man may prefer or even be obligated to look like them, provided his actions brings a religious benefit." Resembling the polytheist in religious appearance is a kind of "necessity permits the forbidden" even though they (forbidden acts) are basically prohibited. Citing verses from the Koran, the justification says in effect that Allah will forgive you for not living the life of a good Muslim, for it is in the service of Allah, in the service of jihad.

The training manual's dedication provides perhaps one of the best insights into the al Qaeda leadership's view of their struggle:

In the name of Allah, the merciful and compassionate
To those champions who avowed the truth day and night...
...And wrote with their blood and sufferings these phrases...

The confrontation that we are calling for with the apostate regimes does not know Socratic debates...Platonic ideals...nor Aristotelian diplomacy.

But it knows the dialogue of bullets, the ideals of assassination, bombing, and destruction, and the diplomacy of the cannon and machine-gun.

Islamic governments have never and will never be established through peaceful solutions and cooperative councils. They are established as they [always] have been

> by pen and gun
>> by word and bullet
>>> by tongue and teeth.

The literary quality and rhetorical force of this dedication is striking. Socratic debates, Platonic ideals, Aristotelian diplomacy—characteristics of a democracy—are dramatically contrasted with the absolutist, uncompromising nature of the confrontation with apostate regimes, referring to the moderate modernizing Islamic nations who have strayed from the Islamist path, who will know only "the dialogue of the bullet, the ideals of assassination, bombing and destruction, and the diplomacy of the cannon and machine gun."

The three dangling last lines, in their pairing of qualities responsible for the establishment of Islamic governments pair words connoting violence (gun, bullet, teeth) with words reflecting persuasive rhetoric (pen, word, tongue). Powerful rhetoric is highly valued in Arab leaders, and a notable aspect of Osama bin Laden's leadership is his capacity to use words to justify and to inspire.

Al Qaeda Version 1.0: Leadership, Structure, and Organization

The organizational structure that follows is that which characterized al Qaeda before 9/11, and what, with apologies to Bill Gates and Microsoft, has been characterized as al Qaeda Version 1.0. Al Qaeda is unique among terrorist groups and organizations in its nonhierarchical structure and organization. Perhaps reflecting his training in business management, bin Laden in effect serves as chairman of the board of a holding company, which can be termed "Radical Islam, Inc.," a loose umbrella organization of semiautonomous terrorist groups and organizations with bin Laden providing guidance, coordination, and financial and logistical facilitation.

Unlike other charismatically led organizations, such as Guzman's Sendero Luminoso (Shinning Path) of Peru, or Ocalan's PKK (Kurdistan's Workers Party) of Turkey, both of which were mortally wounded when their charismatic and controlling leaders were captured, bin Laden established a flat and dispersed organizational structure in which subordinates were entrusted with clearly designated responsibilities, and their successors were seamlessly promoted to open positions.

Ayman al-Zawahiri, bin laden's second in command, has been designated as his successor. A leading Islamic militant, Zawahiri is a physician who founded the Egyptian Islamic Jihad and its new faction, Talaa'al al Fateh (Vanguard of Conquerors). It was Zawahiri's group that was responsible for the attempted assassination of President Hosni Mubarak of Egypt and is considered responsible for the assassination of President Sadat. Zawahiri, who is responsible for more day-to-day decisions, can be seen as serving as CEO to bin Laden as chairman of the board. Chairman of the Islamic Committee and responsible for many of the fatwas and other official writings of al Qaeda, Zawahiri indeed is reputed to be even more apocalyptic and extreme in his views than bin Laden. There has been speculation about the amount of influence Zawahiri has over bin Laden, with some believing that Zawahiri is the "behind-the-scenes" driving force of al Qaeda.

The then number three, Mohammed Atef, also of the Islamic Jihad of Egypt, was chairman of the military committee and training before his death in Afghanistan in the fall of 2001, during U.S. raids following the September 11 attacks in the United States. In another example of the redundant organizational structure and the successor system, following Atef's death, Abu Zubaydah, formerly head of personnel and recruiting, became head of the military committee until his capture by U.S. and Pakistani forces in Pakistan in the spring of 2001. He was in turn succeeded by Khalid Sheik Mohammad, the alleged mastermind of the 2001 attacks, who has also been captured. No doubt another successor has moved into the vacant position. Despite the fact that bin Laden has not been seen in public since the fall 2001 U.S. attacks in Afghanistan, the fact that al Qaeda's global network continues to operate is testimony to the effective leadership structure of the organization.

Conceptually, al Qaeda differed significantly from other terrorist groups and organizations in its structural composition. Unprecedented in its transnational nature, al Qaeda has proved a challenge to law enforcement officials— its organizational structure, diffuse nature, broad-based ethnic composition, emphasis on training, expansive financial network, and its technological and military capabilities make it not only a formidable force but also one difficult to detect.

Al Qaeda's global network consisted of permanent or independently operating semipermanent cells of al Qaeda-trained militants, established in over 76 countries worldwide, as well as allied Islamist military and political groups globally.[2] The strict adherence to a cell structure has allowed al Qaeda to maintain an impressively high degree of secrecy and security. Moreover, as was the case with the al Qaeda bombings in Kenya and Tanzania, locals who have been trained by but are not official members of al Qaeda may be activated to support outside operatives as needed to carry out attacks by establishing safe houses, procuring cars and local resources, and other means.

Al Qaeda was reorganized in 1998 to enable the organization to more effectively manage its assets and pursue its goals. The revamped al Qaeda structure had four distinct but interconnected elements: a pyramidal structure to facilitate strategic and tactical direction; a global terrorist network; a base force of guerrilla warfare inside Afghanistan; and a loose coalition of transnational terrorist and guerrilla groups.[3] Strategic and tactical direction comes from al Qaeda's Consultation Council (Majlis al-Shura), which consists of five committees—Military, Business, Communications, Islamic Studies, and Media, each headed by a senior leader in the organization—which oversee the operations of the organization.

Al Qaeda also maintained its own guerrilla army, known as the 55th Brigade, an elite body trained in small unit tactics. This group comprising approximately 2,000 fighters was reportedly the "shock troops" of the Taliban, having been integrated into their army in the period 1997–2001.[4]

While bin Laden had developed this elaborate organizational structure and delegated responsibility and authority, he nevertheless watched closely over major operational planning, as exemplified by the following anecdote, which emerged from testimony offered at the 2001 trial of the al Qaeda terrorists responsible for the coordinated bombing attacks on the U.S. embassies in Dar es Salaam, Tanzania and Nairobi, Kenya.

> The embassies had been painstakingly surveyed for more than eighteen months. When photographs of the embassy in Dar es Salaam were brought back to al-Qaeda headquarters in Afghanistan and shown to bin Laden, he reportedly pointed to a location by the embassy and indicated that that was where the explosive laden truck bomb should go.

Al Qaeda's approach of allying itself with various existing terrorist groups around the world enhances the organization's transnational reach. Al Qaeda has worked to establish relationships with diverse groups, not only geographically but ideologically as well; it has developed working relationships with organizations as diverse as Hezbollah and the Liberation Tigers of Tamil Eelam (LTTE), which do not follow the strict Wahhabi al Qaeda version of Salafi/Sunni Islam. Al Qaeda established relationships with at least 30 Islamist terrorist groups, including such well-known groups as the Egyptian Islamic Jihad, Al Gama'a al-Islamiyya (GAI, Egypt), Harakat ul-Ansar (Pakistan); Al-Ittihad al-Islami (AIAI, Somalia); and the Palestinian Islamic Jihad and Hamas. In addition to its primary logistical base in Afghanistan, al Qaeda maintained a direct presence in Sudan, Yemen, Chechnya, Tajikistan, Somalia, and the Philippines through relationships with Islamist organizations that already existed in these countries.[5]

In essence, bin Laden and his senior leaders have "grown" the al Qaeda "corporation" through mergers and acquisitions. Bin Laden has worked to minimize differences between the groups within the organization, emphasizing their similarities and uniting them with the vision of a common enemy—the West.

Having maintained bases in Pakistan, Sudan, Afghanistan, and elsewhere, as well as an ideological doctrine that rings true to much of the Islamic community, al Qaeda's membership base reached every corner of the world, encompassing several dozen constituent nationalities and ethnic groups.[6] Its ideology has allowed al Qaeda to unite the previously unorganized global community of radical Islam, providing leadership and inspiration. Beyond the actual al Qaeda cells maintained in over 60 countries worldwide, al Qaeda sympathizers exist in virtually every country on earth. The sympathizers are not only the disenfranchised youth of impoverished communities, but also include wealthy and successful businessmen in such countries as Saudi Arabia and Egypt.

Like many terrorist organizations, al Qaeda does not have a formal recruitment strategy; rather, it relies on familial ties and relationships, spotters in mosques who identify potential recruits, and the many new members/ recruits volunteering, actively pursuing joining this revered organization. Al Qaeda members recruit from their own family and social groups, and once trained, these new members are often reintegrated into their own communities. Very similar to the Muslim Brotherhood, the concept of "brotherhood" draws on the idea that familial ties in the Islamic world are binding. Al Qaeda members refer to each other as "brother" and tend to view the organization as their extended family.

Al Qaeda training camps trained both formal al Qaeda members as well as members of Islamist organizations allied with al Qaeda. According to reports, al Qaeda training is broken into essentially three separate courses: Basic Training—training specific to guerrilla war and Islamic law; Advanced Training—training in the use of explosives, how to carry out assassinations, and heavy weapons; and Specialized Training—training in surveillance and countersurveillance techniques, forging and adapting identity documents, and conducting maritime or vehicle-based suicide attacks.[7]

Al Qaeda developed extensive training materials used in their camps and other training situations. In addition to paramilitary training, great emphasis is placed on Islamic studies—Islamic law, history, and current politics. These training materials produced by al Qaeda, exemplified by the al Qaeda training manual discussed earlier, clearly demonstrate al Qaeda's twin training goals—the indoctrination of recruits in both military and religious studies.

But all of this centralized management structure was to change in the wake of the 9/11 attacks and the subsequent war against the Taliban regime in Afghanistan that had hosted bin Laden and his organization. Al Qaeda Version 1.0 was no more. In contrast to hierarchical terrorist organizations with authoritarian control, which would have been devastated by such an attack on their command structure, al Qaeda was an adaptive learning organization, and swiftly and effectively reacted to this assault, morphing into al Qaeda Version 2.0 and the global Salafi jihad.

Al Qaeda Version 2.0 and the Global Salafi Jihad

The Afghanistan intervention offensively hobbled, but defensively
benefited al-Qaeda. While al-Qaeda lost a recruiting magnet and a
training, command and operations base, it was compelled to disperse
and become even more decentralized, "virtual" and "invisible."

International Institute for Strategic Studies, 2004

Al Qaeda in the Post-9/11 Era

The unique and far-reaching transnational nature of al Qaeda represents one
of the greatest threats currently facing international security. Following the
September 11 attacks, NATO, for the first time since its founding 52 years ago,
invoked Article V, which states that an attack on one member state of NATO
is considered an attack on all member states of NATO. A massive air and
ground campaign was launched against al Qaeda, its operational bases, and
its Taliban supporters in Afghanistan. As a result of the campaign, al Qaeda
suffered severe losses, including the death and/or capture of several senior
leaders. Despite these losses and the dispersal of members throughout the
world, it is a testament to its organizational structure that al Qaeda remains
operationally intact—severely wounded, but certainly not destroyed.

For many al Qaeda followers, the fall 2001 attacks in Afghanistan only
served to reinforce their sense of righteous belief in their cause and their perception of the West as anti-Islamic aggressors. Although we have not seen a
second large-scale al Qaeda attack, there is nothing to suggest that al Qaeda is
no longer operational. Despite al Qaeda's Afghan base having been destroyed
and its leadership dispersed, its cellular structure remains intact with both
active and sleeper cells throughout the world. It is possible that in setting
the bar so high with 9/11, al Qaeda did not wish to lower their sights, and
the shift from a more centralized command and control to a more dispersed
semiautonomous network delayed plans in track. It is most likely, however,
owing to the highly focused international attention, that the next wave of
al Qaeda attacks will be on a smaller scale and undertaken by cells operating
semi-independently. Yet, as witnessed in the 2006 foiled British, U.S.-bound
airliner plot, in their new semiautonomous form, al Qaeda and the jihadi
network retain the capability of mounting a major coordinated attack, the
hallmark of al Qaeda operations.

With the U.S. tendency to personalize their enmities, there is a wist-
ful hope that the death or capture of bin Laden will end the threat from
al Qaeda. It will not. In the event of bin Laden's death or capture, al Qaeda's
flat, dispersed organizational structure, the presence of a designated successor, the nature of bin Laden's and Zawahiri's leadership and charisma, and
their enshrined religious mission, all indicate that the terrorist network will

survive. Bin Laden's loss would assuredly be a setback, but since Zawahiri is already running al Qaeda's daily operations, his transition to the top job would be virtually seamless. The organization's luster for alienated Muslims would dim, but within the organization, Zawahiri's considerable stature and charismatic attractiveness should permit him to carry on the network's mission. Osama bin Laden has not been seen in public since September 23, 2001, and he is believed by some to have been seriously wounded in the attack on Tora Bora. Bin Laden's death would surely lead to his designation as a martyr in the cause of Islam and might well precipitate terrorist actions. His capture could lead to retaliatory hostage taking or other terrorist actions. In either event, al Qaeda will survive.

While the former U.S. President George W. Bush and British Prime Minister Tony Blair took pains to clarify that the War on Terror is not a war against Muslims, but a war against terrorism, bin Laden, in seeking to frame this as a religious war, has now laid claim to the title of commander in chief of the radical Islamic world, opposing the commander in chief of the Western world, President George W. Bush. Alienated Arab youth find resonance in bin Laden's statements, and see him as a hero. Al Qaeda has become a catalyst for an international jihadist movement that will continue to grow, influenced by, but independent of, the original parent organization.

From al Qaeda Version 1.0 to al Qaeda Version 2.0

No good deed goes unpunished, and as a consequence of the 2001 war in Afghanistan, al Qaeda has progressively morphed from what has been called al Qaeda Version 1.0 into al Qaeda Version 2.0, operating much more autonomously, out of hubs and nodes, but lacking the prior centralized hierarchical control. Al Qaeda 1.0, with centralized planning, staffing, command, and control, was basically destroyed in the campaign in Afghanistan. While retaining a broad-based organization, al Qaeda 2.0 has become an ideology that provides inspiration for the global Salafi jihad movement. The form and function of al Qaeda has significantly changed since 9/11, but more precisely since the massive air and ground campaign was launched against al Qaeda, its operational bases, and its Taliban supporters in Afghanistan in the fall of 2001. While bin Laden does not have a controlling autocratic leadership style, there was nevertheless centralized operational planning, financial management, training, and logistical support before this attack.

Contributing to the resilience of al Qaeda is the fact that it is an adaptive learning organization, regularly reviewing and pursuing lessons learned from both successful and failed operations, such as the inclusion of the lessons from Mossad in the al Qaeda training manual. A less adaptive organization would have been destroyed by the focused attack in Afghanistan. But bin Laden had taken courses in business management at the university in Jeddah and learned about delegation of authority, flat organizations, and dispersal of organizational functions. He sent out a communiqué in the fall of 2002, which dispersed the organization and established a regional command structure, and said, in effect, "we have shown you the way. From now on it is up to you to plan and fund your own operations."

Osama bin Laden's active leadership in formulating specific attacks post-9/11 was transferred to the growing global recruits, who were thereby granted the responsibility to carry on operations against the Western Infidel.[8] Yet bin Laden continued to maintain symbolic leadership control over the organization through his full praise and hailing of attacks by al Qaeda-linked groups. In 2002, he embraced attacks in Bali, Yemen, and Moscow as a "response to what happened to all Muslim brothers around the world": "The incidents that have taken place since the raids on New York and Washington up until now—the recent operation in Moscow and some sporadic operations here and there—are only reactions and reciprocal actions. These actions were carried out by the zealous sons of Islam in defense of their religion and in response to the order of their God and prophet, may God's peace and blessings be upon him." In the audiotape, bin Laden speaks on behalf of all the mujahedin fighters, but more broadly, the nation of Islam: "The Islamic nation, thanks to God, has started to attack you at the hands of its beloved sons, who pledged to God to continue jihad, as long as they are able, through words and weapons, to establish right and expose falsehood."[9]

While the string of attacks in the last few years by al Qaeda-linked groups were probably mounted independently, insofar as the groups indicated that the attacks were in response to bin Laden's guidance and affirmed by him, they added to the luster of al Qaeda rather than being portrayed as a reflection of bin Laden's and al Qaeda's eroding influence and a lack of organizational coherence.

Bin Laden and Zawahiri early recognized the value of the Internet in disseminating their extremist messages. They had posted on one of their Web sites a coherent strategy for utilizing the Internet for recruitment and to disseminate their jihadi messages:

> Due to the advances of modern technology, it is easy to spread news, information, articles and other information over the Internet. We strongly urge Muslim internet professionals to spread and disseminate news and information about the Jihad through e-mail lists, discussion groups, and their own websites. If you fail to do this, and our site closes down before you have done this, you may hold you to account before Allah on the Day of Judgment.... This way, even if our sites are closed down, the material will live on with the Grace of Allah.

An important example of this strategy preceded the March 2004 attack on the Madrid train station. A December 2003 posting on al Qaeda Web sites called for terrorist attacks against Spain on the eve of the election, indicating it would either force the regime to withdraw from Iraq, or would lead to a socialist victory at the polls and the new party would then pull out.[10]

> In order to force the Spanish government to withdraw from Iraq, the resistance should deal painful blows to its forces....It is necessary to make the utmost use of the upcoming general election in March next year. We think that the Spanish government could not tolerate more than two, maximum three blows, after which it will have to withdraw as a result of popular pressure. If its troops remain in Iraq after these blows, the victory of the Socialist Party is almost secured, and the withdrawal of the Spanish forces will be on its electoral program. ("Jihadi Iraq: Hopes and Dangers," al-Qaeda manual published December, 2003)

In this way al Qaeda could legitimately lay claim to inspiring the major March 2004 attack, just before the election, that led to the fall of the government and the decision of the successor socialist government to remove troops from Iraq. The Abu Hafs al Masri Brigade, a European jihad group linked to al Qaeda, claimed responsibility for the Istanbul, Turkey bombings in August 2004, stating that the attack in "Istanbul was only the beginning....[A] group of mujahedeen...did the first attack after all of them [European nations] have refused the truce that was offered by our sheikh,"[11] referring to bin Laden's advice to European states to reject the U.S. War on Terror. (This is an interesting example of the transfer of blame so characteristic of terrorist groups.) This sustained control over the reins of the organization illustrate his ultimate preeminence as leader of al Qaeda while embracing an emerging generation of new blood to carry on the attacks and replace the killed and captured.

Abu Musab Zarqawi, then founding leader of al Qaeda in Mesopotamia, in an October 2004 audiotape, communicated the importance of the new generation to continue on the fight to resist the Infidel: "Oh, young men of Islam, here is our message to you. If we are killed or captured, you should carry on the fight. Don't betray God and His Prophet."[12]

Co-opting Potential Rivals: The Case of Abu Musab al-Zarqawi

Part of al Qaeda's leadership genius under bin Laden and Zawahiri is not to focus on differences, but to co-opt and embrace potential rivals. A striking example was that of Abu Musab al-Zarqawi, whose silent power and barbaric militant ways captivated audiences and proved to rival bin Laden on many levels.

The decision by bin Laden and Zawahari to forge relations with Zarqawi exemplifies the essence of the new global threat of terror—shifting alliances, as well as changing mission and resources. While sheer differences in vision and leadership were apparent, arguably combining resources benefited the overarching jihad mission of al Qaeda and its need for decentralized leadership. Captivating media audiences around the world, Zarqawi's violent unbounded approach to waging war against the infidels on the battlefield of Iraq, including Shia brethren, provided a stark contrast to the deeply ideological principles of Islamic Jihad as espoused by bin Laden. In October 2004 Zarqawi swore allegiance "to the sheikh of the mujaheddin, Osama bin Laden," and thereby recognized bin Laden as the "emir" in Iraq.[13] But this was in words only, and by no means did Zarqawi hand over control. "[This is] a cause [in which] we are cooperating for the good and supporting jihad."[14]

Bin Laden recognized the need to provide Zarqawi relative autonomy to carry out operations in Iraq while attempting to retain influence over the jihad, which was diverging from the path of bin Laden's al Qaeda, as it emphasized sectarian violence and threatened competition as more fighters flocked to Zarqawi's charismatic banner.

A letter intercepted by U.S. forces, dated July 2005, from Zawahiri to Zarqawi attempts to reassert al Qaeda's priorities in Iraq by calling into question Zarqawi's lack of foresight and planning. This was in part due to the extent of the sectarian violence that Zarqawi was leading, with Sunni Muslims killing Shi'ite Muslims, raising questions about the religious justification for the escalating violence. "We are extremely concerned, as are the mujahedeen and all sincere Muslims, about your Jihad and your heroic acts until you reach its intended goal. Therefore, I stress again to you and to all your brothers the need to direct the political action equally with the military action, by the alliance, cooperation and gathering of all leaders of opinion and influence in the Iraqi arena."[15]

Zawahiri attempts to inject an element of reality into Zarqawi's jihadist thinking, which fostered sectarian violence and killing of supporters of the Infidel, and he demonstrates an acute awareness of the power of the media: "Among the things which the feelings of the Muslim populace who love and support you will never find palatable—also—are the scenes of slaughtering the hostages....And your response, while true, might be: Why shouldn't we sow terror in the hearts of the Crusaders and their helpers....However, despite all of this, I say to you: that we are in a battle, and that more than half of this battle is taking place in the battlefield of the media. And that we are in a media battle in a race for the hearts and minds of our Umma." This letter also reflects the acute awareness on Zawahiri's part of the impact of media images on the population they hoped to influence in the "war for hearts and minds," that there was a hazard in disaffecting their supporters by indiscriminate violence.

The Zawahiri letter captured the prevailing frustration at the highest levels of leadership to contain Zarqawi's deviations, which they felt were threatening the reputation of al Qaeda, and in particular were counterproductive for al Qaeda's reputation in the Muslim world.[16]

But Zarqawi did not change his indiscriminate tactics. Shortly after the letter surfaced, Zarqawi's al Qaeda in Iraq claimed responsibility for three suicide attacks in Amman, Jordan in November 2005 that left many Muslims dead, demonstrating that Zarqawi was by no means influenced and certainly was not deterred by the firm tone of Zawahiri's letter.

Despite Zarqawi's defiance, in a June 2006 audio speech eulogizing Zarqawi after his death, bin Laden offers up great respect for "one of our best knights, an Emir who was one of the best Emirs." While the eulogy appears to be an effort to defend Zarqawi's role in sectarian violence in Iraq, in fact it is also an opportunity to reassert al Qaeda's priorities in Iraq and set the record straight. "To those who accuse Abu Musab al-Zarqawi of killing some segments of the Iraqi people, I say…Abu Musab, may God have mercy upon his soul, had clear instructions [implicitly, from bin Laden] to focus his fighting on the occupying invaders, led by the Americans, and not to target whoever wanted to be neutral, but whoever insisted on fighting along with the Crusaders against Muslims should be killed, regardless of their sect or tribe. Supporting the infidels against Muslims is one of the 10 things that nullify Islam, as stipulated by scholars."[17]

One of the difficulties in moving from centralized command and control to a more dispersed, decentralized organization is maintaining overall control and not having actions by assertive, competitive leaders threaten the organization's overall direction and reputation. This was the dilemma for bin Laden in containing the ambitious Zarqawi, whose sectarian excesses were leading to Muslim criticism of the jihad and undermining bin Laden's authority. This problem—how to maintain influence, if not control, and yet claim credit for actions to demonstrate the movement has not left the leader behind—is exacerbated as the organizational shape of al Qaeda has progressively evolved into the global jihad movement

Some would go so far as to say that al Qaeda now provides an overarching ideology for groups and organizations operating independently. The organizational form of Hamas and Hezbollah is much tighter and more authoritarian, with followers in action cells having little say in the conduct of operations. In contrast to these other radical Islamist terrorist organizations, which are quite hierarchical in organizational style, al Qaeda has a much looser organizational form, with distributed decision making, reflecting the leadership style of bin Laden.

The Global Salafi Jihad

One of the more alarming developments, which poses profound counter-terrorism challenges, is the increase in recruitment to the global Salafi jihad of second-generation émigrés to Europe, as exemplified by the March 11, 2004 Madrid train station and the July 7, 2005 London transit bombings as well as the foiled August 2006 coordinated attack on U.S.-bound planes from Heathrow airport in London. Throughout Europe, there is an increased radicalization and recruitment of terrorists from second- and third-generation émigrés to the global Salafi jihad, with estimates reaching as high as 87 percent of the new recruits coming from the diaspora. Although most Muslim immigrants and refugees are not stateless, many suffer from an existential sense of loss, deprivation, and alienation from the countries in which they live. Their families had emigrated to Western Europe to seek a better life, but they and their offspring had not been integrated into the recipient society. They are then exposed to extreme ideologies that increasingly radicalize them and can foster entering the path of terrorism.

Be it in Germany, where Atta and his 9/11 colleagues attended a radical mosque in Hamburg; in Great Britain, where both the 2005 London transit bombing and the 2006 foiled U.S.-bound airliner plot were carried out by Pakistani-British citizens; or the assassination of Dutch playwright Theo van Gogh for mocking the Prophet, there is a growing population of discontented Muslim émigrés who have been secondarily radicalized within their host country, from whose culture they feel excluded and alienated. The Madrid train station bombing of 2004 was conducted by Muslim émigrés and members of the Muslim diaspora originally from countries in North Africa. The London transport bombings of 2005 were carried out by Muslim youth with Pakistani family roots, living in a Muslim diasporic community in Leeds, England. The Muslim diaspora in the Netherlands is mainly of Moroccan origin. Thus there is not a monolithic Muslim diaspora, but rather a pastiche of Muslim diasporic communities.[18]

These events raise concerns about so called "homegrown terrorists": young, second- and even third-generation residents of Western countries driven by alienation and possibly inspired by the global Salafi jihad but carrying out these attacks independently of it. Recent events, however, show that "homegrown" may be too simple a characterization, as exemplified by the British individuals of Pakistani descent who planned the summer 2006 plot to hijack and blow up 10 U.S.-bound airliners. The leaders had traveled back to Pakistan, where apparently they were in contact with al Qaeda members for training in explosives. Dame Eliza Maningham-Butler, the director general of MI-5, Britain's security service, stated they had identified nearly 30 plots that "often have links back to al-Qaeda in Pakistan and through those links al-Qaeda gives training and guidance to its largely British foot soldiers here." She also stated that Spain, France, Canada, and Germany faced similar threats.[19] So while there is a looser control, al Qaeda continues to play a significant role in influencing and guiding the global jihad. The influence and involvement of al Qaeda (which in a sense is also a transnational diasporic entity), suggests that the group inspired and facilitated such acts of the disaffected among Muslim British citizens.

Grounded in the everyday experience of secular Muslim émigrés to Western Europe, European social conditions promoted feelings of alienation among young Muslims who felt excluded from the rigid European social structure. Not particularly religious, they drifted back to the mosque to find companionship, acceptance, and a sense of meaning and significance. This in turn made them vulnerable to extremist religious leaders and their radicalization within Muslim institutions. Based on his study of jihadi networks, Marc Sageman sees one possible path in the movement as moving toward a global leaderless jihad.[20] The challenge for bin Laden, Zawahiri, and the founding generation of al Qaeda will be to continue to provide both inspiration and direction to the jihad under their overall influence. And, given the semiautonomous functioning of the radical cells within the diasporic communities, this poses a profound challenge to international counterterrorism.

Cracks in the Militant Islamist Wall

One of the difficulties the West has faced in countering the extremist militant Islamist messages circulating on the Internet has been the relative muteness of moderate Muslim voices countering the extremist within their own ranks. And messages propagated from the outside are swiftly dismissed as Western propaganda. But in the past several years this has been changing and cracks are appearing in the previously impermeable militant Islamist wall.

Of particular importance was the publication from prison by Dr. Fadl of a detailed refutation of the principles he had outlined earlier in "The Essential Guide for Preparation" that had served as a founding document of al Qaeda providing justification in the sharia for the extreme actions of the Muslim radicals, the essential guidelines for conducting a holy war to defend a Muslim world under attack. He further extended these views in "The Compendium of the Pursuit of Divine Knowledge." Fadl declared that Muslims have a right, indeed an obligation, to attack Muslim leaders who are not fully committed followers of the faith, for they are apostates. But, beginning in the late 1990s, the obligation to strike out violently against enemies of the faith came under increasing scrutiny in what came to be known as "the revision."[21] In his new book, *Rationalizing Jihad in Egypt and the World,* Fadl in effect rebukes al Qaeda for its unlimited violence, especially the lack of justification for killing Muslims and innocents in the struggle, for exceeding boundaries. He was not totally turning away from the path of jihad, but rather specifying that the extremities to which al Qaeda had gone were undermining the very purposes for which jihad was justified. "There is nothing that invokes the anger of God and His wrath like the unwarranted spilling of blood and wrecking of property."[22] This was particularly significant for Fadl, who had been given the title *emir* for his knowledge of the Koran, had provided the very theological principles that animated al Qaeda. In a fax announcing his book, Fadl had declared that "we are prohibited from committing aggression even if the enemies of Islam do that."

This in turn emboldened other Muslim theorists who had been harboring doubts about the extremity of violence that al Qaeda had conducted, questioning whether it was not excessive and undermining the very goals al Qaeda espoused.[23] In an interview with Bergen and Cruickshank, Noman Benotman, leader of the Libyan Islamic Fighting Group, revealed that as early as the summer of 2000 he had informed bin Laden and senior militant leaders in a meeting in Kandahar, "that the jihadist movement had failed. That we had gone from one disaster to another, like in Algeria, because we had not mobilized the people." But it was not until January 2007, stimulated by the rising chorus of questions of the extremity of indiscriminate violence, led by the writings of and discussion of Fadl, that Benotman, now living in exile in London, withdrew the Libyan Islamic Fighting Group from its alliance with al Qaeda, and in November 2007 wrote an open letter to Zawahiri calling on al Qaeda to end all operations in Arab countries and the West. Bergen and Cruickshank see the turning of clerics and militants once seen as allies of al Qaeda as a consequence of the adoption of the doctrine of *takfir*, declaring they (al Qaeda) had the right to decide who was a true Muslim, and to kill those (*takfir*) who were not. A noted Saudi religious leader, Sheik Salman al Oudah, had asked on Middle East TV, "My brother Osama, how much blood as been spilt? How many innocent people, children, elderly and women have been killed...in the name of al-Qaeda? Will you be happy to meet God almighty carrying the burden of these hundreds of thousands or millions [of victims] on your back?"

In the long run, this rising chorus of voices of dissent within Islam will deplete the reservoir of hatred and extremism on which recruiters to radical Islam draw. But while the tide may be turning, the path ahead is a long one, requiring patience and persistence. For all too many, "hatred has been bred in the bone," and the current generation will not easily be turned from the path of extremist violence and terrorism.

Notes

1. See Jerrold M. Post, ed., *Declaration of Jihad against the Country's Tyrants, Military Series: The al-Qaeda Terrorism Manual* (Maxwell Air Force Base: USAF Counterproliferation Center, 2005), in which, based on consultations with experts on Islam, I demonstrate how many of the verses used to justify acts of terrorism are in fact taken out of context or mean something quite different from that which the manual's author, probably Zawahiri, asserts.
2. Countries believed to have active al Qaeda cells include Britain, France, Germany, Bosnia, Croatia, Albania, Bosnia, Spain, Argentina, Brazil, Paraguay, Uruguay, Trinidad & Tobago, Australia, Papua New Guinea, Borneo, Brunei, Nauru, Fiji, Philippines, Indonesia, Malaysia, Singapore, Saudi Arabia, UAE, West

Bank & Gaza, Egypt, Pakistan, Yemen, Somalia, Sudan, Comoros, Ethiopia, Kenya, Libya, South Africa, the United States, Canada, as well as South America, where it has a growing presence; Ibid., 79.

3. Rohan Gunaratna, *Inside Al Qaeda: Global Network of Terror* (New Delhi: Roli Books, 2002), 54–94.

4. Ibid., 58.

5. Ibid., 5–6.

6. Ibid., 96.

7. Ibid., 72.

8. David Johnston and David Sanger, "New Generation of Leaders Is Emerging for Al-Qaeda," *New York Times*, August 10, 2004.

9. "Bin Laden Tape Praises Bali Attack," *Guardian*, November 13, 2002.

10. "Jihadi Iraq: Hopes and Dangers," al Qaeda online manual, December 2003.

11. "Rival Groups Claim Turkey Blast," CNN.com, August, 10, 2004.

12. Michele Catalano, "October Turkey," *Command Post*, October 3, 2004.

13. "Zarqawi's Pledge of Allegiance to al-Qaeda: From Mu'asker al-Battar, Issue 21," *The Jamestown Foundation*, December 16, 2004.

14. "Letter from Zarqawi to bin Laden," January 2004, www.cpa-iraq.org/transcripts/20040212_zarqawi_full.html (accessed March 25, 2009).

15. "Letter from al-Zawahiri to al-Zarqawi," *GlobalSecurity.org*, July 9, 2005, http://www.globalsecurity.org/security/library/report/2005/zawahiri-zarqawi-letter_9jul2005.htm (accessed March 25, 2009).

16. "Al-Qaeda in Iraq: Letter to al-Zarqawi Fake," CNN.com, October 13, 2005.

17. "Bin Laden Seizes Opportunities in His June and July Speeches," *The Jamestown Foundation*, July 5, 2006.

18. A detailed discussion of the alienated Muslim diasporas in Europe can be found in Jerrold Post and Gabriel Sheffer, "The Risk of Radicalization and Terrorism in American Muslim Communities," *Brown Journal of International Affairs*, 2007.

19. Elaine Sciolino and Stephen Gey, "British Terror Trial Traces a Path to Militant Islam," *New York Times*, November 26, 2006.

20. Marc Sageman, *Understanding Terror Networks* (Philadelphia: University of Pennsylvania Press, 2004).

21. The revisionist thinking and decrying of extremity violence in the name of Islam is documented by Lawrence Wright in "The Rebellion Within," *New Yorker*, June 2, 2008.

22. Fadl, quoted by Wright, "The Rebellion Within."

23. Peter Bergen and Paul Cruickshank well document the spread of concern about the extremity of jihad and the further cracks within the previously unassailable wall of militant Islam in "The Unraveling," *New Republic*, June 11, 2008.

Part II

The Impact on War, Peace, and Security

Chapter 9

Countering Terrorism: Beyond Deterrence

Bruno S. Frey and Simon Luechinger[*]

In the wake of the attacks of 9/11, most governments tightened security measures, enacted harsh antiterrorism laws, curtailed the civil rights of suspected terrorists and of normal citizens, and increased the budget of the police, intelligence, and the military. Deterrence (broadly defined to also include preemptive measures etc.) is, and always has been, at the forefront of counterterrorism efforts.

Deterrence has also been the focus of many studies on terrorism by economists.[1] Contrary to a widely held belief, the economic analysis of terrorism rests on the premise that terrorists are rational actors.[2] Rationality does not refer to the goals of the terrorists, but to the means by which the goals are pursued. Terrorists systematically compare the costs and benefits of alternative courses of action; they compare the costs and benefits of achieving their goals by peaceful or by violent means and they compare the costs and benefits of different modes of attacks. There is substantial evidence that terrorists are rational in this sense.[3] In this framework, it can easily be seen why deterrence policy is potentially effective in reducing terrorist activity. By increasing the probability of apprehension and the severity of punishment, deterrence raises the expected costs of terrorism to prospective terrorists and induces them

---

[*]Bruno S. Frey is Professor of Economics at the University of Zurich. He received honorary doctorates in economics from the University of St. Gallen and the University of Goeteborg. He is the author of numerous articles in professional journals and books including *Not Just for the Money* (1997), *Economics as a Science of Human Behaviour* (1999), *The New Democratic Federalism for Europe* (1999), *Arts & Economics* (2000), *Inspiring Economics* (2001), *Successful Management by Motivation* (2001), *Happiness and Economics* (2002), and *Dealing with Terrorism: Stick or Carrot?* (2004). Simon Luechinger is a postdoctoral research fellow at the London School of Economics.

to revert to more peaceful means.[4] In striking contrast to the prominence given to deterrence, the evaluation of this strategy by many renowned terrorism experts is unfavorable. Hoffman, for example, claims, that countless times "attempts by the ruling regime to deter further violence...backfired catastrophically."[5] Fortunately, therefore, the rational choice framework also points to other, alternative policies to deterrence. The framework suggests that terrorist activity can be reduced by either lowering the benefits of terrorism to prospective terrorists or by reducing the costs of alternative courses of action (and thereby increasing the relative costs of terrorism).

We propose three strategies to deal with terrorism. Of these two strategies aim at lowering the benefits of terrorism to terrorists by decentralizing the polity, the economy, and the society (section 2) and by diffusing media attention (section 3). The third strategy attempts to raise the relative or opportunity costs of terrorism by lowering the price of its alternatives (section 4). Section 5 concludes the chapter.

Decentralize the Polity and the Economy

Terrorists seek to destabilize the polity and the economy. For example, in a video message in December 2001, bin Laden identifies the U.S. economy as a target: "It is important to hit the economy [of the United States], which is the base of its military power."[6] In the pages that follow, we argue that decentralization increases the resilience of a country's polity and economy. Again, if the resilience is increased and the effect of terrorist attacks is thereby diminished, prospective terrorists have less incentive to commit attacks in the first place.[7]

Any system with many different centers is more stable because of the ability of the various centers to substitute for each other. When one part of the system is negatively affected, another part or parts can take over. This basic insight also applies to terrorism. A target's vulnerability is lower in a decentralized society than in a centralized society. The more centers of power there are in a country, the less terrorists are able to hurt it. In a decentralized system, terrorists do not know where to strike because they are aware that each part can substitute for the other so that a strike will not achieve much. In contrast, in a centralized system most decision making takes place in one location. This power center is an ideal target for terrorists and therefore is in great danger of being attacked.

As a means of reducing vulnerability, decentralization of the polity and the economy can be achieved in various ways. Political decentralization may take at least two forms, horizontal decentralization or separation of powers, and vertical decentralization or federalism. In the first case, political authority is distributed over a number of different political actors. Most important is the classical separation of power between government, legislature, and courts.

In the second case, political power is spatially decentralized and is divided between various levels of government. According to an empirical analysis of the occurrence of terrorist attacks in 111 countries over the years 1972–2000, fiscal decentralization is found to reduce the number of events in a country; however, it had no effect if found for other indicators of federalism.[8]

A market economy is based on an extreme form of decentralization of decision making and implementation. Under competitive conditions, the suppliers are able to completely substitute for one other. If one of them is eradicated owing to a terrorist attack, the other suppliers are able to fill the void. They are prepared, and have an incentive, to step in. Therefore, the more an economy functions according to market principles, the less vulnerable it is to terrorist attacks.[9]

Diffusing Media Attention

The relationship between terrorists and the media can be described as "symbiotic."[10] The media want to make news to attract readers or viewers and have thus an incentive to sensationalize terrorism. The terrorists on their part rely on the media to spread fear and to publicize their cause. Terrorists have become very skilled in using the media to achieve the maximum effect.[11] They have learned to exploit the media to propagate their political demands to millions and even billions of people. Terrorists have fully adjusted their tactics to accommodate media needs.

Terrorists can be prevented from committing violent acts by reducing the utility gained from such behavior. One way to ensure that terrorists derive lower benefits from terrorism consists in the government ascertaining that a particular terrorist act is not attributed to a particular terrorist group. This prevents terrorists receiving credit for the act, and thereby gaining full public attention for having committed it. The government must see to it that no particular terrorist group is able to monopolize media attention. Therefore, several scholars advocate media censorship, statutory regulations, or voluntary self-restraint.[12] All information on who committed a particular terrorist act is then suppressed. But in an open and free society, it is impossible to withhold the type of information that the public is eager to know. Further, such intervention does not bind the foreign press and news media. Any news about the occurrence of a terrorist act and the likely perpetrators is therefore very likely to leak out. Terrorists seeking publicity can easily inform foreign news agencies. This first strategy must therefore be rejected as being ineffective and incompatible with democracy as the freedom of the press is seriously curtailed.

We propose an alternative way of diffusing media attention without infringing on the freedom of the press.[13] The government can divert attention from terrorist organizations and their goals by supplying more information to the public than desired by the terrorist group responsible for a particular violent act. It must be made known that several terrorist groups could be responsible for a particular terrorist act. Experience shows indeed that in the case of most terrorist attacks several groups of terrorists have claimed responsibility. The authorities have to reveal that they never know with certainty which terrorist group may have committed a violent act. Rather the government must publicly discuss various reasonable hypotheses. As a consequence, the media disperse public attention to many different, and possibly conflicting, political groups and goals.

The information strategy of refusing to attribute a terrorist attack to one particular group can be expected to have systematic effects on the behavior of terrorists. The benefits derived from having committed a terrorist act decreases for the group that undertook it because the group does not reap the public attention hoped for. The political goals it wants to publicize are not propagated as much as desired. This reduction in publicity makes the terrorist act (to a certain degree) senseless, as modern terrorism essentially depends on publicity. Terrorists who are ready to take a high risk, even the risk of death, to put forth their political beliefs, feel deeply dissatisfied. Their frustration is intensified by the feeling that other, not equally as "brave" political groups, are given a free publicity ride. The terrorists become frustrated and will either desist from further activities, or increasingly expose themselves to ordinary counterterrorist measures by the police. The amount of terrorism will decrease; the dissatisfaction with existing political and social conditions will be expressed in different, less violent ways.

Positive Incentives

Positive incentives consist of providing people with previously unattainable opportunities to increase their utility. Since these opportunities are only available for people and groups abstaining from violence, the opportunity costs of remaining or becoming a terrorist are raised. Similarly, by offering nonviolent alternatives to address terrorists' political goals, the relative costs of terrorism increase. At first glance, an obvious possibility to raise opportunity costs would be to increase the income in peaceful occupations. The reasoning is that the more an individual can gain in ordinary activity, the less she or he is inclined to engage in terrorism. However, contrary to popular opinion, the preponderance of evidence suggests that there is no economic foundation for terrorism. Analyzing the characteristics of members of Israeli extremists, the Hezbollah, Hamas, and Palestinian Islamic Jihad, Krueger and Maleckova and Berrebi find that poverty does not increase the propensity to participate in terrorism.[14] If anything, terrorists, including suicide bombers, come from the ranks of the better-off in society. The same pattern reverberates in public opinion data on attitudes toward violence and terrorism. Among the better-educated and better-off respondents, more respondents consider terrorist attacks to be justifiable than among the respondents from lower ranks.[15] Further, opinion polls conducted in the West Bank and Gaza strip find little evidence to suggest that a deteriorating economy increases support for terrorism. Time-series analyses fail to find a significant relationship between terrorism and GDP growth in Israel.[16] Finally, according to cross-country studies, poverty does not increase terrorism risk, as assessed by an international risk agency[17] or as reflected in the number of international terrorist attacks,[18] nor do perpetrators predominantly come from poor countries.[19] The pattern can be explained by understanding that terrorists are not so much motivated by their own material gain as by their political cause. The well-educated and well-off individuals usually have stronger political views than the general population and are more prepared to pursue their political goals—be it with terrorism or other form of political participation.[20] Therefore, in the following pages we propose counterterrorism policies aiming at lowering the relative costs of pursuing political goals by nonviolent means by reintegrating terrorists into mainstream politics and providing access to the political process as well as welcoming repentants.[21]

One of the most fundamental human motivations is the need to belong, and this applies to terrorists also. The isolation from other social entities gives strength to the terrorist group because it has become the only place where a sense of belonging is nurtured. An effective way to overcome terrorism is to break up this isolation. The (potential) terrorists must experience that there are other social bodies able to care for their need to belong. Interaction between groups tends to reduce extremist views, which are more likely to flourish in isolated groups of like-minded people. Segregation reinforces extremism and vice versa.[22] Therefore, breaking up this vicious circle of segregation and extremism should lower terrorists' inclination to participate in violent activities.

Further, terrorists can be granted access to the normal political process and they should be motivated to pursue their political goals by legal means. This approach was effective in Northern Ireland. From the Northern Ireland peace process the *Economist* draws a general lesson: "[O]ffer such people [terrorists] a legitimate way to get what they care about most and they drop the most extreme aims, and give up terrorism too."[23] This evaluation is buttressed by Neumann who writes that "the peace process of the 1990s appeared to set a precedent well beyond Northern Ireland in showing that the main insurgent group—the Republican movement, consisting of the Provisional Irish Republican Army (IRA) and its political front, Sinn Fein—could be persuaded to abandon its military campaign in exchange for nothing but a place at the negotiating table."[24]

If terrorists' and their supporters' inclination to participate in violent activities can be lowered by offering them nonviolent alternatives to address their grievances, one should observe less terrorism in countries with extensive political rights and civil liberties. A growing body of cross-country studies is providing evidence on the relationship between political rights, civil liberties, and terrorism.[25] Several studies investigate differences in the occurrence of terrorism across countries. In these studies, the majority of results points to an inverted u-shaped relationship between terrorism and political freedom or democracy, that is, terrorist activity is most prevalent in countries with an intermediate degree of political freedom or democracy. This is evidence for two countervailing effects: On the one hand, wide-ranging political rights decrease the costs of nonviolent legal activities and increase the relative costs of terrorism, as posited above. On the other hand, freedom of speech, movement, and association facilitate terrorism as they permit parochial interests to get organized and reduce the costs of conducting terrorist activities. However, there is even more direct evidence supporting the positive incentive hypothesis. Krueger and Laitin calculate the average number of terrorist attacks per country based on the origin of the perpetrators.[26] The results strongly support the positive incentive hypothesis: Countries with a lower level of civil liberties or political rights have, on average, a higher participation rate in terrorism. Further, there is also evidence for the positive incentive hypothesis from microdata. MacCulloch and Pezzini analyze the determinants of revolutionary preferences of respondents in three surveys conducted over three periods between 1981 and 1997, containing the answers of 130,000 people living in 61 countries.[27] Revolutionary preferences are elicited by agreement/disagreement to the following statement: "The entire way our society is organized must be radically changed by revolutionary action." The effect of political freedom on support of revolutionary actions is analyzed with a probit regression controlling for individual characteristics, macroeconomic variables, country and time fixed-effects. The coefficient on Freedom House's composite index of political freedom is negative and significant. An individual, living in a country that loses one point in the level of freedom on the three-point scale, demonstrates an increase in the probability of supporting a revolt by three to four percentage points, depending on the specification. Similarly, civil liberties and political rights both have negative and significant effects on revolutionary tastes. Hence, denial of civil liberties and political freedom increases the propensity to undertake terrorist acts. This is shown by both individuals' behavior and stated preferences.

Another policy to increase the opportunity costs of terrorism is to welcome repentants. Persons engaged in terrorist movements can be offered incentives, most importantly reduced punishment and a secure future, if they are prepared to leave the organization they are involved with and are ready to talk about it and its objectives. The prospect of being supported raises a member's opportunity costs of remaining a terrorist. Such an approach has indeed been put into practice with great success. In Italy, a law introduced in 1982, the *legge sui pentiti* (law on repentants), left it up to the discretion of the courts to reduce sentences quite substantially, on condition that convicted terrorists provide tangible information leading to the arrest and conviction of fellow terrorists. The implementation of this principal witness program turned out to be an overwhelming success.[28] It provided the police with detailed information, which helped to crack open the *Brigate Rosse* cells.

Concluding Remarks

Politicians and most academics focus on deterrence and preemption when considering counterterrorism policies. We argue that the application of the economic methodology to the study of terrorism offers a wider range of antiterrorism policies. A first alternative to deterrence is to reduce terrorist attacks by making them less attractive to terrorists. This can be done by immunizing targets through decentralization, or by diffusing media attention once an attack has taken place. Another strategy is to raise the opportunity cost to terrorists. Specifically, we suggest reintegrating terrorists into the mainstream society and providing access to the political process, and welcoming repentants. The strategy of offering positive incentives to terrorists to relinquish violence has been used with good results in the bloody Northern Ireland conflict. Further evidence on the effectiveness of this approach comes from cross-country studies on the relationship between civil liberties, political rights, and terrorism. Terrorists often originate from countries with regimes that suppress the political rights and civil liberties of their citizens. Moreover, countries with an intermediate level of political rights and civil liberties face the highest terrorism risk.

The three policies against terrorism outlined in this chapter support the view that "there is no contradiction between a robust application of constitutional rights and an effective counterterrorism strategy."[29] On the contrary, extensive separation of powers is the cornerstone of the constitution in all democratic countries, as it is of a federalist structure in many. Publicity of terrorists can be reduced without infringing on the freedom of the press, but by the rigid application of the principle that someone is considered innocent until proven guilty. Finally, no trade-off exists between civil liberty (and political rights) and security. The analysis of alternative counterterrorism policies also point at the costs and potentially counterproductive effects of ill-founded counterpolicies. In the fight against terrorism, governments often curtail civil liberties and undermine the separation of powers. As the preceding discussion suggests, such reactions—even if well intentioned—may inspire more people to resort to terrorism than prevent them from doing so.

Notes

1. For general introductions into the economic analysis of terrorism, see Bruno S. Frey, *Dealing with Terrorism- Stick or Carrot?* (Cheltenham, UK, and Northampton,

MA: Edward Elgar, 2004); Walter Enders and Todd Sandler, *The Political Economy of Terrorism* (Cambridge: Cambridge University Press, 2006); Alan B. Krueger, *What Makes a Terrorist? Economics and the Roots of Terrorism* (Princeton, NJ: Princeton University Press, 2007).

2. The opposite and commonly held notion of the irrational terrorists is expressed, for example, by Albert Parry, *Terrorism: From Robespierre to Arafat* (New York: Vanguard Press, 1976), 26: "[I]t is important to establish the mental deviation or sheer aberration of many terrorists."

3. For example, Jon Cauley and Eric Iksoon Im, "Intervention Policy Analysis of Skyjackings and Other Terrorist Incidents," *American Economic Review* 78 (1988): 27–31 and Walter Enders and Todd Sandler, "The Effectiveness of Antiterrorism Policies: A Vector-Autoregression-Intervention Analysis," *American Political Science Review* 87 (1993): 829–844 show that security measures decrease the type of attacks they are designed for but, at the same time, terrorists react by substituting one type of attack with another, often more deadly one.

4. William M. Landes, "An Economic Study of U.S. Aircraft Hijacking, 1961–1976," *Journal of Law and Economics* 21 (1978): 1–31.

5. Bruce Hoffman, *Inside Terrorism* (New York: Columbia University Press, 1998), 61.

6. BBC News, "Bin Laden Video Excerpts," BBC News Transcript, http://news.bbc.co.uk/2/hi/middle_east/1729882.stm (accessed January 21, 2008).

7. Bruno S. Frey and Simon Luechinger, "Decentralization as a Disincentive for Terror," *European Journal of Political Economy* 20 (2004): 509–515.

8. Axel Dreher and Justina A. V. Fischer, "Decentralization as a Disincentive for Terror? An Empirical Test," Mimeo, KOF Swiss Economic Institute, ETH Zurich, 2007.

9. See Bruno S. Frey, Bruno S., Simon Luechinger, and Alois Stutzer, "Calculating Tragedy: Assessing the Costs of Terrorism," *Journal of Economic Surveys* 21(2007): 1–24 and Bruno S. Frey, Simon Luechinger, and Alois Stutzer, "The Life Satisfaction Approach to the Value of Public Goods: The Case of Terrorism," *Public Choice* 138 (2009): 317–345, for a survey on the economic consequences of terrorism and an estimate of the overall consequences of terrorism in France and the British Isles.

10. See Peter Chalk, "The Liberal Democratic Response to Terrorism," *Terrorism and Political Violence* 7 (1995): 10–44; Dominic Rohner and Bruno S. Frey, "Blood and Ink! The Common-Interest-Game between Terrorists and the Media," *Public Choice* 133 (2007): 129–145.

11. Brigitte L. Nacos, *Terrorism and the Media: From the Iran Hostage Crisis to the Oklahoma City Bombing* (New York: Columbia University Press, 1994).

12. Paul Wilkinson, *Terrorism versus Democracy: The Liberal State Response* (London and Portland, OR: Frank Cass, 2000).

13. See also Bruno S. Frey, "Fighting Political Terrorism by Refusing Recognition," *Journal of Public Policy* 7 (1988): 179–188.

14. Alan B. Krueger and Jitka Maleckova, "Education, Poverty and Terrorism: Is There a Causal Connection?" *Journal of Economic Perspectives* 17 (2003): 119–144; Claude Berrebi, "Evidence about the Link between Education, Poverty and Terrorism among Palestinians," *Peace Economics, Peace Science and Public Policy* 13 (2007): article 2.

15. Jitka Maleckova, "Terrorists and the Societies from Which They Come," in *Tangled Roots: Social and Psychological Factors in the Genesis of Terrorism*, ed.

Jeff Victoroff (Washington, DC: IOS Press, 2006), 147–161; Alan B. Krueger, *What Makes a Terrorist? Economics and the Roots of Terrorism* (Princeton, NJ: Princeton University Press).

16. Alan B. Krueger and Jitka Maleckova, "Education, Poverty and Terrorism: Is There a Causal Connection?" *Journal of Economic Perspectives* 17 (2003): 119–144; Claude Berrebi, "Evidence about the Link between Education, Poverty and Terrorism among Palestinians," *Peace Economics, Peace Science and Public Policy* 13 (2007): article 2.

17. Alberto Abadie, Poverty, "Political Freedom, and the Roots of Terrorism," *American Economic Review. Papers and Proceedings* 96 (2006): 50–56.

18. James A. Piazza, "Rooted in Poverty? Terrorism, Poor Economic Development, and Social Cleavages," *Terrorism and Political Violence* 18 (2006): 159–177.

19. Alan B. Krueger and David D. Laitin, "Kto Kogo? A Cross-Country Study of the Origins and Targets of Terrorism," in *Terrorism, Economic Development, and Political Openness*, ed. Philip Keefer and Norman Loayza (Cambridge: Cambridge University Press, 2008): 148–173.

20. Alan B. Krueger, *What Makes a Terrorist? Economics and the Roots of Terrorism* (Princeton, NJ: Princeton University Press).

21. See more fully Bruno S. Frey and Simon Luechinger, "How to Fight Terrorism: Alternatives to Deterrence," *Defence and Peace Economics* 14 (2003): 237–249.

22. Russel Hardin, "The Crippled Epistemology of Extremism," in *Political Extremism and Rationality*, ed. Albert Breton, Gianluigi Galeotti, Pierre Salmon, and Ronald Wintrobe (Cambridge and New York: Cambridge University Press, 2002): 143–160.

23. "Democracy in the Middle East: Mainstreaming Terrorists," *Economist*, June 25, 2005, 15.

24. Peter R. Neumann, "Bringing in the Rogues: Political Violence, the British Government and Sinn Fein," *Terrorism and Political Violence* 15 (2003): 154.

25. The literature is reviewed in Bruno S. Frey, Bruno S., and Simon Luechinger, "Terrorism: Considering New Policies," in *The Economic Costs and Consequences of Terrorism*, ed. Harry W. Richardson, Peter Gordon, and James E. Moore (Cheltenham, UK, and Northampton, MA: Edward Elgar, 2007): 17–37.

26. Alan B. Krueger and David D. Laitin, "Kto Kogo? A Cross-Country Study of the Origins and Targets of Terrorism," in *Terrorism, Economic Development, and Political Openness*, ed. Philip Keefer and Norman Loayza (Cambridge: Cambridge University Press, 2008): 148–173.

27. Robert J. MacCulloch and Silvia Pezzini, "The Role of Freedom, Growth and Religion in the Taste for Revolution," STICERD Working Paper No. 36, London School of Economics and Political Science, 2002.

28. Paul Wilkinson, *Terrorism versus Democracy: The Liberal State Response* (London and Portland, OR: Frank Cass, 2000).

29. David Cole and James X. Dempsey, *Terrorism and the Constitution. Sacrificing Civil Liberties in the Name of National Security* (New York: New Press, 2002), 15.

Chapter 10

Worse than Terror? Nuclear Misdirection after 9/11

*Stephen J. Cimbala**

After 9/11, numerous expert analysts, scholars, media commentators and government officials agreed that nuclear terrorism was the worst danger facing the United States, its allied governments and their societies. The danger of nuclear terrorism is real and should not be discounted. But nuclear terrorism is also related to another danger: that of nuclear first use by states. The problems of nuclear first use by states and nuclear terrorism are joined at the hip. The spread of weapons among countries with outlaw regimes or regional grievances increases the likelihood of a nuclear handoff to nonstate actors, including terrorists, even as states build larger arsenals for coercing or attacking their neighbors. The danger is particularly acute in Asia, where nuclear proliferation threatens to escape political control. A breakdown of nonproliferation in Asia could result in a simultaneous and multiple failure of deterrence with catastrophic effects. This chapter discusses pertinent issues and employs a model for the analysis of deterrence stability within a future nuclear Asia.

In this study, we project to the year 2020 or shortly thereafter: into the second or third decade of the twenty-first century. Are deterrence stability, crisis stability, and arms race stability even conceivable, let alone possible, in a multipolar nuclear Asia? If not, the context for additional 9/11s, perhaps with nuclear or other weapons of mass destruction, becomes more precarious. The political context of an Asian nuclear arms race is obviously

*Stephen J. Cimbala is Distinguished Professor of Political Science at Penn State Brandywine and the author of numerous works in national security policy, nuclear arms control, defense studies, and other fields. Cimbala is a past winner of the University's Eisenhower award for teaching, has served as a consultant to various government agencies and think tanks, and is a frequent media commentator on national security topics.

different from the political context that surrounded U.S.-Soviet competition throughout the cold war. Therefore, the consequences of variations in the performances of various forces may be more significant for crisis and arms race stability in an eight-sided arms competition, compared to the two-way street of the cold war.

Policy Problems and Issues

United States policy has been to support the Nuclear Non-Proliferation Treaty (NPT), requiring nonnuclear state subscribers to the treaty to abjure the option of nuclear weapons. Nonnuclear states have, under the NPT regime, the right to develop a complete nuclear fuel cycle for peaceful purposes: generating electricity, for example. States adhering to the NPT are required to make available their facilities and infrastructure for scheduled inspections or challenge inspections by the International Atomic Energy Agency (IAEA). The IAEA has a mixed track record: depending on the cooperation or resistance of the regime in question, inspectors may obtain an accurate road map of a country's nuclear program, or be misled. In Iraq, for example, regular IAEA inspections before 1991 failed to detect the complete size and character of Saddam Hussein's efforts to develop nuclear weapons.

U.S. intelligence has also performed erratically in ascertaining the extent of WMD, including nuclear, activities in potential proliferators. The CIA assured President Bush and his advisors that the presence of large quantities of WMD in Iraq in 2003 was a "slam dunk." As it turned out, no WMD were found by inspectors after the completion of Operation Iraqi Freedom and the ousting of Hussein from power. The CIA was apparently taken by surprise in 1998 by the nearly simultaneous Indian and Pakistani detonations of nuclear weapons, followed by announcements in New Delhi and Islamabad that each was now an acknowledged nuclear power. The U.S. government signed an agreement with North Korea in 1994 freezing its nuclear development programs, but in 2002 North Korea unexpectedly denounced the agreement; admitted it had been cheating, and marched into the ranks of nuclear powers.

The difficulties in containing the spread of nuclear weapons and delivery systems are further compounded by the possibility that materials or technology could find its way into the hands of terrorists, to deadly effect. Reportedly, al Qaeda has tried to obtain weapons-grade material (enriched uranium and plutonium) and assistance in assembling both true nuclear weapons and radiological bombs (conventional explosives that scatter radioactive debris). Nuclear weapons are in a class by themselves as weapons of "mass destruction." Thus, a miniature nuclear weapon exploded in an urban area could cause much more death and destruction than either biological or chemical weapons similarly located.

In addition to the plausible interest of terrorists in nuclear weapons, there is also the disconcerting evidence of nuclear entrepreneurship resulting in proliferation. The A.Q. Khan network of Pakistani and other government officials, middlemen, scientists, and nondescripts trafficked for several decades in nuclear technology and know-how. The Khan network, described as a Wal-Mart of nuclear proliferation, apparently reached out and touched North Korea, Libya, and Iran, among others.[1] States seeking a nuclear start-up can save enormous time and money by turning to experts in and out of government for help, and the knowledge how to fabricate nuclear weapons is no longer as esoteric as it was in the early days the atomic age.

In response to 9/11 and to the possible failure of nuclear containment in Asia and the Middle East, the Bush administration sought to reinforce traditional nonproliferation with an interest in preemptive attack strategies and missile defenses. U.S. superiority in long-range, precision weapons makes preemption technically feasible, provided the appropriate targets have been identified. U.S. policy guidance apparently also allows for the possible use of nuclear weapons in preemptive attack against hostile states close to acquiring their own nuclear arsenals.[2] Missile defenses are further behind the curve, compared to deep strike, but the first U.S. national missile defense (NMD) deployments took place in 2004, under the Bush administration commitment to deploy defenses based on several technologies against rogue state or terrorist attacks. Preemption strategies and defenses are controversial in their own right.[3] For present purposes, however, they are simply talismans of U.S. government awareness and acknowledgment that containment and deterrence can no longer complete the antiproliferation tool kit.

Uncertainty about the rate of nuclear weapons spread in future Asia is in contrast to the comparative stability of the cold war experience. During the cold war, nuclear weapons spread from state to state at a slower rate than pessimists projected. In part, this was due to the bipolar character of the international system and nuclear preeminence of the Soviet Union and the United States over other contenders. Both superpowers discouraged horizontal proliferation among other state actors, even as they engaged in vertical proliferation by creating larger and more technically advanced arsenals. In addition, the NPT and the regime it established contributed to limitation in the rate of nuclear weapons spread among states that might otherwise have gone nuclear.[4]

The end of the cold war and the demise of the Soviet Union have moved the zone of political uncertainty, and the interest in WMD and missiles, eastward, across the Middle East, South Asia, and the Pacific basin.[5] The states of North America and Western Europe, pacified or at least debellicized by an expanded NATO and a downsized Russia, regard nuclear weapons as dated remnants of the age of mass destruction. The most recent "Revolution in Military Affairs" has created a new hierarchy of powers, based on the application of knowledge and information to military art.[6] Nuclear and other WMD are, from the standpoint of postmodern westerners, the military equivalent of museum pieces, although still dangerous in the wrong hands.

On the other hand, major states in Asia, and in the Middle East within the range of long-range missiles based in Asia, see nuclear weapons and ballistic missiles as potential trumps. The appeal of nuclear weapons and delivery systems for these states is at least threefold. First, they enable "denial of access" strategies for foreign powers who might want to interfere in regional issues. U.S. military success in Afghanistan in 2001 and in Iraq in 2003 only reinforced this rationale of access denial via WMD for aspiring regional hegemons or nervous dictators. Second, nuclear weapons might permit some states to coerce others who lack countermeasures in the form of deterrence. Israel's nuclear weapons, not officially acknowledged but widely known, have appealed to Tel Aviv as a deterrent against provocative behavior by Arab neighbors and as a possible "Samson" option on the cusp of military defeat leading to regime change.

Third, nuclear weapons permit states lacking the resources for advanced technology, conventional military systems to stay in the game of declared major powers. Russia is the most obvious example of this syndrome. Without her nuclear arsenal, Russia would be vulnerable to nuclear blackmail, or even to conventional military aggression, from a variety of strategic directions. Russia's holdover deterrent from the cold war, assuming eventual modernization, guarantees Moscow military respect in Europe and makes its neighbors in Asia more circumspect.

North Korea is another example of a state whose reputation and regard are enhanced by its possible deployment of nuclear weapons and potential deployment of long-range ballistic missiles. In the absence of a nuclear capability, North Korea is a politically isolated outlaw state with a bankrupt economy that would receive almost no international respect. But as an apparent nuclear power, North Korea has played nuclear poker with a five-nation coalition attempting to disarm its program by peaceful means: the United States, Russia, Japan, China, and South Korea.

In an agreement signed with those five powers in February, 2007, North Korea promised to shut down within 60 days its nuclear reactor at Yongbyon and to admit international inspectors into the DPRK (*Democratic People's Republic of Korea*) to verify compliance. For taking this step, North Korea was to receive an emergency shipment of fuel oil from the United States, Russia, China, and South Korea. The first phase of this pact thus froze the North Korean plutonium-based weapons program but left for future discussions its suspended uranium-enrichment program. In September, 2007 North Korea agreed to declare and disable all of its nuclear programs by the end of the calendar year 2007, but negotiations dragged on into 2008.[7]

Failure to contain proliferation in Pyongyang could spread nuclear fever throughout Asia. Japan and South Korea might seek nuclear weapons and missile defenses. A pentagonal configuration of nuclear powers in the Pacific basin

(Russia, China, Japan, and the two Koreas—not including the United States, with its own Pacific interests) could put deterrence at risk and create enormous temptation toward nuclear preemption. Apart from actual use or threat of use, North Korea could exploit the mere existence of an assumed nuclear capability to support is coercive diplomacy. As George H. Quester has noted:

> If the Pyongyang regime plays its cards sensibly and well, therefore, the world will not see its nuclear weapons being used against Japan or South Korea or anyone else, but will rather see this new nuclear arsenal held in reserve (just as the putative Israeli nuclear arsenal has been held in reserve), as a deterrent against the outside world's applying maximal pressure on Pyongyang and as a bargaining chip to extract the economic and political concessions that the DPRK needs if it wishes to avoid giving up its peculiar approach to social engineering.[8]

A five-sided nuclear competition in the Pacific would be linked, in geopolitical deterrence and proliferation space, to the existing nuclear deterrents of India and Pakistan, and to the emerging nuclear weapons status of Iran. An arc of nuclear instability from Tehran to Tokyo could place U.S. proliferation strategies into the ash heap of history and call for more drastic military options, not excluding preemptive war, defenses and counterdeterrent special operations. In addition, an eight-sided nuclear arms race in Asia would increase the likelihood of accidental or inadvertent nuclear war. It would do so because: (1) some of these states already have histories of protracted conflict; (2) states may have politically unreliable or immature command-and-control systems, especially during a crisis involving a decision for nuclear first strike or retaliation; unreliable or immature systems might permit a technical malfunction that caused an unintended launch, or a deliberate, but unauthorized, launch by rogue commanders; and (3) faulty intelligence and warning systems might cause one side to misinterpret the other's defensive moves to forestall attack as offensive preparations for attack, thus triggering a mistaken preemption.

Thus far, we have discussed the problem of an Asian nuclear arms race as an abstract, albeit sufficiently alarming, problem. The sections of the chapter to follow pin down the concept by detailed interrogation of one hypothetical scenario: an eight-sided nuclear polygon of force structures and, therefore, of probable operational performances in deterrence, in crisis management and, if necessary, in war.

States and Forces

Comparative Deployments and Outcomes

What would a nuclear arms race in Asia look like, after the second decade of the present century? If proliferation in Asia is successfully contained or rolled back, by politics or by war, speculation becomes irrelevant. Therefore we will assume a more pessimistic future: proliferation is not contained. The second or third decade of the twenty-first century witnesses an eight-sided nuclear club, to include Russia, China, Japan, North and South Korea, India, Pakistan, and Iran. Although proliferation is not contained under this set of assumptions, it does not automatically result in war. The assumption that nuclear weapons can spread among these states without war will be questioned by some, and with some justification. For example, the United States has declared that an Iranian or a North Korean nuclear capability is presently unacceptable: the former must be prevented, and the latter, must be rolled back. And some experts would surely argue that China would never accept a Japan armed with nuclear weapons.

On the other hand, the rollback of North Korea's nuclear program is not a certainty: a complicated international bargaining process may leave the DPRK as a standing nuclear power, with a trade-off including more glasnost on the part of the regime, a willingness on the part of Pyongyang to adhere to some international arms control agreements, and economic assistance from the United States and other powers to help rebuild North Korea's moribund economy. As for the Iranian nuclear case, both Israel and the United States have obliquely threatened preemption (presumably with conventional weapons) against Iran's nuclear infrastructure and against any nuclear-capable military forces. But the costs of carrying out the threat of preemption against Iran must be factored into the equation. Iran is a large state and cannot be conquered and occupied by outside powers—unlike Iraq. Iran could therefore reconstitute any destroyed nuclear power plants or other infrastructure. An additional consideration is political. An Israeli preemption against Iran becomes a recruitment poster for another holy war by jihadists against Israel. Iran has been one of the major sponsors of Hezbollah and other groups that have carried out past terror attacks in Palestine. An Israeli preemption against Tehran might reignite the intifada or otherwise destabilize the peace process headed toward political devolution and Palestinian self-rule.

The point is that many uncertainties loom, and the exclusion of any specific candidate state from the future nuclear club is not automatic. Therefore, we will include all eight in the analysis and assign to them notional forces. As a benchmark, we assume that the older and newer nuclear forces are deployed within an agreed limit comparable to the agreed ceilings of the Moscow Treaty between the United States and Russia: a ceiling of 2,200 warheads on launchers of "strategic" or intercontinental range, with freedom to mix various types of launch platforms among land-based, sea-based, and air-launched weapons. However, given the geography of the situation, it is not necessary for some states to have missiles or aircraft of transcontinental range to inflict strategic, that is, catastrophic and decisive, damage on one or more adversaries. Therefore, nuclear-capable missiles of intermediate or medium range, and bombers with comparable combat radii, might qualify as strategic launchers, depending on who is actually threatening, or shooting at, whom. For analytical purposes, we will simply stipulate that "ICBM" or "bomber" could also include ballistic missile or fixed wing aircraft of less than transcontinental range. (Cruise missiles are omitted from the present analysis for purposes of simplification, but the reader should be alerted that, as cruise missiles become smarter, stealthier, and more widely available, they could be a preferred weapon for some states if capped with nuclear charges, compared to ballistic missiles).

States in the analysis include Russia, China, India, Pakistan, North Korea, South Korea, Iran, and Japan. Some might object to the inclusion of Japan, whose current policy abjures any nuclear weapons capability. However, unless North Korea's nuclear arsenal is verifiably dismantled, incentives for South Korea or Japan to go nuclear increase, especially if North Korea deploys additional ballistic missiles of longer range.

Figure 10.1 below summarizes the forces deployed and available to the various state parties, under the agreed (formal or tacit) ceiling of 2,200 warheads.[9]

Each nation would have to plan for the likelihood that only a portion of its forces would survive a nuclear first strike, retaliate, and arrive at their assigned targets. The relationship between each state's initially deployed forces and its survivable and retaliating forces is summarized in figures 10.2 and 10.3, below. In addition, the numbers of surviving and retaliating warheads are grouped by the alert status and launch doctrines for each military. Forces may be on either of two alert statuses (generated or day alert), and they may be planning for prompt or delayed launch after attack.

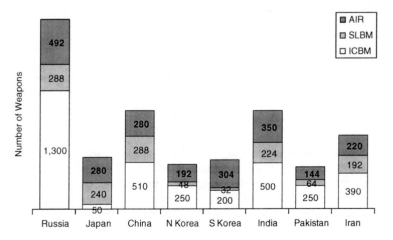

Figure 10.1   Total Strategic Weapons

Source: AWSM@ model by Dr. James Scouras. Note that Dr. Scouras is not responsible for the database nor for arguments or opinions in this study.

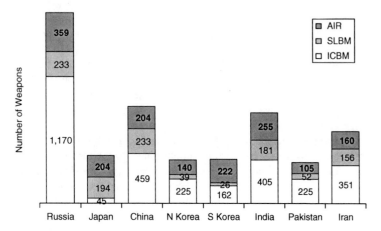

Figure 10.2 Maximum Retaliation

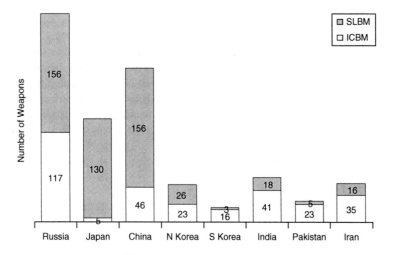

Figure 10.3 Minimum or Assured Retaliation

Several findings of significance are already apparent, and some are coun-terintuitive for advocates of nonproliferation. From the standpoint of deter-rence stability, there is no clear metric by which one can say that "so many additional nuclear powers equate to such-and-such a decline in deterrence." First, it is not impossible for a many-sided nuclear rivalry, even as regionally robust as this case is, to be stable. Provided it has the resources and the tech-nical know-how to do so, each state could deploy sufficient numbers of "first strike survivable" forces to guarantee the "minimum deterrent" mission, and perhaps the "assured destruction" mission as well.

Both "minimum deterrence" and "assured destruction" are terms of art that overlap in practice. Assured destruction (or assured retaliation) forces are second strike forces sufficient under all conditions of attack to inflict "unacceptable" societal damage. The term "unacceptable" varies with the recipient of the damage and depends on cultural values and political priorities. But it would be safe to assume that the decapitation of the regime and the loss of at least 25 percent of its population and/or one half its industrial base would satisfy the requirements of assured destruction for "rational" attackers (defining "rationality" is a separate problem; see below).

Minimum deterrence is a standard presumably less ambitious than assured destruction: it requires only that the defender inflict costs on the attacker that would create enough pain to make the gamble of an attack insufficiently appealing. For example, during the cold war, the French nuclear retaliatory forces were not sufficient by themselves to deter a Soviet attack on NATO, but they might have deterred nuclear blackmail against France separately by threatening Moscow with the prospect of "tearing an arm off," or destroying several Soviet cities.

To see the preceding arguments more clearly, let us compare the outcomes for two sets of operational assumptions. First, figure 10.2 summarizes the performance of each state's forces under the most favorable operational conditions: the retaliator has forces on generated alert and decides in favor of prompt launch. This maximum condition for each state's forces is compared to the minimum condition of alertness and launch readiness, summarized in figure 10.3.

Some of the states' forces perform more effectively than others do. Much depends on force mix as well as alertness and launch protocols. States more dependent upon land-based missiles in fixed basing modes, as opposed to submarines and bombers, will find themselves more dependent upon prompt as opposed to delayed launch for survivability. And bombers are not nearly as assuredly survivable as submarines. On the other hand, the complexity of operating submarine missile forces is daunting: ballistic missile-firing submarines require advanced construction techniques, sophisticated command-and-control systems, and highly educated officers and enlisted personnel. Political reliability is also necessary: submarine forces cause problems for dictatorships, since once at sea, captains and crews can resist micromanagement better than land-based forces can. The Soviet Union attempted to solve this problem during the cold war by assigning special political officers to each boat, watching over the political reliability of the captain and crew and having to acquiesce to any orders that required other than routine business.

Nor should the complexity of operating bombers as nuclear retaliatory forces be underestimated. Bombers have the advantage that they can be scrambled, or even launched, to signal firm intent, but then recalled short of attack. They are less first strike survivable than submarines, but more so than silo-based missiles. Bombers also have men in the loop who have considerable discretion once they are in flight and en route to "fail safe" points before final attack confirmation. Bombers would probably exist in so many varieties among the various states that no single standard of readiness, flight training, or technological performance would serve as an adequate basis for deterrence planning. A number of states included in our analysis might still rely on tactical fighter-bombers instead of "true" special purpose strategic bombers for the delivery of nuclear munitions by air-to-ground missiles or gravity bombs. As "slow flyers" compared to missiles, bombers pose less of a threat of preemptive attack provided early warning is obtained: the quality of air defenses throughout the region and among our states of interest varies considerably.

The preceding discussion is only the tip of the iceberg, however. The stability of the Asian balance of terror rests more on the political intentions of the actors than it does on the characteristics of their forces. Their forces can support a policy of adventurism and brinkmanship or one of adherence to the political status quo and "live and let live," or a range of policies in between. In international systems terms, stability is enhanced when the power of states favoring the status quo exceeds the power of states or other actors in favor of systemic overthrow. The "status quo" here refers to the existing number of major actors, their relative military and other power positions, and the polarities that create tension and possible conflicts among them. These matters can be unpredictable and surprising even for heads of state and military planners whose business it is to avoid systemic surprise. As an example, the process by which the July crisis of 1914 avoided diplomatic resolution and led the great powers into World War I, involved preexisting alliance commitments, ill-considered diplomatic demarches, and inappropriate military plans highly dependent upon rapid mobilization and deployment immediately before the war. Leaders saw hasty mobilization as a deterrent, but overlapping mobilizations, combined with political alarms in late July and early August, created a vortex of suspicion that leaders seeking an "out" were unable to control.

Although the projection of past events into future scenarios is always perilous, something like the July 1914 crisis in Europe could erupt in Asia once nuclear weapons have been distributed among eight states and in numbers sufficient to tempt crisis-bound leaders. National, religious, or other cultural hatreds could be combined with the memory of past wrongs and the fear of preemptive attack. This could occur not only between dyads of states but between alliances, as it did on the eve of World War I. Coalitions might form among a nuclear-armed China, Pakistan, North Korea, and Iran—lined up against Russia, Japan, South Korea, and India. This would be an alignment of market democracies of various stripes against dictatorships or authoritarian regimes of sorts. Another possibility would be conflicts between dyads within, or across, democratic and dictatorial coalitions: for example, rivalry between Japan and China, between the two Koreas, or between India and Pakistan. Russia might find itself in bilateral competition or conflict with China or with Japan. Iran might use its nuclear capability for coercion against U.S. allies, such as Saudi Arabia or Israel, drawing American political commitments and military power directly into a regional crisis. China might coerce or attack Taiwan, with the same result.

Stability and Sensitivity

We noted previously that decisions for war or nuclear blackmail will probably be driven by political variables more than military ones. Nevertheless, even in the case of nuclear forces that are intended more for coercion than for actual use, it can matter a great deal how they are deployed, and operated, short of war. The deployments and operational modes for nuclear forces may seem as if they are "hard" or "objective" facts, and to some extent they are: whether weapons are to be land- or sea-based, how many warheads or reentry vehicles are carried by a particular missile, and so forth. On the other hand, nuclear force deployments and operational characteristics also have subjective properties. Weapons, launchers, and command-and-control protocols "communicate" intentions with respect to the probable or possible behaviors of states and their leaders: intentions that might not be correctly interpreted or understood by other states. During a crisis in which one or more states contemplate the possibility of nuclear attack, countries will not only listen to one another's diplomatic statements, they will also watch what the other country is doing, including its military capabilities and maneuvers, for clues about its future behavior.

Regardless of force size, force characteristics and operational assumptions make a considerable difference for crisis and arms race stability. Most states in Asia will depend on land-based missiles and/or bomber-delivered weapons as the bulwark of their deterrents. Few if any will be capable of operating fleets of ballistic missile submarines as does the United States. Thus, ICBM- or IRBM/MRBM-dependent countries in Asia will rely on alerted forces and prompt launch to guarantee survivability. Hair triggers may be more the rule than the exception. In addition, many of the land-based missiles available to Asian powers for use as "strategic" launchers will be of medium or intermediate range: theater, as opposed to intercontinental, missiles. These theater-range missiles will have shorter flight times than true ICBMs, allowing less time for the defender's launch detection, decision making and response. Errors in launch detection, in the estimation of enemy intentions, and in choice of response are more likely with shorter-range compared to longer-range missiles.

The high dependency of Asian forces on land-based missiles will be compounded by command-and-control systems that may be accident prone or politically ambiguous. In democratic states, political control over the military is guaranteed by checks and balances and by constitutional fiat. In authoritarian polities, the military may operate as a political tool of the ruling clique or it may be an autonomous political force, subject to intrigue and coup plotting. The possibility of political overthrow or military usurpation during a nuclear crisis cannot be ruled out in systems lacking constitutional or other political safeguards. The danger is not only that of Bonapartism on the part of disgruntled officers. It is also the danger of panic in the face of nuclear threats and an institutional military bias for getting in the first blow to maximize the possibility of military victory and avoid defeat.

The performance of forces in our illustrative and hypothetical case is also influenced by the command-and-control systems that connect political and military leaders with force operators, and with one another. Although command-and-control variables have not been built into the model, the implications for command decision making, and for the problem of control during crisis management, are clear enough. The forces most dependent on land-based ballistic missiles show the most discrepancy between hair-trigger and slow-trigger responses. On the other hand, states with balanced forces such as Russia, or with major reliance upon sea-based as opposed to land-based missiles (Japan), are comparatively less reliant on jumpy warning and fast firing. If hair-trigger responses are necessary for survivability, then policymakers and commanders will have few minutes in which to make life-and-death decisions for entire societies. And missiles of theater or shorter range offer even fewer minutes of decision time than ICBMs, whose intercontinental reach requires 20 minutes or so from silo to silo.

Faced with this analysis, states might decide to supplement vulnerable and potentially provocative land-based ballistic missiles with cruise missiles. Cruise missiles can be based in various environments; on land, at sea, and in the air. They can be moved on relatively short notice and can attack from various azimuths with high accuracy. Other states cannot have failed to notice the U.S. use of cruise missiles to great effect during the Gulf War of 1991 and in punitive strike campaigns throughout the 1990s, as well as during Operation Enduring Freedom in Afghanistan and in Operation Iraqi Freedom in 2003. Cruise missiles can be fitted with conventional or nuclear warheads: the choice obviously depends on the target and mission, and the decision whether to arm the missile with nuclear or nonnuclear munitions affects its operational range. But it is certainly conceivable that various states in our mix will turn to ALCMs (air-launched cruise missiles), SLCMs (sea launched), and GLCMs (ground launched) as weapons of choice for high priority conventional, or nuclear, missions. The absence of air defenses of any consequence, in many states, invites their opponents to explore this option if they can.

The analysis performed here also underlines the truth of the old saying that "everything old is new again." The end of the cold war did not repeal the nuclear revolution, although it did make deterrence calculations more complicated. Nuclear weapons are in a class by themselves as instruments of mass destruction: very small numbers can produce historically unprecedented destruction and social chaos almost anywhere. What is important about these differences is *not* the numbers and percentages, however, but the possible effect of leaders' *perceptions* that higher alerts and faster launches are necessary to avoid catastrophic defeat, should war occur. There are no "winnable" nuclear wars depicted here: nor would there be, even if agreed levels among the powers were reduced to several hundreds of warheads.[10] The danger is that a war might begin, not so much from deliberation, but from desperation: states may feel that their nuclear deterrents were threatened, and therefore coerced to make a yes-no decision on a time line that permits neither reflection nor appropriate vetting of the information at hand.

Conclusions

A nuclear version of 9/11 is among the worst possible threats facing the United States and its allies in the present century. This threat is embedded in a larger context. Nuclear proliferation, especially in Asia, increases the probability of more 9/11s *and* raises the likelihood of nuclear wars between states. More boys with nuclear toys may not use them exclusively for state-to-state brinkmanship. Leaders may also use nonstate actors such as terrorists as nuclear surrogates for deniable attacks on enemy governments or societies. Regional rivalries, including ethnonationalist and religiously inspired disagreements, combine dangerously with weapons of mass destruction, from the standpoint of international security and stability.

States' nuclear forces may be deployed and operated with more, or less, sensitivity to the problem of provocative crisis behavior. Asian states with high dependency on land-based missiles for their retaliatory forces may find their freedom of action constrained by the "lose or use" quality of these launchers. Coupled to command-and-control and warning systems with insufficient fidelity, ballistic missiles armed with nuclear weapons invite irrevocable decisions based on insufficient evidence and desperate hopes. And, on account of their shorter flight times compared to intercontinental missiles, theater- or shorter-range ballistic missiles may have greater potential for triggering inadvertent or accidental nuclear war.

Notes

1. Graham Allison, *Nuclear Terrorism: The Ultimate Preventable Catastrophe* (New York: Henry Holt, Times Books, 2004), 61–63.
2. Lawrence Korb, with Peter Ogden, *The Road to Nuclear Security* (Washington, DC: Center for American Progress, December 2004), 5.
3. See Karl P. Mueller et al., *Striking First: Preemptive and Preventive Attack in U.S. National Security Policy* (Santa Monica, CA: RAND, 2006), for an assessment of past and present U.S. experience. Unnecessary confusion in the American policy

debate about preemption and preventive war strategies is noted in Colin S. Gray, *The Implications of Preemptive and Preventive War Doctrines: A Reconsideration* (Carlisle, PA: Strategic Studied Institute, U.S. Army War College, July 2007).

4. Joseph Cirincione, *Bomb Scare: The History and Future of Nuclear Weapons* (New York: Columbia University Press, 2007), 43. According to Cirincione, the following states have abandoned nuclear weapons programs, nuclear weapons, or both since the NPT entered into force: Argentina, Australia, Belarus, Brazil, Canada, Iraq, Kazakhstan, Libya, Rumania, South Africa, South Korea, Spain, Switzerland, Taiwan, Ukraine, and Yugoslavia (Ibid., 43).

5. Paul Bracken, *Fire in the East: The Rise of Asian Military Power and the Second Nuclear Age* (New York: HarperCollins, 1999), esp. 95–124.

6. Michael O'Hanlon, *Technological Change and the Future of Warfare* (Washington, DC: Brookings Institution, 2000), 7–31.

7. For optimistic and pessimistic appraisals, respectively, see David Albright and Jacqueline Shire, "Slowly, but Surely, Pyongyang Is Moving," *Washington Post*, January 24, 2008, A19, and Art Brown, "North Korea's Stacked Deck," *New York Times*, July 15, 2008, http://www.nytimes.com/2008/07/15/opinion/15brown. html. Partial progress, in the form of an agreement to disable North Korea's main reactor by the end of October, 2008 was reported in July, 2008 by the five states negotiating with the DPRK. See Tini Tran, Associated Press, "Korea Agrees in Talks to Disable Nuclear Reactor," July 12, 2008, http://www.wtopnews. com/?nid=105&sid=584989.

8. George H. Quester, *Nuclear First Strike: Consequences of a Broken Taboo* (Baltimore, MD: Johns Hopkins University Press, 2006), 49.

9. I am grateful to Dr. James Scouras for the use of his AWSM@ model in this analysis. He is not responsible for any arguments and conclusions in this study.

10. This point is made in the larger context of an argument for further Russian and American nuclear arms reductions, and for strengthening the nuclear nonproliferation regime, by Wolfgang K. H. Panofsky, "Nuclear Insecurity," *Foreign Affairs*, September–October 2007, in Johnson's Russia List 2007-#180, August 23, 2007.

Chapter 11

The 9/11 Attacks and U.S. Grand Strategy: The Peril or Prudence of the Bush Doctrine

*Robert G. Kaufman**

September 11, 2001, transformed the consciousness of this generation of Americans, just as December 7, 1941, did for what became the World War II generation. The attacks homicide bombers perpetrated on the World Trade Center and the Pentagon shattered the illusions of the 1990s: that the collapse of the Soviet Union spelled the end of history, with democracy irrevocably triumphant and catastrophic wars a relic of the past. Instead, Americans rudely discovered that the United States faced another existential threat to its freedom, reminiscent of the threats fascism and communism posed during the twentieth century.

This chapter reflects on the significant continuities and discontinuities of the Bush administration's strategic response to 9/11, known as the Bush Doctrine. It focuses largely on the two most controversial premises of the this doctrine; namely, the United States must include military preemption in its repertoire of options, because of the dangerous convergence between the spread of radicalism and the spread of weapons of mass destruction; and, the United States must promote stable liberal democracy in the Middle East, because the root cause of 9/11 and similarly inspired aggression is the region's lamentable political culture, which exalts tyranny, fanaticism, and oppression.[1]

Four major themes run through these reflections: First, the Bush Doctrine's framework for the preventive use of force ranks as the most fundamental

---

* Robert G. Kaufman is Professor of Public Policy at Pepperdine University and author of *In Defense of the Bush Doctrine*.

change 9/11 has wrought on American grand strategy. Despite intense opposition to the administration's decision to wage war in Iraq, this aspect of the Bush Doctrine will endure for decades to come. Second, the events of 9/11 and its aftermath offer a sobering lesson about the limited capacity of multilateral institutions such as the United Nations (UN) to act as substitutes for American power. Third, the Bush Doctrine's embrace of democratic regime change as a war aim has a long, deep, and successful pedigree in the annals of American grand strategy. What has changed profoundly since 9/11 is the administration's determination to promote stable liberal democracy in the Middle East: the region where previous generations of American statesmen rated the prospects for well-ordered liberty as dismal. Fourth, the Bush administration's emphasis on regime type has profound implications for identifying friends, foes, threats, and opportunities for the United States in areas beyond the Middle East.

Preventive Use of Force

No feature of the Bush Doctrine has elicited more widespread and scathing criticism than the president's repudiation of the main trends in modern just war theory, which make the use of force categorically a last resort.[2] Such discord is normal in times of peril: war has often served as the catalyst for fundamental transformations of American grand strategy. The wars of the French Revolution and Napoleon, lasting from 1792 to 1815, triggered a ferocious debate in the United States over foreign policy, which culminated in President Washington's dictum of no entangling alliances or commitments outside the Western Hemisphere that entailed the cost or risk of war. This strategy of isolationism, or armed neutrality, reigned supreme in American diplomacy for nearly 150 years; the discredited American intervention in World War I was the exception that proved the rule. It took the Japanese attack on Pearl Harbor on December 7, 1941, and Nazi Germany's declaration of war against the United States days later to convince a generation of American statesmen once and for all that isolationism no longer sufficed to protect the American national interest in the changing circumstances of the twentieth century.[3]

After World War II, the Truman administration devised a new grand strategy of vigilant containment in response to the emergence of the Soviet threat and the advent of nuclear weapons. This strategy aimed to wear down and, ultimately, to defeat Soviet totalitarianism through robust forward deterrence and through the establishment of a worldwide American alliance system, with the democracies of Western Europe and Japan as the lynchpins.[4] During the 1970s, the agonizing debate over the Vietnam War impelled the United States again to recast its grand strategy. The unanticipated outcome of this debate was the election of Ronald Reagan, who contributed mightily to winning the cold war during the 1980s by reviving and intensifying President Truman's original concept of robust containment.[5]

Likewise, the attacks on 9/11 had a seismic impact on President George W. Bush's strategic outlook. Earlier, he had sounded more like the Republican realist critics of the Bush Doctrine, such as Brent Scowcroft, than the principle architect of it. During the 2000 presidential campaign, candidate Bush called for the United States to pursue a more humble foreign policy. The attacks on 9/11 convinced President Bush that the United States could not rely on the strategy of containment and deterrence, which served us well during the cold war, against certain types of threats emanating from certain types of actors.[6]

The president's post-9/11 outlook owes much to the traditional war thinking of St. Thomas Aquinas, which was silent on the question of whether force should be used as a last resort or sooner.[7] There is no presumption against war in Aquinas that one finds in modern versions of just war theory. Whether one resorts to force sooner or later is a prudential judgment, not a categorical one. It depends on the gravity of the danger, the probability of its realization, the availability of alternative means, and the prospects for success.[8]

Moreover, the president grounded his philosophical and practical defense of preemption in the lesson of history: using force sooner sometimes averts a greater moral and geopolitical disaster. No statesman speaks more authoritatively on this subject than Winston Churchill. We know that, had the democracies heeded Churchill's advice and stopped Hitler at various watersheds during the 1930s, we could have avoided the worst war in history. During the Cuban Missile Crisis, President Kennedy rightly contemplated launching a preemptive strike against Soviet nuclear missiles deployed in Cuba, had not the Soviet Union conceded under pressure to remove them. In May 1981, Israel rightly launched a preventive strike against Iraq's nuclear reactor at Osirik, preventing an Iraqi nuclear capability when Saddam Hussein invaded Kuwait in the summer of 1990, which may have deterred the United States from responding decisively or raised the cost and risk of such a response.[9] Conversely, the major powers during the 1990s made a terrible mistake, waiting too long to respond to the genocide in Rwanda and the ethnic cleansing in the Balkans, which exponentially increased the slaughter there.[10]

This writer considers the case for the president's decision to remove Saddam, his execution of the war, and the probabilities of a successful outcome vastly more compelling than the arguments of the administration's critics.[11] Yet the modes of thinking about when to wage war that the Bush Doctrine employs will survive robustly, whatever position one takes on the controversy surrounding the Iraq War and whatever the war's outcome. Like the Truman Doctrine with regard to the cold war, the Bush Doctrine will not end debate; it will set the terms of the debate. Democratic President Barack Obama has begun with a stronger presumption against the preemptive or preventive use of force than what the Bush Doctrine establishes.[12] A future

Republican president may even have a lower threshold than President Bush for gathering dangers such as Iran.[13] Yet the homicide bombings of 9/11 offered a chilling preview of the massive destruction that rogue states and their terrorist clients could inflict with weapons of mass destruction. In these circumstances, the United States will retain explicitly the Bush Doctrine's option of preemptive action to counter a sufficient threat to our national security. No future president will rule out the preemptive or preventive use of force as a categorical imperative.

Limited Capacity of Multilateral Institutions

Nor will any future presidents make the UN or the North Atlantic Treaty Organization (NATO) the arbiter of legitimacy for using force for the foreseeable future. In this case, America's reaction has restored the more modest expectation for collective security that reigned until the end of the cold war, before the apparent success of the UN in reversing Iraq's invasion of Kuwait in 1990 caused hopes to soar that it could deal effectively with dangerous aggressors.

The UN's failure to deal effectively with Saddam in the aftermath of 9/11 came on the heels of mounting UN gridlock in the face of multiple gathering dangers.

UN intervention in Bosnia during the 1990s was too weak to succeed, but large enough to curtail effective action until stronger NATO forces replaced the hapless UN contingents. The UN intervention in Somalia ended in a debacle in 1993. The UN bungled even worse in Rwanda in 1994, doing nothing to prevent that sad nation's holocaust, in which 800,000 Rwandans were killed in one hundred days. Another terrible display of UN impotence occurred in the Balkans during the summer of 1995 when Dutch peacekeepers merely watched as Serbs murdered seven thousand Muslim men in Srebrenica, an area that the United Nations had designated as a safe zone. In 1999, the United Nation's and its NATO allies, including France, decided to ignore rather than rely on the United Nations to wage war in Kosovo, which Serbian atrocities had precipitated. The UN intervention is Somalia ended in a debacle in 1993.[14]

The record of the UN in Sudan is little better. By February 2004, more than one million refugees had fled their homes in fear of government-sponsored Arab militias known as Janjaweed, which raped and killed at will. Yet the UN responded only belatedly, tepidly, and ineffectively because permanent members of the Security Council such as France and China thwarted efforts to impose tough sanctions on the Sudanese government.[15] Add to these failures the UN's appalling performance in Lebanon: Hezbollah flouted UN Resolution 1559 that requires the disarming and dismantling of this murderous terrorist organization. UN peacekeepers did not lift a finger to stop

Hezbollah and its Syrian and Iranian sponsors from raising and equipping a veritable army, with thousands of missiles.[16]

This impotence is not contingent, but intrinsic to the institution. The UN founders created a Security Council (UNSC), composed of five great permanent policemen (the United States, the Soviet Union, France, Great Britain, and China), plus a rotating pool of temporary members. Each of the five great powers possesses a veto, which could thwart any collective UN action it opposes.

Nothing revealed the deficiencies of the UN more vividly in the aftermath of 9/11 than its inability to enforce a total of 17 UN resolutions that Saddam defied with impunity before President Bush determined to remove him. The rampant corruption of the UN's oil for food program, which Saddam exploited to bribe members of the UNSC, was merely the symptom of a deeper and more fundamental problem: those who oppose the assertion of American power—at home and abroad—strive to use the UN instrumentally as a means to shackle it. Consequently, the UN's collective security system can do little to restrain a rising, authoritarian China, rogue states such as Iran, and North Korea, or a host of other major potential aggressors looming on the horizon. In the case of the Iranian mullahs' brazen determination to build nuclear weapons, the UN is unlikely to agree beyond the lowest common denominator of ineffective action.[17]

Expanding the Security Council to include other members—particularly democratic India and Japan as the Bush administration wisely proposes—has considerable merit for other reasons: equity, to reflect the changing distribution of power since World War II; and a compelling U.S. interest in having two major democratic allies with complementary strategic outlooks as members. Nevertheless, this will only intensify the already powerful gravitational pull of the UNSC to gridlock because of the divergent interests of the council's members. Eliminating the UNSC's veto is an even worse idea, because it merely would repeat the mistake of the UN's predecessor, the League of Nations, which severed power from responsibility. The veto remains essential for preventing the UN to run amok, as it is often inclined to do because of the large number of tyrannies represented at the UN and their enablers who appease them.[18]

In light of the dangerous intersection between radicalism and the spread of WMD, the 9/11 generation of American statesmen cannot delude themselves about the contributions the UN can make to U.S. security. Ultimately, the robustness of American power, unconstrained by the UNSC veto, remains a necessary if not sufficient condition for sustaining an international environment conducive to peace, freedom, security, and prosperity. Muscular multilateralism is difficult enough to attain even among stable liberal democracies with shared values and largely complementary perceptions of interests. It becomes prohibitively dangerous in a forum structurally inclined to paralysis, such as the United Nations.

Although the United States should pay more attention to the view of our allies than to the UN, 9/11 reminds us that no nation, no alliance, no international organization can have a veto on American action. The NATO alliance of 27 members is too large and cumbersome to generate an effective consensus in areas outside of Europe. This holds especially true for issues involving the Middle East, where American and European perspectives have diverged sharply since the Suez Crisis of 1956. Typically, for example, the United States and our European allies have found themselves at odds over the Arab-Israeli dispute and its broader implications. American presidents from Nixon through President George W. Bush (with Carter as the exception) saw the Palestinian extremism and rejectionism as the major source of the problem, whereas our Western European allies (wrongly, in this writer's view) favored accommodating rather than confronting radical Palestinians and other Middle Eastern tyrannies. So even the NATO alliance cannot always serve as an effective substitute for American power, asserted either unilaterally or in collaboration with a coalition of the willing that usually will include many though not all of our democratic allies.[19]

Promotion of Stable Democracies

President Bush's commitment to spreading stable liberal democracy to the Middle East arises from his well-founded conviction that regime type, ideology, and the propensities of individual leaders account for substantial variations in how states behave in matters of international relations. On the positive side, stable liberal democracies do not go to war with one another, have a higher convergence of interests with each other than with other types of regimes, and invariably resolve the disagreements that do occur among themselves without violence.[20] On the negative side, tyranny animated by malevolent ideology often breeds dangerous and catastrophic aggression.

This regime analysis integral to the Bush Doctrine is not new, but it represents one of the most venerable and successful traditions in American diplomacy. In every war the United States has fought since World War I, American presidents have defined the regime type of our adversary as the root cause of the conflict, and insisted on democratic regime change as a war aim to address that root cause. The tragedy of World War I is that the United States left Europe too soon, with democracy in Germany precarious and Germans unreconciled to their defeat. Franklin Roosevelt and Winston Churchill did not repeat that mistake during and after World War II. The United States and Great Britain demanded the unconditional surrender and total defeat of the Nazi regime, in a manner so devastating that the German people could not deny it; thus, they imposed democratic regime change on Germany and were determined to enforce it to create a rightly ordered peace. In the early days of the cold war, the Truman administration identified the malevolent nature of the Soviet regime as the root cause of the conflict; thus, the Truman Doctrine called for relentless political, military, and economic pressure on the Soviet Union with the object of precipitating its collapse. That strategy succeeded magnificently, especially during the final phase of the cold war under Ronald Reagan.[21]

One of the major causes of the Iraq War of 2003 was the ambiguous outcome of the Gulf War of 1990–1991 that left Saddam and his brutal Baath regime in power. After 9/11, President George W. Bush did not make the same mistake. He insisted that a just and durable peace in the Middle East required Saddam Hussein's unmitigated defeat and democratic regime change, which the United States must have the foresight and perseverance to enforce. After a difficult period between the end of the conventional military phase of the Iraq War in May 2003 and the advent of the surge in June 2007, the United States seems to be within hailing distance of creating an open democratic Iraq decent to its people and its neighbors. Such an outcome could have the hugely positive effect of emboldening democratic forces in the Middle East—a region that sorely needs freedom—to address the real root cause of terror.[22]

Granted, many thoughtful people who rightly accept the validity of the democratic peace argument predict that the Bush Doctrine will fail in the Middle East: that the conditions are not propitious for democracy to succeed; that it must emerge, if at all, organically, not by force. These critics point not only to the difficulties in Iraq but also to the electoral success of terrorist organizations such as Hamas as evidence of the Bush administration's folly.[23] Yet even if democracy does not succeed swiftly and in all places in the Middle East and even though Americans elected Barack Obama, who is opposed to the war in Iraq and committed to an early exit from it, the Bush administration's response to 9/11 and rationale for it have irrevocably altered the way in which the United States defines and pursues its interest in the Middle East. The issue has become not whether, but how, to induce the toxic political culture of this troubled, dangerous, and volatile region to evolve in a more benign direction.

No future administration should or will rely on authoritarian regimes in the Middle East as the bulwark of stability. During the cold war, this policy made sense as the lesser moral and strategic evil, because, besides Israel, conditions in the Middle East held out no plausible hope for constructing the democratic alliance systems so successful in the more important geopolitical theaters of Europe and East Asia. The synergistic effects of globalization and technological dynamism have changed this equation. Many autocratic regimes such as Saudi Arabia's are neither durable in the long term nor all that reliably moderate. Even in places such as the Palestinian territories, where elections have yielded results we justifiably deplore, a brutal and corrupt Palestine Liberation Organization under Yasser Arafat offered no better alternative for achieving a tolerable Arab-Israeli peace. A more decent and responsible leadership will never emerge in Palestine without the necessary, if insufficient, conditions of elections and transparency in the Palestinian Authority. Meanwhile, the dangers inherent in the dissemination of the potential for developing WMDs will mount ominously, until the emergence of decent, stable, liberal democratic regimes in the Middle East.

Of course, spreading democracy and choosing a stable liberal democratic ally are not always prudentially available options. In some cases, the United States must continue to engage with regimes that fall far short of our ultimate preferences. Yet most Americans after 9/11 grasp the profound truth of Natan Sharansky's aphorism: you are always better off with a stable liberal democracy, even one that hates you, than a dictatorship that loves you.[24] For all the differences that Americans will surely have on how to promote and sustain democracy prudentially, there is a post-9/11 consensus that alliances and alignments with stable liberal democratic regimes rest on a far more durable foundation than tactical arrangements with dictators. Convergences of enlightened self-interest among stable, liberal democracies are much more likely to transcend changes in time and circumstances—to become permanent rather than tactical interests.

Emphasis on Regime Type

Beyond the Middle East, the continuities since 9/11 are in many ways more significant than the discontinuities. The world has witnessed the resurgence of great power rivalry normal in world politics, which the end of the cold war ephemerally suspended for merely a decade. This rivalry has ideological and regime-type dimensions as well. An autocratic China and an increasingly authoritarian Russia are less menacing adversaries to the United States than the totalitarian dictatorships of Nazi Germany and the Soviet Union were during the twentieth century. The current Chinese and Russian regimes also are less organically and unremittingly hostile to the United States than the Islamo-Fascist theocracy of Iran and its regional surrogates. Nevertheless, an illiberal China and Russia are significantly greater threats to the United States than liberal democratic regimes there would be.[25]

In this respect, the Bush Doctrine incorporates many of the main tenets of American grand strategy since World War II: History has not ended. Nor will it end with man's contrivance alone. There is always a devil in international relations lurking, even in the best of times. No generation of Americans can take peace or freedom for granted. The United States must remain unremittingly vigilant to preserve its ideals and self-interest, rightly understood. Geopolitically, the United States must continue to prevent any single hostile power of combination of powers from dominating Europe, East Asia, or the Middle East: these are major power centers, from which potentially grave and perhaps mortal threats to America's national interest could arise.[26]

If 9/11 revealed that winning the War on Terror remains the most immediate priority for American foreign policy, constructively reacting to the rise
of China looms as the largest priority for the near future. A dynamic but
authoritarian China growing at an annual rate of more than 9 percent may
develop the capability and ambition to dominate East Asia, the world's paramount power center now and for the remainder of the twenty-first century.
The range of opinion on how to deal with China spans a narrower spectrum
than most fundamental debates over American foreign policy. Consensus
exists on the need to retain a strong American presence in East Asia. Unlike
Western Europe, where regional institutions buttress the zone of democratic
peace, East Asia remains a highly competitive, fractious, and ideologically
diverse region. Nor are there adequate regional substitutes for American
power to forge an effective balancing coalition should China embark on an
expansionist course.[27]

Consensus also exists that trade with China is largely desirable. Even those
most wary of Chinese ambitions distinguish between the effects of engagement with China and the failed policy of détente with the Soviet Union, which
rested on many of the same premises but operated in less felicitous circumstances. Engagement with the Soviet Union failed because it was a totalitarian
state, with no private sector. Thus, Western trade and credits subsidized the
very Soviet military apparatus so menacing to the United States and lessened
the pressure for fundamental political reform. Trade with China could have
a more benign result by strengthening and emboldening China's burgeoning
private sector. Eventually, China's entrepreneurial class may demand political rights commensurate with their new status, which could lead to regime
change that could tame Chinese ambitions.[28]

The logic of the Bush Doctrine dictates a mixed strategy toward an autocratic China—continuing to engage it economically while containing it militarily. A democratic alliance system, with Japan and India as core members,
is a vital element of such a containment strategy. One of the most significant
developments that 9/11 has catalyzed is the emerging strategic partnership
between the United States and democratic India. As Fareed Zakaria has aptly
put it, the two countries "know and understand each other the way the United
States has developed a relationship that was strategic, but also with much
more—with the United States, and later with Israel."[29] Likewise, as Robert
Blackwell, America's ambassador to India between 2001 and 2003 observed,
India may lead the list of nations "which share with us vital national interests
and the willingness to do something about threats to these interests," that is,
preventing China from dominating East Asia, and defeating radical Islam,
which also menaces the Indian state.[30]

To conclude, the events of 9/11 have had a paradoxical effect on the
perception and reality of America's role in the world. The most profound
change has occurred in American policy toward the Middle East. Elsewhere,
the continuities in American grand strategy before and after 9/11 loom as

large as the discontinuities. For all the problems that confront the United States, the Bush Doctrine has diagnosed the danger we face and prescribed the remedy for it more presciently than any of the plausible alternatives. The principles of the Bush Doctrine will dominate the discourse about American foreign policy for the next several American presidential elections to come. The homicide bombing of the World Trade Center and the Pentagon precipitated a global conflict that will take decades to unfold. The Bush Doctrine stands as the most immediate, the most controversial, the most durable, and perhaps the most beneficial legacy of that day of infamy Americans now know as 9/11.

Notes

1. Robert G. Kaufman, *In Defense of the Bush Doctrine* (Lexington and London: University Press of Kentucky, 2007), 157–183.
2. See, for example, Jimmy Carter, "Just War—or a Just War," *New York Times*, March 9, 2003, 13; Michael Walzer, *Arguing about War* (New Haven: Yale University Press, 2004).
3. John Lewis Gaddis, *Surprise, Security, and the American Experience* (Cambridge, MA: Harvard University Press, 2004).
4. For a recent book that explains this brilliantly from Truman's perspective, see Elizabeth Edwards Spalding, *The First Cold Warrior: Harry Truman, Containment, and the Remaking of Liberal Internationalism* (Lexington and London: University Press of Kentucky, 2006).
5. Paul Kengor, *The Crusader: Ronald Reagan and the Fall of Communism* (New York: Regan Books, 2006).
6. For a solid journalistic account that captures the evolution of the president's thinking and his decisive impact on the decision to invade Iraq, see Bob Woodward, *Plan of Attack* (New York: Simon & Schuster, 2004).
7. Thomas Aquinas, *Summa Theologica*, vol. 2, trans. The Fathers of the English Dominican Province (Chicago and London: Encyclopedia Britannica, 1948), 577–81.
8. James Turner Johnson, "Just War as It Was and Is," *First Things* (January 2005): 14–24.
9. Kaufman, *In Defense of the Bush Doctrine*, 68–74, 91–93.
10. For a scathing account of the UN's role in Rwanda, see Michael Bartlett, *Eyewitness to Genocide: The United Nations and Rwanda* (Ithaca: Cornell University Press, 2002).
11. For the best of these critics, see Michael. R. Gordon and Bernard. E. Trainor, *Cobra II: The Inside Story of the Invasion and Occupation of Iraq* (New York: Pantheon Books, 2006); Jeffrey Record, *Dark Victory: America's Second War Against Iraq* (Annapolis: Naval Institute Press, 2004).
12. Barack Obama, "Renewing American Leadership," *Foreign Affairs* 86, no. 4 (July–August 2007): 2–16.
13. John McCain, "U.S. Foreign Policy: Where Do We Go from Here," *World Affairs Journal* 20, no. 9 (March 26, 2008): 1–7.

14. Joshua Muravchik, *The Future of the United Nations: Understanding the Past to Chart a Way Forward* (Washington, DC: American Enterprise Institute Press, 2005), 117–72.

15. Martin Meredith, *The Fate of Africa: From Hopes of Freedom to the Heart of Despair* (New York: Public Affairs, 2005), 517–19.

16. Kaufman, *In Defense of the Bush Doctrine*, 72.

17. For an excellent account of this grim story, see William Schawcross, *Allies: The U.S., Britain, Europe, and the War in Iraq* (New York: Public Affairs, 2004).

18. Arch Puddington, "The Wages of Durban," *Commentary* 112, no. 4 (November 2001): 29.

19. Rober Kagan, *Of Paradise and Power: America and Europe in the New World Order* (New York: Vintage, 2004); M. Boot, "A Transatlantic Truce: Isn't It Pragmatic?" *Los Angeles Times*, February 17, 2005, B13.

20. Spencer Weart, *Never at War: Why Democracies Will Not Fight One Another* (New Haven: Yale University Press, 1977).

21. Kaufman, *In Defense of the Bush Doctrine*, 23–62.

22. Peter Feaver, "Anatomy of the Surge," *Commentary* 125, no. 4 (April 2008): 24–28.

23. Francis Fukuyama, *America at the Crossroads: Democracy, Power and the Neoconservative Legacy* (New Haven: Yale University Press, 2006).

24. Natan Sharansky, *The Case for Democracy: The Power of Freedom to Overcome Tyranny and Terror* (New York: Public Affairs, 2004).

25. Robert Kagan, *The Return of History and the End of Dreams* (New York: Alfred A. Knopf, 2008).

26. Eugene Rostow, *Toward Managed Peace* (New Haven: Yale University Press, 1993), 3–18.

27. For a well-respected account of a more soft line approach to China, see Avery Goldstein, *Rising to the Challenge: China's Grand Strategy and International Security* (Palo Alto: Stanford University Press, 2005). For an account more congenial to this writer's more stern view of the Chinese regime and its ambitions, see Ross Terrill, *The New Chinese Empire and What It Means for the United States* (New York: Basic Books, 2003).

28. See a nice summary in this regard by Robert G. Sutter, *China's Rise in Asia: Promises and Peril* (Lanham, MD: Rowman and Littlefield, 2005).

29. Fareed Zakaria, "India's Rising," *Newsweek*, March 6, 2006, 32–42.

30. Robert D. Blackwill, "The India Imperative," *National Interest* 80 (Summer 2005): 10.

Chapter 12

Grand Strategy Transformed: 9/11 and the Birth of Crusading Realism

*Lamont Colucci**

My interest in the Bush Doctrine had a single inspiration: the smoking twin towers. The event was a catalyst that created the single most important shift in American national security strategy in 50 years by returning us to our revolutionary war roots. The purpose of my research is to explain and illustrate this shift in what many have labeled the Bush Doctrine. There have been many books and articles on the Bush Doctrine, but none that make the argument herein. I argue that the Bush Doctrine, and thus Crusading Realism, returns the United States to the very cornerstone of American values, the ideas of the Declaration of Independence and natural law. In other words, the natural law arguments of the eighteenth century are reborn in twenty-first-century America caused by Islamic extremism, the threat of WMD, and the presence of rogue regimes—the toxic nexus.

The title of my own book—*Crusading Realism*—became the argument. Crusading Realism bridges the gap between the traditional ideas in international relations and foreign policy that have rested in the United States primarily on liberalism and realism. The 1990s, the years of strategic drift, were an appalling disaster for American national security, in many ways creating the conditions for the catastrophic events in and around 9/11. It is this unique reaction by President Bush to this dangerous problem that becomes Crusading Realism. My book, *Crusading Realism: The Bush Doctrine and*

*Lamont Colucci, a former diplomat with the U.S. State Department, is Assistant Professor of Politics and Government at Ripon College. He is the coordinator for an interdisciplinary national security studies program and teaches courses on national security, foreign policy, intelligence, terrorism, and international relations.

American Core Values after 9/11 was the culmination of three years of research concerning this question and had a definite beginning and an end culminating immediately following the first shots fired in the war against Saddam Hussein's Baathist dictatorship. This examination is therefore not about the invasion or liberation of Iraq, but rather, the reasons that led to the invasion and the general War on Terror and Islamic Bolshevism. Critics may hang on to this in a desperate attempt to deconstruct the arguments made here in a further effort to caricature President Bush, Vice President Cheney, and their administration rather than deal with serious issues of national security policy and philosophy.

The Beginning

"A second plane hit the second tower. America is under attack."[1] This statement, made by Chief of Staff Andrew Card to President George W. Bush at 9:05 a.m. on September 11, 2001, served as the opening line for a profound change in modern American foreign policy.

This chapter examines the extent to which the Global War on Terror, announced that day, was the catalyst for a foreign and national security policy that has come to be known as the Bush Doctrine. The Bush Doctrine represents a fundamental shift in modern American foreign policy and national security, affecting national well-being, national values, homeland security, diplomacy, foreign relations, defense, and military issues. There have been many attempts to describe the Bush Doctrine within the landscape of international relations theory, using such terms as Democratic Realism, Democratic Imperialism, Republican Realism, Expansive Internationalism, Conservative Internationalism, and Liberal Internationalism. Although each of these has its own appeal, a more fitting descriptive term would be that of "Crusading Realism." Such a term encapsulates the unique features of the Bush Doctrine, developed in a spirit of idealism that motivates the push toward democracy, yet simultaneously constrained within the bounds of *realpolitik* and *machtpolitik*.

The term "crusade" is admittedly a controversial one. Moreover, President Bush's use of it following the attacks was widely criticized, both at home and abroad. Still, it has a recent precedent, in World War II, when Eisenhower, as the commanding general of the allied forces, asked American and British soldiers about to land at Normandy to "embark on a great crusade" for the liberation of France.

The Bush Doctrine reflects a belief that American civilization is the highest achievement and aspiration for mankind, an attempt to build an American cosmopolis. While ancient Rome's foreign policy assertiveness took the form of "expansive defense" for the purpose of securing and stabilizing its own empire, America's recent foreign policy assertiveness may be understood as a crusade to secure and stabilize democracy both at home and abroad. Furthermore, while the Bush Doctrine amounts to a significant change in modern American national security and foreign policy, it is also an organic development of what came before it; it is the full maturation of policies that have grounded the United States of America and were part of its original building blocks.

9/11 as a Watershed Event

The morning of September 11, 2001, was as routine and mundane as any other. The sky over New York was blue; people set about their business in a habitual way and the basic aspects of life were unchanged. True, there were tensions in the air: the international scene was unsettled; and the system of international relations created by World War II was crumbling. Americans, however, seemed almost oblivious, and with this sense of detachment came an unexpressed feeling of invulnerability. America was far away from the world of trouble; America was safe and secure within its own borders; and Americans pursued an economic life focused on prosperity and choice.

The attack by Japan on Pearl Harbor was the watershed event in twentieth-century American foreign policy. It defined the very nature of American military and political involvement in international relations, catapulting the United States into the position of reluctant superpower. It caused an unquestionable shift in the manner in which the United States engaged the world, and such a shift, such a watershed event, had occurred on only two previous occasions in the republic's history: the very founding of the republic and the sinking of the USS Maine. Although the Spanish-American War would shatter the *perception* of a semipermanent isolationism, and America would thereafter act upon the stage as a world power, it would take the Japanese surprise attack at Pearl Harbor to create the conditions for her to become a superpower. It was there that the postwar world system was shaped and United States foreign policy thenceforth directed against the Soviet Union and international Communism. This international system, on which so many other things were dependent, came crashing down in 1991. The United States, seeing no threat equivalent to the Soviets on the horizon, relaxed, oblivious to the new threats that existed. Former CIA director James Woolsey said it best: "We have slain a large dragon, but we now live in a jungle filled with a bewildering variety of poisonous snakes. And, in many ways, the dragon was easier to keep track of."[2] Few were paying attention to the slithering, the biting, and the plotting.

The sequence of events leading up to September 11, 2001, is well known. Suffice it to note here that the 1993 attack on the World Trade Center, the attacks made on American forces in Somalia, the 1996 bombing of the Khobar towers in Saudi Arabia, the 1998 destruction of the two American embassies in East Africa, and the attack on the USS Cole in 2000 were just a few of the major events that could have changed American foreign policy but did not. That change would take place only after the events of 9/11. The Bush administration, coming into office in one of the closest elections in American history, had few major foreign policy goals. There was talk of repairing the relationship with Japan, containing (or at least constraining) Chinese aggression, building a national missile defense, and reorienting U.S. relationships with its allies. Nevertheless, there was no great vision of foreign policy before to 9/11.

The crux of the post-9/11 change in foreign policy is the notion of a distinctive Bush Doctrine. Some may ask whether the Bush Doctrine indeed represents a watershed in United States foreign policy comparable with those seen in 1898 and 1947, or whether it is simply a reexpression of the historically constant elements in American foreign policy. In fact, the Bush Doctrine is not only a fundamental shift in United States foreign policy, but it has even created new regimes in American foreign policy and in the elements of international relations.

It is clear that most serious students and scholars of this period saw the actions taken by the Bush administration from September 11, 2001, onward as a significant shift in strategic doctrine.[3] Moreover, the 9/11 attacks became the lens through which the Bush administration saw all elements of American foreign policy.

Past administrations, especially under Clinton, perceived the threat of terrorist actions as primarily a law enforcement problem. That meant they would analyze a terrorist attack, focusing on the specific individuals who committed the act, and then pursue them or act with allies to do so to capture them and bring them to some sort of justice (preferably an American jail). This policy succeeded in removing from some specific individuals the opportunity to commit specific terrorist acts. However, the policy could not address the systemic problem of international terrorism itself. During the Clinton years the threat was understood as concerning law enforcement, not as military and intelligence matters. In as far as the military and intelligence were employed before 9/11, the approach was one of constraint and very narrow rules of engagement, even including, and perhaps especially, the First Gulf War. The intelligence and security services, including the CIA, were hamstrung by both Vietnam War and cold war era rules and procedures that produced faulty intelligence and (even when accurate) few actions. Richard Haas wrote, when he was Bush's director of the Office of Policy Planning in 2002, "The tragic events of September 11, 2001, the attacks on the World Trade Center and the Pentagon did not create the post-post Cold War world. But they helped end the decade of complacency."[4]

In some ways, the Bush Doctrine can be seen as a repudiation of multilateralism, but this misses the point. There was never a desire to act alone but rather, a desire to act. If that meant unilaterally, then Bush's answer was "so be it." Further, the doctrine not only changed the way in which the world's only superpower engaged the world, but it also changed the policy of that superpower toward its major allies and opponents. Whether we look at relations with such great powers as Russia, China, Japan, the United Kingdom, or Germany or at those with such pivotal powers as Turkey, North Korea, or Indonesia, 9/11 and the Bush Doctrine have certainly created climactic changes in all of these interactions.[5]

In doing so, they used the event to define a new and bold strategy for the twenty-first century.[6] Pro-democracy activist and former Soviet dissident Natan Sharansky concurs, but argues that the significance of 9/11 was that it provided the catalyst for the democracy promotion aspects of the Bush Doctrine. His book *The Case for Democracy* is one that President Bush cites as pivotal to his intellectual and policy development, and Sharansky contends that the groundwork of the democracy promotion aspect of the Bush Doctrine occurred within days of the 9/11 attack.[7]

Sharansky, together with the architects of the Bush Doctrine and their intellectual allies, is scathing in his criticism of those in the West who argue that democracy is only suitable for certain kinds of people or societies. They cite examples such as Japan, Germany, and Russia to prove their point.[8] To understand President Bush and those who subscribe to the Bush Doctrine, it is essential to see that they fundamentally believe that democracy is a universal good, a universal desire, and a universal goal, and that it is part and parcel of a universal natural law. Yet a major issue in the Bush Doctrine and throughout American foreign policy is the tension and duality between the principles of the republic and the use of power: the problem of national self-interest and idealism.[9] The Bush Doctrine can be seen as an attempt to reconcile these two in a new formula for the twenty-first century.

The full flavor of the Bush Doctrine comes out in the 2005 inaugural address:

America's vital interests and our deepest beliefs are now one. From the day of our founding, we have proclaimed that every man and woman on this earth has rights and dignity, and matchless value, because they bear the image of the maker of heaven and earth.... We are led, by events and common sense, to one conclusion: the survival of liberty in our land increasingly depends on the success of liberty in other lands. The best hope for peace in our world is the expansion of freedom in all the world.... There is only one force of history that can break the reign of hatred and resentment, and expose the pretensions of tyrants and reward the hopes of the decent and tolerant, and that is the force of human freedom.... History has an ebb and flow of justice, but history also has a visible direction, set by liberty and the author of liberty.... We will persistently clarify the choice before every ruler and every nation: The moral choice between oppression, which is always wrong, and freedom, which is eternally right.[10]

Here is the most forceful expression of an American foreign policy doctrine in the entire history of the republic. It is more sweeping in scope than that of even Theodore Roosevelt or Ronald Reagan, more committed than that of George Washington, Thomas Jefferson, or James Monroe, more forceful than that of Woodrow Wilson, Harry Truman, or Bill Clinton, and more absolutist than that of all these presidents. It is appropriate here to sketch its principal components.

There were three stages to the Bush Doctrine. Stage I relates to those events immediately following the September 11, 2001, attacks upon the United States, with initial statements about the United States making no distinction between the terrorists and those that harbor them. Stage II concerns the decisions that surround the October 2001 invasion of Afghanistan, which is the first real test of the doctrine itself. Stage III begins with the president's speech at West Point military academy in 2002, outlining what can be distilled down to five major aspects of the mature doctrine:

1. *Preemption*—This is the willingness for the United States to determine in advance if an imminent, clear, and present danger and credible threat exists, before an attack from a rogue state, terrorist group, or state sponsor, and to act to eliminate that threat. The threat of WMDs plays a major role in this part of the doctrine.
2. *Self-Defense*—This encompasses changes related to homeland security, from the revamping of bureaucracy to the Patriot Act.
3. *Preventative War*—This is the boldest aspect of the Bush Doctrine, and it should *not* be confused with preemption. Preventative war is when no imminent threat exists, but the United States discerns a definite potential danger to its vital or national interests that must be destroyed. Iraq provides our case study for this aspect.
4. *Unilateralism*—This is the idea that if the United States must act alone, it will do so with neither guilt nor hesitation.
5. *Democracy*—This encapsulates the belief that it is only through promoting democracy (by military means, if necessary) that the United States will not only be safe but also fulfill its international moral obligations.

In terms of practical policy, it aims to instill democracy and freedom in places that are tyrannical, in the expectation that doing so will eliminate terrorist aggression and forestall WMD proliferation.[11] This represents a return to the first principles of American Security strategy,[12] a return made possible by four specific conditions: the end of the cold war, the 9/11 attacks on the United States, the preeminence of American power, and the people who came to power in 2000, especially President Bush.

As the Bush Doctrine took shape, it encountered criticism across the whole political spectrum. It is evident that the U.S. foreign policy apparatus itself has problems coming to terms with the Bush Doctrine.

Understanding "Crusading Realism"

On the argument put forward here that 9/11 was a trigger is in itself a neces-sary but not a sufficient condition for the formulation of the distinctively new Bush Doctrine. The change of president in a heated and highly partisan politi-cal atmosphere was likely to bring about a new emphasis in foreign policy, and this was apparent early on, in the face of what has been termed here Assertive Nationalism. The response to 9/11, however, clearly transcended the limits of Assertive Nationalism and propelled the United States into a new era of inter-ventionism, characterized by a commitment to primacy, preemption, preven-tion, and (democracy) promotion. Thus, it is clear that without 9/11, the Bush administration would have embraced Assertive Nationalism and not the ideal-ism and refinements of Crusading Realism. This is not to say that 9/11 created Crusading Realism in a vacuum. Rather, 9/11 created the catalyst to allow the prior, existing thinking of President Bush and the Crusading Realists to come to fruition. The 9/11 attacks provided the impetus, the reason, and the need for a presidency on the road to Assertive Nationalism to embrace the totality of its own beliefs in mankind, God, justice, philosophy, and therefore policy. The 9/11 attacks served as the trigger to restart American foreign policy based on the historic and philosophic traditions of the United States—the merger of Americanism with American foreign policy.

Contemporary judgment, as well as the long-term assessment of the Bush Doctrine, rest upon how this new era is to be interpreted. It is apparent that the conventional, binary distinction between realism and idealism cannot do justice to the change. My interpretation shows the Bush Doctrine as radical in the true sense of that term: as not just innovatory, but as a return to the roots of American thought in terms of natural law concepts that are "writ-ten on the heart." Finally, the Bush Doctrine must be understood also in the context of a general change in international relations. The Bush administra-tion was reacting to a new paradigm of doom. The potential triangular rela-tionship between transnational apocalyptic terrorist groups (al Qaeda and Islamo-Bolshevism), WMDs, and rogue states presented the Bush adminis-tration with a threat to vital national security interests never before imagined in American foreign policy.

The Bush Doctrine as a Return to the Roots

The Bush Doctrine does not exist in a political or historical vacuum. The culmination of two hundred years of United States foreign policy, it is a natural outgrowth of the tensions, rivalries, and debates that have bedeviled American foreign policy since the founding of the nation. The founders who created the United States were products of the Western Enlightenment. They were rooted in the idealism and rationalism of philosophers such as John

Locke and believed that human progress was not only possible but necessary.[13] Thus, the idealism of "human rights" and the pragmatism of national interest have been present in the conduct of the United States' foreign affairs since the outset.[14] It is in these terms that the Bush Doctrine is best understood.

Consider two such declarations:

> So it is the policy of the United States to seek and support the growth of democratic movements and institutions in every nation and culture, with the ultimate goal of ending tyranny in our world–and to provide new guards for their future security.[15]

And:

> But when a long train of abuses and usurpation, pursuing invariably the same object evinces a design to reduce them under absolute despotism, it is their right, it is their duty, to throw off such government.[16]

Were it not for the archaic and poetic language of the second quotation, it would be easy to conclude that these two statements came from the same document. These two bookends mark both the beginning and the present culmination of United States foreign policy. The first quotation is the declaration of principles of the Bush Doctrine, finally outlined in full formality in President Bush's 2005 inauguration speech. The second is arguably the most powerful sentence in American English, from the Declaration of Independence.

It is clear from the primary and secondary sources, the minutes of meetings, the interviews, the rhetoric, and the speeches, that President Bush had embraced his personal belief in Christian morality together with the Lockean concepts that birthed the republic. Whether he or others spoke of the "freedom agenda," "God's gift to humanity," or the "non-negotiable demands of human dignity" as the cornerstone of this new doctrine, it is all the same—a fundamental return to the founding of the nation. These are the expressed tenets of natural law come full circle to create American foreign policy of the twenty-first century. It is the universal belief that there is a standard to which no man or nation can measure, but can only aspire. It is the belief that policy must follow from morality and ethics.

However, just as the revolutionaries could not have won the day without cannon or shot, neither could the Crusading Realists win the day without muscle and toil. In this way, there is contempt for both the realists and the Wilsonians for missing half of the universe. It is this that makes Crusading Realism unique and potentially permanent. What presidential candidate who is serious could repudiate the philosophy behind Crusading Realism without abandoning the very essence of Americanism? It is quite possible that a future president may not practice Crusading Realism in reality, but it would be political suicide to go openly against the principles therein expressed. Thus, we may have candidates dodge, weave, and tack, but never will they be able to embrace Crusading Realism's antithesis. The twinning of natural law—the very legitimacy of being of the United States—with practical policy is now the touchstone awaiting a future president to pull the sword from that stone.

It seems clear that the philosophy of the Declaration of Independence, marked by a firm and steadfast belief in natural law, the divine entitlement of liberty, and special providence stakes out a pathway to the change in American foreign policy that was made flesh by the Bush Doctrine. That doctrine would never have taken hold without the catalyst of 9/11. It is so striking that it took 229 years for the Declaration of Independence to become a foreign policy document. In between those bookends, the debates that raged in American foreign policy were manifold: declineists versus triumphalists, unilateralists versus multilateralists, and isolationists versus internationalists.[17] And so they battled on to capture the spirit of American foreign affairs for over two centuries.

In conclusion, the roots of what is here termed Crusading Realism are to be found in many of the distinct eras of American history: the founding of the nation, the rise of Manifest Destiny, American exceptionalism, the gunboat diplomacy of Theodore Roosevelt, the rollback doctrines of the Eisenhower years, the Reagan crusade against Communism, and the Crusading Realist's contempt for the Clinton era. The key, and the continuing thread, is the promotion of democracy. Democracy promotion is truly revolutionary for two reasons: because of its scope of change and because it returns American foreign policy to its revolutionary roots. The founding of the United States was based on republican liberty under law, a law grounded in natural law, "written on the heart" of every human being born. Natural law must be a universal law for it to be justified in any way. The Bush Doctrine is, then, a break from the immediate past by being far and away the only comprehensive doctrine to return to the natural law principles of the founding of the nation as a strategy of United States foreign policy. Unlike the Monroe Doctrine, which was targeted against the Western Europeans, and unlike the Truman and Reagan Doctrines, which addressed the Communist threat, the Bush Doctrine has a comprehensive quality, standing as a warning to rogue states like Iraq, to groups like al Qaeda, and to the rulers in Beijing alike.

Notes

1. Andrew Card, *Ask the White House* (Washington, DC: White House, 2003). This was the statement that Card whispered into President Bush's ear at 9:05 a.m. on 9/11 at Emma F. Booker Elementary School.
2. United States Senate, R. James Woolsey, in Testimony before the SSCI, February 2, 1993.

3. Dunn David Hastings, "A Doctrine Worthy of a Name? George W. Bush and the Limits of Pre-Emption, Pre-Eminence, and Unilateralism," *Diplomacy and Statecraft* (New York: Routledge, 2006), 4–5.

4. Richard Haas, *Defining U.S. Foreign Policy in a Post-Post-Cold War World* (New York: Foreign Policy Association, 2002), 31.

5. Mary Buckley and Robert Singh, eds., *The Bush Doctrine and the War on Terrorism* (London: Routledge, 2006). This is illustrated by scholars such as George Blazyca writing about Poland and Central Europe and Brendon O'Connor writing about Australia.

6. Colin Gray, *The Sheriff* (Lexington, KY: University Press of Kentucky, 2004), 11.

7. Natan Sharansky, *The Case for Democracy* (New York: Perseus Books Group, 2004), 19–20.

8. Sharansky, *The Case for Democracy*, 6.

9. Thomas Magstadt, *An Empire If You Can Keep It* (Washington, DC: CQ Press, 2004), 1.

10. George W. Bush, Second Inaugural Address. Washington, DC, January 18, 2005.

11. Max Boot, "Neither New Nor Nefarious: The Liberal Empire Strikes Back," *Current History* 1–2, no. 67 (2003): 1–7.

12. Thomas Donnelly, *The Underpinnings of the Bush Doctrine* (Washington, DC: American Enterprise Institute, February 1, 2003), http://www.aei.org/publications/pubID.15845/pub_detail.asp (accessed on March 23, 2009).

13. Magstadt, *An Empire If You Can Keep It*, 24.

14. Ralph Peters, *New Glory: Expanding America's Global Supremacy* (New York: Penguin Books, 2005), 10.

15. George W. Bush, Second Inaugural Address.

16. United States Congress, *Declaration of Independence*, 1776.

17. Joseph Nye, *The Paradox of American Power: Why the World's Only Superpower Can't Go It Alone* (Oxford: Oxford University Press, 2002), 3–4.

Chapter 13

Three Blocks, Two Towers, One Trend: Civil-Military Cooperation Before and After 9/11

*Christopher Ankersen and David J. Betz**

Winning wars accomplishes little if we cannot also win the peace. The strategic goals for which the wars are fought can only be achieved if the follow-on mission leaves an occupied territory more stable and democratic than before. Civil-military cooperation (CIMIC) is the key to achieving such stability.

Douglas C. Lovelace, Jr., Director,
United States Army War College Strategic Studies Institute

The American army exists to fight and win the nation's wars. To entertain other ideas is dangerous, as it detracts from this primary mission. As Condoleezza Rice stated in 2000, "[C]arrying out civil administration and police functions is simply going to degrade the American capability to do the things America has to do. We don't need to have the 82nd Airborne escorting kids to kindergarten."[1] Put more succinctly, if somewhat more crudely, by Charles Krauthammer, "[P]eacekeeping is for chumps."[2] All this,

*Christopher Ankersen is Course Tutor at King's College London and editor of two books, *Civil-Military Cooperation in Post-Conflict Operations* and *Understanding Global Terror*. David J. Betz is Senior Lecturer of War Studies at King's College London, where he heads the Insurgency Research Group and is Academic Director of the online master's degree, War in the Modern World. He is the author of *Civil-Military Relations in Russia and Eastern Europe, Army and State in Post-Communist Europe*, and numerous journal articles.

of course, changed with the events of 9/11. Now, the U.S. Army plays a key role in Provincial Reconstruction Teams (PRTs), which are "providing security, democratic governance, economic and reconstruction assistance to local and provincial governments across Afghanistan."[3] In the army's latest capstone field manual, General William S. Wallace claims that there has been a revolutionary departure from past doctrine. It describes an operational concept where commanders employ offensive, defensive, and *stability or civil support operations* simultaneously as part of an interdependent joint force to seize, retain, and exploit the initiative, accepting prudent risk to create opportunities to achieve decisive results. Just as the 1976 edition of FM 100–5 began to take the army from the rice paddies of Vietnam to the battlefield of Western Europe, this edition will take us into the twenty-first-century urban battlefields among the people without losing our capabilities to dominate the higher conventional end of the spectrum of conflict.[4]

A remarkable turnaround in such a short period of time.

Or so it seems. Contrary to the image sketched above, American involvement in civil-military cooperation (or CIMIC) has a long history and was not born in the aftermath of the attacks on the World Trade Center and Pentagon in September 2001.[5] Rather, it is part of nuanced and sophisticated approach to conflict developed within the American military. What is true, though, is that it has neither been fully understood nor flawlessly implemented in the events that followed 9/11. The aim of this chapter is to trace the evolution of American conceptual thinking and actual practice as it relates to civil-military cooperation.

Three Blocks Emerged from a Yellow Wood

America has had a long and but sometimes meandering involvement with civil-military cooperation, for a number of reasons and in a number of guises.[6] Perhaps the seminal encapsulation of the American experience with these types of military operations can be found in the United States Marine Corps *Small Wars Manual*. Written in 1940, it defined "small wars" as

> Operations undertaken…wherein military force is combined with diplomatic pressure in the *internal or external* affairs of another state whose government is unstable, inadequate or unsatisfactory for the preservation of life and of such interests as are determined by the foreign policy of our Nation.[7]

In these small wars "measures will be taken to…break the resistance to law and order by a combination of effort of physical and moral means."[8] It was well understood by the authors of the *Small Wars Manual* that military involvement had to encompass more than mere combat operations.

The moniker of small wars eventually faded away, but the concept remained. By 1966, based on the experience gained by American forces and the example demonstrated by the Viet Cong, General Westmoreland concluded, "It is abundantly clear that all political, military, economic, and security (police) programs must be completely integrated in order to attain any kind of success in a country which has been greatly weakened by prolonged conflict."[9] The following year, the U.S. Army labeled these kinds of integrated actions as stability operations, which it defined as

Internal defense and *internal development* operations and assistance provided by the armed forces to maintain, restore, or establish a climate of order within which responsible government can function effectively and without, which progress cannot be achieved.[10]

After the Vietnam experience, American commitment to *any* form of irregular warfare was at its nadir. Instead, army leaders decided to focus the conventional, high-intensity operations, which marked the European theater, at the expense of counterinsurgency and its supporting activities, such as civil-military cooperation. Critics believe that this was an unvarnished "attempt to prepare to refight the last satisfactory war, World War II."[11] Counterinsurgency is barely mentioned in the capstone field manuals of 1976, 1980, or 1986. Instead, counterinsurgency and its constitutive activities, such as civil-military cooperation, were assigned to Special or Reserve forces; essentially, they were taken out of the mainstream military's repertoire and turned into specialized functions.

However, events in the real world conspired against the ghettoization of civil-military cooperation. The American military participated in numerous UN peacekeeping (e.g., Somalia and Haiti) and NATO peace support operations (e.g., Bosnia and Kosovo) over the course of the 1990s and the U.S. Army briefly introduced a thin doctrinal volume on such operations, but this referred to "traditional peacekeeping" and did not allow for intrusive actions, such as civil-military cooperation.[12] Perhaps not surprisingly the conceptual encapsulation of what conflict had become by the middle of the 1990s did not take doctrinal form. Rather the Commandant of the United States Marine Corps, General Krulak, expressed it as a metaphor. In 1999 he described a world where the armed forces would find themselves fighting a Three Block War, a situation where they would be "confronted by the entire spectrum of tactical challenges in the span of a few hours and within the space of three contiguous city blocks," forced to conduct "humanitarian assistance, peace-keeping, or traditional warfighting" virtually at the same time.[13] This imagery captured the imagination of military commanders for two key reasons. First, for those soldiers who had been deployed on peace operations, it reflected their reality. Despite the dominant images of *Blackhawk Down* that remain, the U.S. mission in Somalia included a large degree of civil-military cooperation, conducted and coordinated by the army and Marine Corps.[14] Second, Krulak's vision was not one of despair, but one of opportunity. Because soldiers found themselves within a Three Block War, they could escape the notion that they were tied to older, now-defunct images, such as " NATO's Central Front." In places ranging from northern Iraq to Haiti, to Bosnia, to Kosovo, civil-military cooperation was a significant—even defining—aspect of American military involvement.[15] Moreover, as Adam Seigle points out, far from being a peripheral activity, civil-military cooperation was an essential element for success.[16]

Despite Krulak's allegorical tale, the transition from a Democrat to a Republican administration in the United States in 2001 was marked, as a part of Secretary of Defense Donald Rumsfeld's campaign of transformation, by a strong opposition to the idea of peacekeeping, which was associated with "nation-building."[17] This can be seen in the decision to close the United States Army War College's Peacekeeping Institute by the summer of 2003.[18]

However, the necessity of stability operations was reinforced following the invasions of Afghanistan and Iraq. Despite the attention placed on the "combat phase" of operations there, there was a realization at many levels before the invasion that some form of stability operation, including activities centered on law-and-order provision and reconstruction, would be necessary. For instance, two professors from the United States Army War College, Conrad Crane and Andrew Terrill, drawing on historical examples, concluded in a report published in February 2003 that "[t]o be successful, an occupation such as that contemplated after any hostilities in Iraq requires much detailed interagency planning, many forces, multi-year military commitment, and a national commitment to nation building."[19] Accordingly, they produced detailed planning considerations for American forces in Iraq after the combat phase was to be complete. Their report identified a number of tasks, across a wide spectrum of responsibility, including public administration, legal issues, public safety, public health, historical, cultural and recreational matters as well as economic and commercial activities.[20] In the end, as is now clear, these concepts were never transformed into action.

The evidence suggests that the United States had neither the people nor the plans in place to handle the situation that arose after the fall of Saddam Hussein. Looters took to the streets, damaging much of Iraq's infrastructure that had remained intact throughout major combat. Iraqi police and military units were nowhere to be found, having largely dispersed during combat. U.S. military forces in Baghdad and elsewhere in the country were not prepared to respond rapidly to the initial looting and subsequent large-scale public unrest. These conditions enabled the insurgency to take root, and the army and Marine Corps have been battling the insurgents ever since.[21]

Indeed, the result was similar to that noted by the commander of the U.S. Third Army responsible for postcombat activities following the First Gulf War. Expressing his reaction in a colorful language, he said that owing to the lack of planning on the part of the Department of Defense, he had been handed a "dripping bag of manure that no one else wanted to deal with."[22]

In light of the inadequate response to postwar planning, the doomed Peacekeeping Institute was reborn, now as the Peacekeeping and Stability Operations Institute.[23] In doctrinal terms, the U.S. Army was prepared to conduct " Stability Operations and Support Operations" (SASO), which made provision for active involvement in the internal workings of the countries targeted.[24] Stability Operations became the popular term of art used by government officials and civilian observers. It provided a way out of discussing peacekeeping, and the equally problematic term "nation-building,"[25] but was to a large degree congruent with peace support doctrine, as conceived by NATO and other Allied militaries.

Events continued to shape American thinking. The realities of military operations in Iraq and Afghanistan prompted the Joint Staff to abandon the term Stability Operations in favor of the more descriptive " security, transition, and reconstruction operations":

> Formerly, operations similar to these were referred to as stability operations. Stability can be a misleading word....Stability understood as *"status quo antebellum"* will not often be our strategic goal. Rather, the United States (and its coalition partners) will seek a new, better *status quo*—a *status quo* in which civilians are better off than they were before conflict erupted. In fact, transition to a new and better *status quo* will often involve instability.[26]

Security, transition, and reconstruction operations would see "the joint force commander, as part of a multinational and integrated multiagency operation...provid[ing] initial humanitarian assistance, limited governance, restoration of essential public services, and other reconstruction assistance." Furthermore, the document stressed that these kinds of operations "are essential for the ultimate achievement of strategic aims. [They] are a *core mission* of the military services and civilian agencies."[27]

The U.S. Army lagged behind the Joint Staff in their move to distance itself from the idea of "stability." However, drawing on the older concept of counterinsurgency, something that had traditionally been the domain of special operations forces, they began to see the need to revitalize their thinking.[28] David Kilcullen claims that counterinsurgency "is armed social work, an attempt to redress basic social and political problems while being shot at. Max Boot, in his historical account *The Savage Wars of Peace*, agrees, stating that American military operations in the twenty-first century will be characterized in part as "wars in which U.S. soldiers act as 'social workers.'"[29] This makes operations such as civil-military cooperation "a central CI [counter insurgency] activity, not an afterthought."[30] This has been formally enshrined in the latest American army and Marine Corps doctrine. Written under the aegis of Lieutenant General David Petreaus, *Counterinsurgency* states that

> A counterinsurgency campaign is...a mix of offensive, defensive and stability operations.... It requires soldiers and marines to employ a mix of familiar combat tasks and skills more associated with non-military agencies. [These include] civil security; civil control; [the provision of] essential services; governance; [and] economic and infrastructure development.[31]

In the contemporary jargon, successful military operations require a mix of both kinetic (hard combat activities) and nonkinetic (softer activities, such as civil-military cooperation and information operations). Counterinsurgency, then, as the latest manifestation of Western military doctrine, is an extension of a much earlier and well-established trajectory.

Deep Roots for a New Tree

It is important to regard this uneven evolution against the backdrop of other events, not just the thinking of the American defense establishment. The idea that civil-military cooperation is a key to success on the battlefield is not merely the product of trial and error and experience by the U.S. armed forces. Krulak's metaphor stands out as an attempt to think seriously about the changes in the nature of conflict, but there are other equally thoughtful attempts to do so. Over the course of the 1990s, the West "discovered" the reality of intrastate conflicts, characterized by the confluence of communal violence: humanitarian suffering (be it in the form of population displacement, famine, or abject poverty); and opportunistic, criminal economic exploitation.[32] As if this were not enough, intrastate conflicts tended to occur in places noted for the absence of indigenous state-based structures and institutions, labeled as failed, failing, fragile, collapsed, or disrupted states.[33] Solutions to these "complex emergencies" would have to come from outside.[34] The new interventions—into situations of complex, multidimensional problems—would require complex, multifaceted solutions. Indeed, it can be said that peace support operations are meant as a corrective to the unidimensional approach of traditional peacekeeping. Rather than dealing with conflicts only at the systemic level, and with separate, often conflicting instruments (such as diplomacy, military action, and development), peace support operations have been "characterized by [their] complex, multilevel, multidimensional nature...[and] signify the attempt to create an operational, normative, just, democratic fabric...in and between civil societies."[35]

The British general Rupert Smith understood this characterization of the contemporary battlefield and believed that beginning in the 1990s and into the future, the West would fight 'Wars amongst the People." Smith holds "a view of the world as one of confrontations and conflicts rather than war, and therefore one in which military force has a role to play; but that role is not a detached one, nor one which will achieve the strategic objective itself."[36] In this world, Smith believes that "the job of the military alongside all agencies conducting the operation is to defeat the opponent and win the will of the majority of the people for the future." Informed by his experience as a commander in the Balkans, Smith asserts that armies are not enough: commanders must understand that they fight amongst—but more importantly, *for*—people: the societies within the failed or fragile states in which they operate.

This thinking necessarily leads to new kinds of force structures and new kinds of tactics. As David Betz has summarized elsewhere, "You cannot fight 'wars amongst the people' without actually being amongst them, which means being able to maintain sustained contact with the local population to restore security and enable the re-emergence of civil life in areas disrupted by combat operations."[37] Similarly, David Last holds that to be effective in ending conflicts, militaries must possess not only combat acumen, but also *contact* skills: the kinds of activities that allow soldiers to build trust with their interlocutors and the population at large.[38] Civil-military cooperation is an example of that kind of contact.

But Does It Work?

As we have demonstrated, civil-military cooperation is neither a new idea nor a new activity for the American armed forces. Civil-military cooperation was not born on September 11, 2001: it has an intimate history with both peace support and counterinsurgency operations. That said, since 9/11, civil-military cooperation has not always been applied appropriately, in accordance with the lessons learned from previous experience.

Perhaps what is more interesting, by way of a concluding question, is to wonder to what extent civil-military cooperation is an effective tool for commanders in the current environment? To answer this effectively, we must also ask what the purpose of civil-military cooperation is: why do commanders carry it out? Broadly speaking, there are two main categories of reasons for civil-military cooperation. The first is force protection. Commanders believe that a population that is "cared for" by intervening military forces will not bite the hands that feed them. In this sense, every school that is rebuilt and each bag of flour that is distributed become a shield. The second reason why civil military cooperation is carried out is an extension of the first. Beyond merely "not shooting," it is hoped that populations who receive the benefit of military generosity will actively provide information—intelligence—on the insurgents in their midst. In exchange for a new well or some clothing, the local populace is supposed to inform the military of impending insurgent operations. Both these reasons rely on the idea that it is possible to change people's behavior through the conduct of influential operations. This is the basis of the much-lauded but poorly defined "hearts and minds" campaigns, of which civil-military cooperation is a part.

In reality, however, relying on civil-military cooperation in this way can be misleading. In Afghanistan, survival often means that villagers hurry to leave the scene of an upcoming ambush, rather than risk reporting to news to NATO or American troops.[39] At the beginning of the Falujah uprising in the spring of 2004, a CNN reporter asked a bewildered U.S. Army captain why the Iraqis were shooting at his company. He responded by saying that he had no idea; he and his men had recently completed over one hundred community improvement projects and the Iraqis should not have been reacting the way they were.[40] The captain is not alone. Many people also believe that reconstruction (of schools, wells, roads, etc.) is the key to victory in the wars in Afghanistan and Iraq. However logical they may appear, the reality is that these assumptions are unproven. How do we know that this kind of (re)construction works, either at the strategic or the tactical level? Is counterinsurgency really "armed social work"? Or have we merely fallen in love with an activity that can be easily measured and that makes good copy back home? Has the "body count" of old been replaced by the "new school count" as some proxy for success?

Believing that a "softer" approach to operations, including contact as well as combat, is somehow new is folly. So is pretending that civil-military cooperation is a panacea for the problem of insurgency. Drawing on the macroexamples of the "reconstruction" of Germany and Japan after World War II cannot be used as a basis for the current exercises that are miniscule by comparison; indeed, as the authors of a landmark study admit, "The post-World War II occupations of Germany and Japan set standards for postconflict nation-building that have not since been matched."[41] Instead, the U.S. armed forces—primarily the army and the Marine Corps—should build on their experience gained in places like Haiti, Bosnia, and Kosovo. Those situations highlight the utility and the limitations of civil-military cooperation in complex situations. Of course, historical analogies are never perfect: Afghanistan is not Haiti; Iraq is not Kosovo. One thing is clear: Krulak's "Three Block Wars" and Smith's "Wars amongst the People" are likely to make up a significant part of the future battlefield. Learning to fight and win *these* wars is of utmost importance.

Notes

1. Condoleeza Rice, cited in Michael R. Gordon, "The 2000 Campaign: The Military; Bush Would Stop U.S. Peacekeeping in Balkan Fights," *New York Times*, October 21, 2000.
2. Charles Krauthammer, "Peacekeeping Is for Chumps," *Saturday Night* (November. 1995): 73.

3. The White House, Office of the Press Secretary, "Helping Afghanistan Achieve Sustainable Progress," Fact Sheet, March 13, 2008, http://www.america.gov/st/texttrans-english/2008/March/20080313170136xjsnommis0.3274652.html (accessed July 20, 2008).

4. United States, *United States Army Field Manual 3-0. Operations* (Washington, DC: United States Government Publishing Office, 2008), foreword. Emphasis added.

5. The term civil-military cooperation is used throughout this chapter because it has the widest applicability (in terms of geographical scope and academic study). However, with specific regard to the armed forces of the United States, the term civil-military operations is more appropriate. Its definition is applied in this chapter to denote civil-military cooperation. It is defined as "The activities of a commander that establish, maintain, influence, or exploit relations between military forces, governmental and nongovernmental civilian organizations and authorities, and the civilian populace in a friendly, neutral, or hostile operational area in order to facilitate military operations, to consolidate and achieve operational U.S. objectives. Civil-military operations may include performance by military forces of activities and functions normally the responsibility of the local, regional, or national government. These activities may occur prior to, during, or subsequent to other military actions. They may also occur, if directed, in the absence of other military operations. Civil-military operations may be performed by designated civil affairs, by other military forces, or by a combination of civil affairs and other forces." *Department of Defense Dictionary of Military and Associated Terms*, Joint Publication 1–02, April 12, 2001 (as amended through August 26, 2008), 90.

6. This section draws on Christopher Ankersen, "Civil-Military Cooperation in the Canadian Army," unpublished PhD thesis, London School of Economics and Political Science, January 2008.

7. United States. *United States Marine Corps Small Wars Manual* (Washington, DC: United States Government Printing Office, 1940), 1. Emphasis added.

8. United States, *Small Wars Manual*, 7.

9. Dale Andrade and James H. Willbanks, "CORDS/Phoenix: Counterinsurgency Lessons from Vietnam for the Future," *Military Review* (March–April 2006): 10.

10. United States, *United States Army Field Manual 31-23. Stability Operations.* (Washington, DC: United States Government Publishing Office, 1967), 1. Emphasis added.

11. Conrad Crane, *Avoiding Vietnam: The U.S. Army's Response to Defeat in Southeast Asia* (Carlisle, PA: United States Army War College Strategic Studies Institute, 2002), 9.

12. United States, *United States Army Field Manual 100-23. Peace Operations.* (Washington, DC: United States Government Publishing Office, 1994).

13. Charles C. Krulak, "The Strategic Corporal: Leadership in the Three Block War," *Marines Magazine*, January 1999.

14. Kevin M. Kennedy, "The Relationship between the Military and Humanitarian Organizations in Operation Restore Hope," in *Learning from Somalia: The Lessons of Armed Humanitarian Intervention*, ed. Walter M. Clarke and Jeffrey M. Herbst (Boulder, CO: Westview, 1997): 104–105.

15. See, for instance, Chris Seiple, *The U.S. Military/NGO Relationship in Humanitarian Interventions* (Carlisle, PA: United States Army Peacekeeping

Institute, 1996); James J. Landon, "CIMIC: Civil Military Coordination," in *Lessons from Bosnia: The IFOR Experience,* ed. Larry Wentz (Washington, DC: National Defense University Press, 1997); Robert C. DiPrizio, *Armed Humanitarians: U.S. Interventions from Northern Iraq to Kosovo* (Baltimore: Johns Hopkins University Press, 2002); Thomas R. Mockaitis, *Civil-Military Cooperation In Peace Operations: The Case Of Kosovo* (Carlisle, PA: United States Army War College Strategic Studies Institute, 2004).

16. Adam Siegel, "Mission Creep…or Mission Understood?" *Joint Force Quarterly* (Summer 2000): 112–115.

17. During the presidential candidate debate with Al Gore, George W. Bush declared, "we can't be all things to all people in the world. I am worried about over-committing our military around the world. I want to be judicious in its use. I don't think nation-building missions are worthwhile." Presidential Debate at Wake Forest University October 11, 2000, http://www.issues2000.org/2004/ George_W_Bush_Foreign_Policy.htm (accessed March 5, 2007).

18. Douglas Holt, "Peacekeeping Institute to Close," *Chicago Tribune,* April 15, 2003, http://www.sourcewatch.org/index.php?title=Peacekeeping_Institute (accessed March 6, 2007).

19. Conrad C. Crane and W. Andrew Terrill, *Reconstructing Iraq: Insights, Challenges, and Missions for Military Forces in a Post-Conflict Scenario* (Carlisle, PA: Strategic Studies Institute, 2003), 1.

20. Ibid., 63–72.

21. Nora Bensahel, Olga Oliker, Keith Crane, Richard R. Brennan, Jr., Heather S. Gregg, Thomas Sullivan, and Andrew Rathmell, *After Saddam: Prewar Planning and the Occupation of Iraq* (Santa Monica: RAND Corporation, 2008), xvii.

22. Crane and Terrill, *Reconstructing Iraq,* 2.

23. United States, Department of the Army, "Army to Retain and Expand Peacekeeping Institute," press release, October 28, 2003, http://press.arrivenet. com/government/article.php/113279.html (accessed March 7, 2007).

24. United States, *United States Army Field Manual 3–07. Stability Operations and Support Operations* (Washington, DC: United States Government Printing Office, 2003). The doctrinal manual was reissued in October 2004.

25. Even though, by this time, the U.S. administration had softened somewhat on the term, as evinced by statements by officials such as the then national security adviser Condoleeza Rice. Jay Nordlinger, "'Power and Values': A Conversation with Condoleezza Rice," *National Review,* September 18, 2002, http://www. nationalreview.com/flashback/flashback-nordlinger091802.asp (accessed March 7, 2007).

26. United States, *Security, Transition, and Reconstruction Operations.* Joint Operating Concept. Version 1.06 (Washington, DC: Office of the Joint Staff, Department of Defence, 2004), 2. Emphasis in the original. This was published in June 2004 and it superseded the existing thinking of November 2003 contained in United States, *Stability Operations.* Joint Operating Concept (Washington, DC: Office of the Joint Staff, Department of Defense, 2003).

27. United States, *Security, Transition and Reconstruction Operations,* iii–v. Observers had been calling for such an integrated approach for some time. See, for instance, Adam Siegel, "Mission Creep…or Mission Understood?" *Joint Force Quarterly* (Summer 2000): 112–115.

28. For a good overview of the U.S. counterinsurgency thinking up to 2004, see International Institute of Strategic Studies, *Strategic Survey 2003/4: An Evaluation and Forecast of World Affairs* (Oxford: Oxford University Press, 2004), 38–48. For an eclectic collection of counterinsurgency articles, launched to coincide with the publication of the new doctrine, see the United States Army Combined Arms Center, *Counterinsurgency Reader: Special Edition of Military Review* (October 2006). Robert R. Tomes provides a connection to earlier thinking and practice in counterinsurgency, which has proven to be popular with American military, in Robert R. Tomes, "Relearning Counterinsurgency Warfare," *Parameters* (Spring 2004): 16–28.

29. Max Boot, *The Savage Wars of Peace: Small Wars and the Rise of American Power,* (New York: Basic Books, 2002), 338.

30. David Kilcullen, "Twenty-eight Articles: Fundamentals of Company-Level Counter-insurgency," *Military Journal* (May/June 2006): 107. Killcullen is a retired regular Australian army officer, now acting as a special advisor on counterinsurgency within the U.S. Department of Defense.

31. United States, *United States Army Field Manual 2-24. Counterinsurgency.* (Washington, DC: United States Government Printing Office, 2006), chapter 1, page 19. This manual is simultaneously published as *United States Marine Corps Warfighting Publication 3-33.5. Counterinsurgency.*

32. See Mary Kaldor. *New and Old Wars: Organised Violence in a Global Era.* 2nd ed. (Cambridge: Polity Press, 2006); Mark Duffield, *Global Governance and the New Wars* (London: Zed Books, 2001); and Amin Saikal, "The Dimensions of State Disruption," in *From Civil Strife to Civil Society: Civil and Military Responsibilities in Disrupted States,* ed. William Maley, Charles Sampford, and Ramesh Thakur (Tokyo: UNU Press, 2003), 17–30.

33. Hugh Miall, Oliver Ramsbotham, and Tom Woodhouse, *Contemporary Conflict Resolution* (Cambridge: Polity Press, 1999), 4.

34. Michael Ignatieff, "State-Failure and Nation-Building," in *Humanitarian Intervention: Ethical, Legal and Political Dilemmas,* ed. J. L. Holzgrefe and Robert O. Keohane (Cambridge: Cambridge University Press, 2003), 299–321.

35. Oliver P. Richmond. *Maintaining Order, Making Peace* (Basingstoke: Palgrave Macmillan, 2002), 11–12.

36. Rupert Smith, *The Utility of Force: The Art of War in the Modern World* (London: Penguin, 2006), 394. Emphasis added.

37. David Betz, "Redesigning Land Forces for Wars amongst the People," *Contemporary Security Policy* 28, no. 2 (2007): 221.

38. "Winning the Savage Wars of Peace: What the Manwaring Paradigm Tells Us," in *The Savage Wars of Peace,* ed. John T. Fishel (Boulder, CO: Westview, 1998).

39. Anthony Loyd, "Villagers Flee Valley as Taleban Dig In to Face Allied Onslaught," *Times,* June 17, 2008, A1.

40. CNN, World News Today, 0703 (Central Mountain Time), April 8, 2004.

41. James Dobbins, John G. McGinn, Keith Crane, Seth G. Jones, Rollie Lal, Andrew Rathmell, Rachel M. Swanger, and Anga R. Timilsina, *America's Role in Nation-Building from Germany to Iraq* (Santa Monica, CA: RAND, 2003), xix.

Chapter 14

More Catalyst than Cause

F. Lincoln Grahlfs*

When I was awakened, on September 11, 2001, with the report of the assault on the World Trade Towers, I had two spontaneous reactions. First, I was concerned about my brother, who worked in the New York financial district, and second, I said, "I hope the government doesn't react in a misguided and foolhardy way." While it is true that things have changed considerably since then, it makes sense to view the events of that day more as a catalyst than as a primary cause.

It took three days before we found out that my brother was all right. But my second concern was based on my feeling that the government had for some time been on a trajectory that might very well produce an overly aggressive, and in my estimation unwise, reaction to the events of that morning. Unfortunately, my fears were realized. As early as nine days later, when he addressed a joint session of the Congress, President Bush identified the events of September 11 as "an act of war" and declared that we were henceforth engaged in a "War against Terror." In doing so he was ascribing to himself the far-reaching powers of a wartime president.

The American Heritage Dictionary defines terrorism as "acts of violence committed by groups that view themselves as victimized by some notable historical wrong."[1] Although these groups have no formal connection with governments, they usually have the financial and moral backing of sympathetic governments. Typically, they stage unexpected attacks on civilian targets, including embassies and airliners, with the aim of sowing fear and

---

* F. Lincoln Grahlfs is Professor Emeritus at the University of Wisconsin Colleges, where he served as chairman of the Department of Anthropology and Sociology for the thirteen campus system at the time of his retirement, in 1988. He is a veteran of World War II and taught sociology and anthropology for 32 years. He is the author of two books, *Voices From Ground Zero: Recollections and Feelings of Nuclear Test Veterans* and *Undaunted: The Story of a United States Navy Tug and Her Crew in World War II.*

confusion. Israel has been a frequent target of terrorism, but the United States has increasingly become its main target.

Terrorism, moreover, is hardly something new; it has been used, among others, by the Irish against British rule, the Jews against the British in Palestine and the Basque in Spain. Terrorism, moreover, could easily be construed to include the Detroit riots of 1967, and the incident in which four Puerto Rican nationalists fired automatic weapons into the chamber of the U.S. House of Representatives in 1954, wounding five of the legislators, as well as the 1972 bombing of a Pan-American plane at the airport in Rome, in which a number of innocent Americans lost their lives.

Indeed, the most contentious period of the French Revolution is identified as "the reign of terror." Terror, in this instance, is regarded by many as an appropriate response to persecution. It was in reference to these circumstances that Robespierre, in a 1794 address, said "If the basis of a popular government in peacetime is virtue, its basis in a time of revolution is virtue and terror—virtue without which terror would be barbaric and terror without which virtue would be impotent."

It should also be noted than great numbers of people die frequently in natural disasters. But whether it be from a natural disaster or from an act of terrorism, in spite of great losses our lives go on and we trust those in a position of authority to take the necessary steps to minimize the dangers.

There are, essentially, two characteristics that particularly distinguish the September 11, 2001, assault on the World Trade Towers and on the Pentagon. First, it was highly organized and planned, and second, it was of a far greater scale than most Americans would have anticipated. It was, however, a criminal act and the perpetrators should have been sought out and punished by legal means. Furthermore, no punishment for the act should have been administered by anyone before a clear determination of guilt or complicity was made. Anything else is tantamount to vigilantism.

Given this context, it seems reasonable to assume that a sensible government would react rationally to terrorist acts by (1) taking all possible steps *in cooperation with other governments* to identify and apprehend those responsible for the acts and to bring them before a *legal tribunal*, (2) engaging in reasonable efforts to identify the concerns underlying the terrorist activity and to seek workable solutions to those conditions, and (3) reassuring the public and taking all possible steps to see that conditions and activities are maintained at as nearly normal level as possible. How, then, can one explain the much more extreme response on the part of the United States government? To do so it is appropriate that we take a look both at the historical background and at the recent evolution of the American presidency.

Among the particulars, one must understand that a considerable part of today's unrest in the Middle East had its roots in circumstances associated with the breakup of the Ottoman Empire at the time of World War I. From the beginning of the twentieth century, oil became increasingly important to the growing industrial economies of the Western world. There were, more-over, large reserves of petroleum in the Middle East. So, with the demise of the Ottoman Empire at the end of World War I, the victorious European allies assumed a significant role in Middle Eastern affairs. By the terms of the Versailles Treaty, France was granted a mandate over Syria and Lebanon and Great Britain over Mesopotamia (Iraq), Palestine, and Trans-Jordan.

The language of the British mandate specifically recognized the "his-torical connection of the Jewish people with Palestine." Additionally, Jewish immigration into the area was to be encouraged without, however, compromising the rights of other peoples in the area. Accordingly, English, Arabic, and Hebrew were all three to be recognized as official languages in the area. But by 1922, on the basis of pledges that had been made to the Arabs during the war, the British government, in action approved by the League of Nations, specifically excluded Jewish settlement from the area of the Palestine Mandate referred to as Trans-Jordan. This area consti-tuted about three-quarters of the mandate. It must be noted, however, that although United States President Wilson played a major role in negotiation of the Versailles Treaty and establishment of the League of Nations, the U.S. Senate never ratified the treaty. Essentially, ratification was blocked because certain influential senators with strong isolationist tendencies suggested that membership in the League would undermine American sovereignty. At the end of World War II, though, the United States held a much stronger hand in world affairs and, as one of the principal architects of the successor to the League of Nations, the United Nations, our diplomats assumed that the presumed threat to its sovereignty would be eliminated by granting veto power over major UN pronouncements to certain major powers, including, of course, the United States.

By the 1940s the Middle East once again was taking on increasing sig-nificance in the world. There were two principal reasons for this. One, of course, was the ever-growing dependence of the civilized world on the use of petroleum. The other was the increased persecution of Jews in much of Europe during the 1930s and 1940s. This persecution had precipitated mass migrations of refugees, leading, in turn, to an increase both in the already significant Jewish population in key American cities and a consid-erable influx of Jews into Palestine. The ensuing strife led, ultimately, to the establishment of the nation of Israel, which was formally recognized by the United Nations in 1948. Because both Judaism and Islam had their origins in the Middle East, the adherents of both faiths laid claim to a homeland in the area.

From its inception the State of Israel has been viewed by its Islamic neigh-bors as an encroachment and a threat. Over the six decades of its existence this has resulted in a number of wars and skirmishes. Throughout this period, the United States has remained one of Israel's strongest supporters, and our political leaders have put much effort into attempting to broker a lasting peace in that part of the world. Thus, it is hardly surprising that we are resented by some of the more extreme factions in the area.

*   *   *

The United States, of course, was not a stranger to controversy. This nation got its start, essentially, with a small collection of migrants from Europe who were motivated by the challenge of adventure and opportunity and had the drive and the ambition to build a new life. These pioneers succeeded in building a strong nation with a stable political system and a dynamic economy. But they lacked the history and traditions of the "old world" whose people, for a long time, considered the United States to be "an upstart."

By the end of the nineteenth century, however, our society had spread from a collection of settlements on the eastern edge of North America, across the continent and, ultimately across the Pacific. And, along with this, there arose an increasing motivation to play a major role in world affairs. This was magnified by the fact that in the two major conflicts taking place in the first half of the twentieth century it was the overwhelming productive capacity of American industry that scored decisive victory and achieved a degree of dominance for the United States in world affairs. Along with these events there occurred a gradual accretion of power in the office of the U.S. president. This trend reached a point during the presidencies of Richard Nixon and Ronald Reagan that led some to affix the label "imperial presidency." What really seems to have emerged at this time was an administrative style with the characteristics of a kind of national "authoritarian personality." The characteristics of the authoritarian personality, as delineated by Theodor Adorno, emphasize excessive conformity; submissiveness to authority; intolerance; insecurity; superstition; and rigid, stereotyped, thought patterns.[2] Thus, key persons in those administrations seemed unable to recognize the validity of any culture, or view of the world, that differed from theirs. They tended to overreact to any deviation from what they perceived to be right, and were somewhat resistant to change. This had a tendency to be translated into a desire to remake the rest of the world in our image.

During the years 1990 to 2000, the atmosphere in Washington was a trifle more relaxed. But, when George W. Bush assumed the presidency, in January of 2001, there were, once again, definite signs of authoritarianism. It seemed evident that his administration would pursue a somewhat aggressive foreign policy, particularly in the Middle East. In spite of his self-declaration as a "compassionate conservative," George W. Bush was known to have a pronounced aggressive streak and a tendency, on occasion, toward vindictiveness. When he was campaigning for the presidency, Mr. Bush promised a robust foreign policy, using the phrase "a touch of iron and a sharpened sword" to characterize his policy. On more than one occasion he stated quite clearly that, as president, he would not hesitate to use force if he thought it was in our interest. When he was pushed to clarify what he defined as "in our interest," his response included the phrase, "if our friends in the Middle East are threatened." Given this country's strong support, over the years, of the nation of Israel, it was quite predictable that many of Israel's neighbors would perceive this statement as threatening.

*   *   *

From the beginning, Mr. Bush demonstrated an almost defiant attitude, stating on a number of occasions that he would retain the sanctions in force against Cuba, he would not rule out the use of force in the Middle East, and pledging "firmness with regimes like North Korea and Iraq." In this connection he invoked Teddy Roosevelt's "speak softly but carry a big stick." He also asserted that he wanted to scrap the antiballistics missile treaty and he was opposed to the Comprehensive Test Ban Treaty; he very much favored the development of an antimissile shield.

Lest anyone conclude that all this was simply campaign rhetoric, fully five months after moving into the Oval Office President Bush served notice that he was a firm leader. In that assertion he stated, "I'm intent on doing what I think is the right thing (with an emphasis on the word "I")."[3] It was, in fact, quite apparent to observers that unilateral action would pretty much typify this administration. Jacob Weisberg, in fact, notes that just a month after Bush took office, *Time* correspondent Charles Krauthammer described his approach as "Don't ask; Tell."[4]

Much is revealed, also, by an examination of the people that a president chooses to serve with him. Even a casual look at the appointed personnel in the administration of George W. Bush leaves one with the clear impression that he was surrounded by hawks and saber rattlers. Let us begin with the vice president. Dick Cheney's government career began with a number of staff positions in the administration of Richard Nixon. When President Nixon resigned, Mr. Cheney served on President Ford's transition team, then in his administration, rising ultimately to be Mr. Ford's chief of staff. Following the election of President Jimmy Carter, Mr. Cheney was elected to Congress from the State of Wyoming. After five terms in Congress, he resigned in 1989 to become secretary of defense in the administration of President George H. W. Bush. With the election of a Democratic president in 1992, he left government and ultimately became the chief executive officer of the Halliburton Corporation. Throughout his government service, and particularly after the resignation of President Nixon, Mr. Cheney consistently advocated for autonomy of the chief executive. His voting record as a member of Congress, moreover, demonstrates strong support for both a strong military and an independent presidency.

In addition, for the post of secretary of defense, a longtime associate of Cheney's, Donald Rumsfeld, was chosen. In the course of eight years as a congressman from Illinois, Rumsfeld came to be recognized as tough, aggressive, and blunt. His support of Richard Nixon's campaign for the presidency was ultimately rewarded by appointment, in 1969, to direct the Office of Economic Opportunity where, in turn, he hired Dick Cheney to be his executive assistant. In 1974 Rumsfeld was appointed ambassador to NATO (the North Atlantic Treaty Organization). Frustration with the diplomatic maneuvering he encountered during his year in that position no doubt contributed significantly to his increasingly hawkish tendencies.

When Nixon resigned and Gerald Ford became president, he called upon Rumsfeld to chair his transition team and, ultimately, to be his chief of staff. Rumsfeld, in turn, tapped his old associate, Dick Cheney, as his assistant. Late in 1975 a shake-up occurred in the Ford administration with Rumsfeld emerging as secretary of defense and Cheney as White House chief of staff. At the time the armed forces were in considerably weakened condition as a consequence of the lengthy Vietnam War. Not only did Rumsfeld perceive an immediate need to rebuild the country's armed strength, but he also felt strongly that there should be stronger civilian control over the military.

In 1997, a group of individuals from recent Republican administrations organized the Project for the New American Century. The *Statement of Principles* of this project, which arrogantly proclaimed the United States to be "the world's preeminent power" and advocated both a strong military and the "shap[ing of] circumstances before crises emerge," was signed by both Cheney and Rumsfeld as well as young President Bush's brother, Jeb, and significant members of the future Bush administration, such as Elliott Abrams (Special Assistant to the President), I. Lewis (Scooter) Libby (Chief of Staff to the Vice President), Paul Wolfowitz (Deputy Secretary of Defense), Henry S. Rowen (Member of the Secretary of Defense's Policy Advisory Board), Peter W. Rodman (Assistant Secretary of Defense for International Security), and Zalmay Khalilzad (Head of the Bush-Cheney Transition Team for the Department of Defense).

The extreme orientation of the Project for the New American Century is dramatically laid out in its report entitled *Rebuilding America's Defenses: Strategy, Forces and Resources for a New Century,* which was published in September, 2000 and was largely adopted by the president after the events of the following year. What this document proposes is the perpetuation, essentially, of a *Pax Americana.* It advocates that the United States maintain a strong nuclear arsenal as well as erect a robust missile defense shield. It calls upon the nation to maintain military forces sufficient to pursue and win "multiple simultaneous large-scale wars," and it mandates absolute American domination of both outer space and cyber space. Furthermore, it speaks for usurpation of the powers of the United Nations. It specifically advocates the manipulation of "regime change" in the promotion of American interests and it speaks to a de facto permanent American military presence in the Persian Gulf region.

In 1991, when the forces of Saddam Hussein had entered Kuwait, the United States retaliated with an all-out assault on Iraq, designated as "Operation Desert Storm." After a relatively quick victory George H.W. Bush, who was president at the time, opted, instead of overthrowing Saddam Hussein and occupying the country, to impose our will by means of a strict embargo and constant aerial surveillance. The embargo and aerial surveillance continued throughout the following administration of President Clinton. However, there were strong indications that when George W. Bush, the son of the previous President Bush, took office in the year 2000, key members of his administration thought that we should have "gone all the way" in 1991 and saw the ousting of Saddam Hussein as "unfinished business."

It will be recalled that in 1933, following the destruction of the German Reichstag by fire, the Nazis launched an intense propaganda program designed to make the people believe they were in constant danger of attack. It worked like a charm, and Hitler was given free rein by the majority of German citizens to pursue his global agenda. After all, Adolph Hitler's own second-in-command, Hermann Goering, observed that people can always be brought to the bidding of the leaders simply by telling them they are being attacked, and denouncing the peacemakers for lack of patriotism and for exposing the country to danger.

Given all this history, President George W. Bush seemed to have been just a trifle ingenuous in acting until September 10, 2001, as though there was even a hint of any danger to the country. Then, in a matter of days after the assault on the World Trade Towers, members of the administration were able to identify just whom to blame, and to begin planning retaliation. This suggests strongly that there already existed, in the Bush administration, a predisposition toward war in the Middle East as well as a predetermination of opponents.

For some time, moreover, there had been a quite evident tendency on the part of Bush and his administration to cut off diplomatic relations with some nations; espouse a "go it alone" agenda; abrogate treaties; favor arming space; cast doubt on the Geneva Conventions; favor "preemptive war"; identify certain nations as constituting a menace; and, in general, strut and exude bravado. All that was needed was to convince the American public that danger was imminent. In this light I would suggest that the events of September 11 did not change the world; rather, they had the catalytic effect of providing a rationale for the promotion of fear, imposition of extreme control, and promotion of hostile action.

Notes

1. *The American Heritage New Dictionary of Cultural Literacy,* 3rd ed. (New York: Houghton Mifflin, 2005).
2. Theodor Adorno, *The Authoritarian Personality* (New York: Harper & Row, 1950).
3. *New York Times,* April 14, 2001.
4. Jacob Weisberg, *The Bush Tragedy* (New York: Random House, 2008), 187.

Chapter 15

Imprisoning Politics: The Logic of Security and the Undermining of Democracy

Saul Newman*

Ever since that global event, September 11, there has been—under the dubious banner of "security"—an unprecedented accumulation of state powers of control, detention and surveillance, and a severe curtailment of what were formally seen as vital civil liberties, legal protections, and democratic rights. Everything from the expansion of electronic and biometric surveillance, to the indefinite detention without charge of terrorist suspects, to the formalization of "shoot to kill" powers for police forces, to the use of torture in interrogation—all suggest that a fundamental transformation is taking place in modern liberal democracies. That these regimes are uncannily coming to resemble the very authoritarian police states and fundamentalist societies that Western governments like to distinguish themselves from, points to a kind of mutation in modern political life.

In this chapter, I propose to explore the contours of a new "security" paradigm—by which I mean an *episteme* of discourses, speech acts, power relations, ideological mystifications, institutional practices, and concrete measures of control and surveillance organized around, and given intelligibility through, the amorphous notion of "security." In other words, with the declaration of the Global War on Terror "security" has become a kind of global signifier that authorizes measures and policies—both internally and externally—which would not hitherto have been seen as legitimate in liberal

---

*Saul Newman is Reader in Political Theory at the University of London and author of three books including *Unstable Universalities*.

democracies. A number of paradoxes are central to this discourse of security: while the discourse of security takes as its seeming prerogative the protection of citizens from terrorist attacks, it provokes a permanent state of fear, vulnerability, and insecurity; and perhaps more fundamentally, while it is instigated by formally elected democratic governments in response, partly, to perceived democratic pressures and fears about terrorism, presenting itself, moreover, as being necessary to protect democracies against their external enemies, in its application and its potential, it is profoundly antidemocratic. We have, then, a discourse and politicoideological paradigm which emerges from within the liberal-democratic space and yet which is profoundly hostile to liberal-democratic principles and practices.

The Securitization of Everyday Life

The notion of "security" is central to the War on Terror. This is a war, after all, that is being prosecuted to guarantee our security from future terrorist attacks: as the former president Bush was fond of reminding us, we must combat the terrorists abroad so that we do not have to do so on our own shores. So the War on Terror is to be both an external and internal war to guarantee our security. Moreover, the War on Terror that was declared in the days following the September 11 attacks, raised the idea of "security" to an almost metaphysical level—protecting citizens from a terrorist attack has now come to be seen as the central function of government, perhaps even the only one given the privatization or abandonment of many of the state's traditional functions such as the provision of social services and welfare. Moreover, a new ideological consensus has now formed around the priority of "security," with politicians from across the political spectrum trumpeting their national security credentials. The claim to be tough on "national security"—along with immigration and border control—forms the essential part of any political platform. There is usually strong bipartisan support in democratic assemblies for increased security and "counterterrorism" measures.

It is these measures and laws, moreover, which represent the most striking examples of the political transformation I am exploring here. The USA Patriot Act, which was passed rapidly through Congress in the weeks following September 11, and which was renewed in 2006, allowed for widespread executive powers of electronic surveillance, detention without charge, immigration and border control, the regulation of financial transactions; as well as authorization of extrajudicial military tribunals and special powers of interrogation, undermining, in effect, existing legal precedents, notions of due process, rules of evidence, and so on.[1] Moreover, the illegal NSA wiretaps on U.S. citizens ordered by President Bush shows the willingness of governments to act outside the boundaries of their constitutional authority under the pretext of security. Other liberal democracies have seen their own, similarly draconian, counterterrorism legislation. In the United Kingdom, various antiterrorist bills enacted since the September 11 and July 7 terrorist attacks, have allowed for the imposition of "control orders," under which terrorist suspects can be detained without charge, and without even the suspicion of having committed any crime—without, in many cases, even knowing the specific nature of the allegations against them. Legislation has also been introduced which criminalizes public statements that could be construed as an incitement toward terrorism, as well as giving the police and intelligence agencies widespread powers of search, arrest, and surveillance.

While some of these laws and measures have provoked an outcry from civil liberties groups, they have generally been accepted as normal, legitimate and necessary, and there has been little debate amongst the public about the clear threat they pose to democratic rights and freedoms.[2] Despite the unprecedented concentration of government and police powers, the restrictions on freedom of speech and protest, the constant intrusions into personal privacy, the undermining of well-established legal traditions, and the expansion of bureaucracy, opposition to these security measures has been relatively muted. There seems to be a sort of ideological chimera of "normality" here, as if what is utterly exceptional and previously unthinkable has now assumed an almost everyday appearance of normalcy and acceptability.

To understand this phenomenon we must look at the way in which the discourse of security has permeated society at all levels, functioning as an ideology that plays upon—and deliberately incites—people's fears and anxieties about terrorism. However, this fear is mingled, in a paradoxical way, with the fear of government itself. The discourse of security becomes internalized in the form of a self-censorship—the fear one experiences in passing through airport security; the awareness of the omnipresence of surveillance; the heightened climate of suspicion and paranoia; the sense of intimidation now felt by protesters and dissidents; the government messages encouraging us to spy on our fellow citizens and report signs of "suspicious activity"; the laws that limit the freedom of speech, imposing severe penalties for statements that can be perceived as supporting terrorism; the reticence, even on the part of academics in the United States, about not towing the official line in the months following September 11—and the persecution of those courageous enough to speak out. Within this new security paradigm we have all become subjects of permanent risk—both as targets for terrorist attacks, as well as potential terrorists ourselves. Thus we are subject to a constant suspicion and surveillance—positioned both as subjects requiring the overbearing protection of the state, and at the same time as potential threats to the security of the state.

As Ulrich Beck shows, the perceived threat of terrorism has now become the defining feature of risk societies—societies that see themselves as permanently threatened by uncontrollable disasters, such as global warming, nuclear accidents, mad cow disease, or global financial meltdowns.

What characterizes these risk-obsessed societies is an all-pervasive sense of distrust:

> The perception of terrorist threats replaces *active trust* with *active mistrust*. It therefore undermines the trust in fellow citizens, foreigners and governments all over the world. Since the dissolution of trust multiplies risks, the terrorist threat triggers a self-multiplication of risks by the de-bounding of risk-perceptions and fantasies.[3]

However, the logic of risk and security is more complex than Beck allows. It is not simply that governments respond to the risk of terrorism with well-intentioned, though misguided, measures of control that are designed to allay our fears. It is, rather, that the security paradigm actually works by deliberately perpetuating a constant and ubiquitous sense of anxiety, in which the fear of terrorism blurs into an obscure fear of the antiterrorist state itself. The constant directives issued by the Department of Homeland Security in the United States, advising people on what to do in case of a terrorist attack, as well as encouraging people to report "signs of suspicions activity" and to organize surveillance in their local neighborhoods, had the deliberate effect of inculcating a certain level of anxiety and suspicion. There can be little doubt that the state has a certain interest in maintaining this climate of fear, in promoting an all-pervasive sense of insecurity: at the most superficial level, one thinks of the government warnings about terrorism and the infamous (and ultimately meaningless) color-coded terror alerts that were used so effectively in the run-up to the 2004 presidential election in the United States; or the way that fears about security and terrorism were deliberately manipulated and played upon by both the U.S. and UK governments to give legitimacy to the invasion of Iraq in 2003. Moreover, the enormous powers accrued by police and security agencies, the centralization of security functions under new and enormously expensive superbureaucracies such as the Department of Homeland Security, and the massive growth in military spending in the United States since the declaration of the War on Terror suggest that certain vested interests are at stake here.[4]

So there is something in the very logic of security itself that provokes insecurity, and even incites further terrorist threats. The danger with the principle of security becoming coextensive with political life, as Giorgio Agamben argues, is that counterterrorism and terrorism will merge into one deadly circuit of mutual incitement and provocation, in which terrorist attacks provoke an even more violent and terroristic response from the state.[5] Can we not see signs of this happening already? The disastrous interventions in Iraq and Afghanistan—undertaken in the name of combating the terrorist threat—seem only to have increased it, now serving as the ultimate recruiting tool for future terrorists around the world. Moreover, the state's response to perceived terrorist threats seems more and more violent and terroristic: the execution-style killing of an innocent commuter on the London subway system, along with the tortures in Abu Ghraib, the arbitrary detention of terrorist suspects, the indiscriminate killing of civilians in Iraq and Afghanistan, show that the democratic state is in danger of becoming terroristic.

The potential—and indeed actual—violence of the new politics of security is further evident in its targeting of certain groups in society as "enemies." While the discourse of security constructs everyone as subjects of risk (rather than as citizens with rights), it also isolates specific groups—particularly Muslim communities—subjecting them to constant police harassment and surveillance. Indeed, a fragile sense of social unity is achieved through the production of the figure of the "terrorist enemy," an enemy who is both external and internal, who must be combated abroad and rooted out at home. In other words, the figure of the terrorist enemy—with all the racial stereotypes attached to it—serves to unite the rest of society in opposition to it. The central ideological message of this discourse is the following: Western society, which stands for freedom, democracy, human rights, openness and tolerance, must stand firm against the fanatical, fundamentalist, violent, barbaric, women-oppressing enemies who "hate our freedom and envy our prosperity," as Blair and Bush liked to remind us. Apart from questioning the hypocrisy and childish simplicity of this message—pointing out that it is precisely these Western societies who are undermining their own much-vaunted freedoms and openly violating human rights norms—it is also important to see its deeply racist undertones. It plays on, mobilizes, and incites, in quite a deliberate although concealed way, racial prejudices and xenophobic anxieties in Western societies about immigration, multiculturalism, and border control.

Security and Democracy

The ubiquity of the politics of security raises important questions about democracy: the discourse of security in Western (post)liberal democracies attempts to justify itself through the notion of democracy—that is, the idea that democratic regimes must use all available means to protect themselves against those who seek to undermine them. Furthermore, the War on Terror was seen—particularly by the neoconservatives in the Bush administration, but also by Tony Blair—as being part of a U.S.-led mission to spread democracy around the world. Here, democracy is seen as an antidote to terrorism. While it might be true, of course, that some form of democracy would be desired by those living under authoritarian regimes in the Middle East, such as those in Saudi Arabia, Egypt, as well as Pakistan, the fact that the United States continues to support these very regimes, in their open violation of democratic rights, highlights the hypocrisy of this global "democratic" mission. Nevertheless, the point is that democracy operates as the ideological standard-bearer of the War on Terror.

However, it is clear that the War on Terror and the politics of security are actually undermining in a very real sense, the democratic rights that they claim to derive their legitimacy from. The danger with the security paradigm in which we are living is that the exercise of democratic rights—particularly those of protest, dissent, public assembly, even militant trade union activity—are coming to be seen as threats to security that must be restricted. The only response to the mass protests in 2003—where over a million people marched through London to demonstrate against the impending war on Iraq—was for the British government to ban protests within a 1-km radius of Westminster. Security concerns have been used as a pretext to clamp down on protests and mass gatherings all around the world, including and especially antiglobalization demonstrations. It would seem, moreover, that "terrorism" is a mobile signifier that is being used to criminalize ever wider forms of social protest. Counterterrorist legislation in the United Kingdom and United States, for instance, is so broad and vague as to include potentially any form of protest within the definition of "terrorism." Indeed, such legislation has been used specifically against animal rights activists and militant environmentalist groups. So the politics of security is something that seriously threatens the full expression of democratic politics, leaving the largely meaningless ritual of voting once every four to five years as the only permissible democratic act.

Therefore it is crucial to examine the relationship between security and democracy. However, the difficulty here is that while, on the one hand, the politics of security is limiting democracy, at the same time it emerges from a democratic space and is given impetus, to a large extent, by democratic electorates. In other words, it would be all too easy to suggest that the security measures that seem to so imperil democracy are instigated by governments entirely against the will of their own people: we have to acknowledge that there is also a popular demand for greater security—for more draconian measures of detention, surveillance, and control—which is driven by fears and anxieties about future terrorist attacks. These anxieties coincide with and blend into more general fears about crime and illegal immigration. The politics of security is only possible in a climate of fear, and while it is true that this fear is deliberately manufactured and perpetuated by the politics of security itself, we also have to recognize the way it is partly legitimized by what is perceived by governments to be wishes of the electorate. The reason why the issue of "national security" has become such a major part of any electoral platform—to the point where it would be almost impossible to be elected without appearing to take this issue seriously—is because the politics of fear and the desire for greater security have deeply permeated the psyche of democratic polities. The reelection of Bush in 2004, for instance, at a time of heightened fears about terrorism, shows the intense desire for security on the part of many people, and the appeal of conservative political forces that appear to respond to this desire with even "tougher" security measures.[6]

The politics of security therefore works by creating a climate of fear and anxiety, and then responds to this with ever more restrictive and draconian controls, thus creating a tenuous and largely illusory sense of public safety. Here we see a kind of infantilizing of the democratic politic: it is no longer a body politic composed of citizens with rights and liberties, but rather a Hobbesian body politic composed of subjects, driven by fears for their security into seeking the overbearing protection of the state. Tocqueville, in his study of American democracy in the early nineteenth century, perceived a new form of despotism there, one that could not be characterized as the tyranny of antiquity, but that had a distinctly modern and democratic character:

> Over this kind of men stands an immense, protective power which is alone responsible for securing their enjoyment and watching over their fate. That power is absolute, thoughtful of detail, orderly, provident, and gentle. It would resemble parental authority if, fatherlike, it tried to prepare its charges for a man's life, but on the contrary, it only tries to keep them in perpetual childhood.... Having thus taken each citizen in turn in its powerful grasp and shaped him to his will, government then extends its embrace to include the whole of society. It covers the whole of social life with a network of petty, complicated rules that are both minute and uniform.... It does not break men's will, but softens, bends, and guides it;...it is not at all tyrannical, but it hinders, restrains, enervates, stifles, and stultifies so much that in the end each nation is no more than a flock of timid and hardworking animals with the government as its shepherd.[7]

What Tocqueville is describing here is a state of servitude that comes with an almost total dependence of people on their governments: the state exercises control no longer through an overt and tyrannical oppression, but by working itself into the social fabric at the most infinitesimal level. By facilitating their happiness and providing for their security, the state manages the lives of its people in the minutest detail. In the contemporary context, we see the myriad of petty rules, laws, and policies that democratic governments implement—which are designed to regulate the conduct of people in virtually every social act, and protect them against potential harms. This is a democratic system of power and social control in which the state alone becomes responsible for our happiness, health, and security, giving us succor and punishing our deviations. Securitization against terrorist threats is simply the latest and most intense articulation of this democratic despotism. The point is, however, that this sort of interaction between the state and society that characterizes modern societies, creates such a level of dependency of people on their government, and erodes their autonomy and responsibility to such an extent, that there is demand for even greater government intervention and control, particularly when people are faced with an all-pervasive sense of threat.

Furthermore, as Tocqueville detected, there was a majoritarian impulse in democracies that threatened to become tyrannical and stifle the rights of individuals and minorities. Once again we can see this today in the War on Terror: there is a willingness on the part of democratic majorities to violate the rights and liberties of certain ethnic minorities because they are seen to pose a greater risk of terrorism. Muslim minorities have become the targets of police surveillance and harassment, and deliberate policies of racial profiling—something non-Muslim majorities in Western democracies generally tend to accept and approve of. This readiness to sacrifice the rights of the few to protect and secure, or more accurately, to provide the *illusion* of protecting and securing the many, has become one of the most disturbing features of the War on Terror and the obsession with security.

Perhaps, as Jacques Derrida suggests, there is something in democracy itself that works against it—something in its own structural logic that threatens to undermine it from within. He refers to this suicidal quality of democracy as *autoimmunity*—a metaphor derived from the AIDS virus, in which, in response to the virus, the body produces antibodies that at the same time attack its own immune system. This self-destructive logic can be seen in the way that governments, in the name of protecting and securing their democracies from terrorist forces that threaten it, introduce measures and laws that undermine democracy from within: "It must thus come to resemble these enemies, to corrupt itself and threaten itself in order to protect itself against their threats."[8]

In other words, in attempting to immunize itself against a terrorist threat, democracy undermines itself from within. One might, then, legitimately ask those governments who insist that the terrorists want to destroy our democratic rights and freedoms, why they are essentially doing the job for them. The point made by Derrida is that there is a constitutive openness in democracy which is essential to it, and which at the same time leaves it vulnerable to attack. But if one tries to secure democracy against such attacks, one ends up undermining it. I would suggest, then, that security and democracy are principles that are in tension with one another: while the latter embodies an openness, pluralism, and indeterminacy, the former seeks only control, regulation, and the delimitation of freedom. Securitization always does a certain violence to the very thing one is attempting to secure. Politics—and particularly democratic politics—embodies the principle of openness and indeterminacy. The logic of security, by contrast, attempts to totalize the social space, to establish fixed coordinates for social identity which are determined by the state and by its security apparatuses, to create some imaginary social unity through the construction of the figure of the terrorist enemy who threatens society. And yet, as we have seen, this attempt to stabilize the social body—to restore the social bond that has forever been severed—brings with it an all-pervasive sense of fear and insecurity. Security is, in reality, the attempt to securitize politics itself—to shut down an autonomous space for politics, and to control and police the conditions upon which genuine politics depends. By submitting social life to technical control and regulation, the discourse of security seeks an evacuation of politics itself. The idea of a life that can be completely secured against threats and risks is also a life without politics.

Moreover, the antidemocratic tendencies that emerge from within the democratic space can only be resisted through a rigorous contestation of this very logic of security. Not only must its efficacy be questioned—the sense in which it creates only the illusion of security, while actually increasing insecurity, in both real and imaginary terms—but also the way that it threatens the democratic spaces and institutions that it supposedly seeks to protect.

Liberty and Security

What must be questioned also is the notion of a *balance* between security and liberty/democracy. Western governments today claim, after passing legislation that in actual fact severely limits civil liberties and democratic rights, that they have struck the "right balance" between these two principles: that they have made some minor concessions in order that democracy and liberty may be better protected in the long run. In other words, the assumption here is that certain civil liberties and democratic rights can be restricted without affecting liberal democracy in its essence. This is the same argument that people such as Alan Dershowitz and Michael Ignatieff have pursued. Dershowitz suggests that in a War on Terror, it is justifiable to use even torture, given the right conditions, and provided the right legal safeguards are applied.[9] In a more toned-down argument, Ignatieff, who rejects Dershowitz's rationalization of torture, nevertheless claims that the sacrifice of certain rights and liberties can be justified as a lesser evil, provided we get greater security in return. The suggestion here is that there are certain measures, such as preventative detention without trial, that can be justified in exceptional circumstances without undermining liberal-democratic principles; and that, moreover, it is precisely the liberal-democratic framework that applies such measures that can best control them and prevent their abuse.[10] There are a number of problems with this argument, however. It is at best questionable whether security measures actually give us greater security. Many security experts have suggested, for instance, that the majority of new security and surveillance measures are expensive, worthless, and ultimately counter-productive. Second, the idea that existing liberal democratic frameworks— because of the systems of checks and balances they enshrine—can adequately control and limit the coercive security measures that they implement, is also questionable: the United States, which has the most developed system of constitutional checks and balances in the world, was patently unable to control executive power in its rounding up of hundreds of Arab Americans, its illegal wiretapping of U.S. citizens, and its administration of Guantanamo Bay. We cannot be so naïve as to imagine that when virtually arbitrary power is placed in the hands of security and military agencies, that this power can be controlled with constitutions. As I have suggested, we can no longer intelligibly talk about liberal democracies as though they still exist in an untainted form: they have largely given way to a postliberal regime of power, coercion, and surveillance.

What is really at issue here, then, is this idea of a trade-off between security and liberty—the idea that certain rights and liberties can be curtailed while leaving intact the liberal-democratic paradigm that we are intending to secure. According to Jeremy Waldron, the very notion of a balance or trade-off between liberty and security, particularly the "new image of balance" post-September 11, must be questioned. It is doubtful whether any real gains to security ensue from sacrificing hard-earned rights and civil liberties, despite what our governments tell us, and despite the psychological sense of security that these sacrifices might bring.[11] Often the only thing that comes with such "trade-offs" is an inordinate increase in the power of the state, something that any liberal should be worried about.

Therefore, the problem for liberal theory today is not how to strike a "balance" between liberty and security in the War on Terror. It is obvious that there is no balance here, that the scales have been tipped too far in favor of security already. Rather, it is to develop ways of protecting, reinforcing and expanding the realm of rights, liberty, individual autonomy and personal privacy against the incursions by the state. We are faced today with a situation in which the very idea of security has become hostile and dangerous to that of liberty. Perhaps to combat this threat, the notion of "security" needs to be reinvented, or rather its origins rediscovered: security can perhaps once again mean security *from* the state—rather than a fragile, tenuous, and paradoxical security that can only be provided *by* the state. In other words, security might be seen as way of protecting the integrity and autonomy of individuals from the excesses of sovereign power: security *against* detention without charge; security *against* arbitrary police powers of search and arrest; a protection of a realm of personal privacy and autonomy against increasingly sophisticated electronic surveillance technology used by governments and corporations alike; a limitation of executive power through ever more rigorous and expansive articulations of rights. Perhaps, in other words, there might be a way of weakening the exclusive link between security and the principle of state sovereignty. Maybe security can come to be seen in terms of a genuine defense and even expansion of liberty—for individuals and collective bodies—rather than something in whose name liberty must be miserably bartered away. Perhaps what is needed is a democratization of security—not only at the domestic level, but at the international level as well. In other words, genuine security from terrorism comes not from undermining democratic rights and civil liberties, and still less from the sovereign exceptionalism of U.S. foreign policy and its total disregard for the international community and its laws. On the contrary, such measures have only dramatically increased our insecurity. Moreover, real security in a world where millions of people live and die in abject poverty, suffer from disease, and where there are massive and growing inequalities in wealth and power, is impossible. Therefore, the notion of security must be radically reconfigured to include security from poverty, political oppression, economic exploitation, as well as new forms of collective security through a strengthening and expansion of international law, juridical institutions, and human rights norms.

Notes

1. See Robert Abele, *A User's Guide to the Patriot Act* (Lanham, MD: University Press of America, 2004) and Katherine Darmer, Robert Baird, and Stuart Rosenbaum, eds., *Civil Liberties vs. National Security in a Post-9/11 World* (Amherst, NY: Prometheus Books, 2004).

2. See Richard Leone and Greg Anrig, eds., *The War on Our Freedoms: Civil Liberties in the Age of Terrorism* (New York: Public Affairs, 2003).

3. See Ulrich Beck, "The Terrorist Threat: World Risk Society Revisited," *Theory, Culture & Society* 19, no. 4 (2002): 39–55, see 44. Emphasis in original.

4. The budget expenditure for the Department of Homeland Security in 2003 was $33.7 billion. See Bruce Schneier, *Beyond Fear: Thinking Sensibly about Security in an Uncertain World* (New York: Copernicus Books, 2003).

5. See Giorgio Agamben, "Security and Terror," *Theory & Event* 5, no. 4 (2002).

6. See David Domke, *God Willing? Political Fundamentalism in the White House, the "War on Terror," and the Echoing Press* (London: Pluto Press, 2004).

7. Alexis de Tocqueville, *Democracy in America*, trans. George Lawrence, ed. J. P. Mayer (London: Fontana Press, 1994), 692.

8. Jacques Derrida, *Rogues: Two Essays on Reason*, trans. Pascale-Anne Brault and Michel Naas (Stanford, CA: Stanford University Press, 2005), 40.

9. Alan Dershowitz, *Why Terrorism Works: Understanding the Threat, Responding to the Challenge* (New Haven, CT: Yale University Press, 2002). Also see Alan Dershowitz's chapter "The Preventative State: Uncharted Waters after 9/11" in *The Impact of 9/11 and the New Legal Landscape*, Matthew J. Morgan, ed. (New York: Palgrave Macmillan, 2009).

10. See Michael Ignatieff, *The Lesser Evil: Political Ethics in an Age of Terror* (Edinburgh: Edinburgh University Press, 2005).

11. Jeremy Waldron, "Security and Liberty: the Image of Balance," *Journal of Political Philosophy* 11, no. 2 (2003): 191–210, see 210.

Part III

Regional Impacts

Chapter 16

America and Europe after 9/11: The Great Divide

*Sarwar A. Kashmeri**

Nothing explains the long-term impact of 9/11 on United States-European relations better than two headlines from the French daily newspaper *Le Monde*. "We Are All Americans," was the headline in the newspaper the day after 9/11. "In this tragic moment, when words seem so inadequate to express the shock people feel, the first thing that comes to mind is this: We are all Americans," wrote Jean-Marie Colombani, reflecting the massive European outpouring of sympathy and support for America. But, just a few months later, on March 9, 2004, Colombani wrote an editorial for the *Wall Street Journal* that was headlined: "Are We Still Americans?" This time, he wasn't so sure.

In the three and a half years that had elapsed between the two editorials, America and Europe had slowly but surely parted company. The transatlantic alliance had ruptured. In this break the American invasion of Iraq that followed 9/11 had been the primary catalyst.

"For Old Friends, Iraq Crisis Bares a Deep Rift in Views," headlined the *New York Times* on February 11, 2003. "Now something deep and fundamental in the different views of Europe and the United States seems to have been brought to the surface by the Iraqi crisis," the article said. "How did transatlantic relations which were so good recently, get so bad so quickly?"

While the crack in this erstwhile rock solid alliance had been widening for some time, the Iraqi crisis brought it to the breaking point. The transatlantic

* Sarwar A. Kashmeri, strategic communications consultant and Fellow of the Foreign Policy Association, has been recognized on both sides of the Atlantic as an observer and commentator on U.S.-European business and foreign policy issues for over a decade. He is the author of *America and Europe after 9/11 and Iraq: The Great Divide*, which recently released its third printing.

bloodletting that took place during the Iraqi discussions within the United Nations Security Council was sobering for the insight it provided into the extent of damage that had already been done to the European-American relationship. The alliance that just a few years earlier had forced an end to the Soviet Empire without firing a shot, and freed millions of people from brutal tyranny, now appeared on the verge of disintegrating.

With the passage of time, it is increasingly clear that the transatlantic rift that burst open after 9/11 and the invasions of Afghanistan and Iraq is quite different from the many transatlantic rifts that preceded it, such as the decision in 1979 to deploy intermediate-range ballistic missiles in Europe, or the 1986 decision by the United States to bomb Libya. Unlike the previous rifts, the existing rift is structural in nature and a simple change of personalities—Nicholas Sarkozy in France, or Barack Obama in the United States for instance—will not be sufficient to fix it. In fact, the relationship (in this essay I speak of the political relationship, not the business ties that thankfully are stronger than ever) cannot just be fixed, it will have to be rebuilt.

To fully understand the legacy of 9/11 and its aftermath, it is important to remember the monumental changes that were taking place in Europe over the past half century as its nation-states transformed themselves into the European Union, and to recall the lack of attention that this sea change in geopolitics received from the United States. Put the emergence of the European Union (EU) and a lack of American understanding of the strategic implications of the EU together and it becomes easier to understand the legacy of 9/11. Let me illustrate with a personal example.

In May 2003, two months into the Iraq War, New York's Foreign Policy Association held its annual dinner, a glittering black-tie event at which the guests of honor, United States Secretary of State Colin Powell and his European Union counterpart, Xavier Solana, were to speak on the importance of the transatlantic alliance. America and Europe had engaged in a bitter and divisive debate at the United Nations, and the guests at this dinner looked at the event as a timely and unusually important fence-mending opportunity.

Flanked by the American and European Union flags, the band of the United States Military Academy at West Point struck up a resounding version of the American anthem and the assembled guests rose to their feet. As the last note of the anthem faded, many guests turned to the European Union flag to await the opening bars of Beethoven's Ninth Symphony, the European Union's anthem. The customary short pause before the anthem gave way to a longer pause, and then the West Point band sat down. The European Union's national anthem was not to be played that evening—the United States, it turned out, does not officially recognize it. I later learned that it would have been permissible to play a recording of the anthem, an equally insulting choice the Europeans had politely waived. I am sure somewhere deep within the United States Department of State and the Defense

Department is an official who can explain why it was acceptable to display the flag of the European Union, but improper to play the anthem associated with it.

Power politics of course played a part in the American neglect of the European Union. Why give it the recognition it merits, if it might only ensure the success of a potential competitor? After all, who knows what an integrated Europe, with its own currency, military, and security policies might mean for America's traditional role as leader of the Western alliance?

To a large extent, however, this neglect of European integration was a result, in my opinion, of viewing the European Union's successes and failures through Anglo-tinted glasses, through the filter of America's "special relationship" with Britain.

As an illustration of this attitude, consider the widespread lack of attention in the United States to the strategic importance of the euro's introduction. The British government had decided not to adopt the euro, but to keep its pound sterling. To win this domestic battle, important British political leaders—Margaret Thatcher, for instance—spoke on both sides of the Atlantic about the ostensible flaws in the very concept of the euro: why it would never come to be, and were it to ever become a reality, why it would not last very long before it imploded.

That the euro and European economic and monetary union would totally transform the European business landscape, and create a range of business threats, but also new opportunities, was virtually ignored by most American corporations, government leaders, and the media. The British were America's bridge to Europe. Surely, if they refused to adopt the euro, there must be something wrong with it, and it would never get off the ground. This was the prevailing American attitude.

The American disconnect with the European Union meant that America did not fully appreciate the role that the competition between France (a founder of the EU) and Britain (an EU skeptic) for the leadership of Europe played in the transatlantic rift that was ostensibly only over Iraq.

This became quite clear in conversations I had with a number of transatlantic leaders during the writing of my book, *America and Europe after 9/11 and Iraq: The Great Divide*. Generals Brent Scowcroft and Wesley Clark as well as former chairman of the Federal Reserve Paul Volcker shared the opinion that the French have always wanted to be the leaders in Europe. "They have always had the self consciousness about their own grandeur and place in the world and they thought here was an opportunity to assert that even more forcibly," Volcker told me speaking about the French veto of the American-British led United Nations Security Council resolution threatening force against Iraq.

Scowcroft believed the French have had the notion for some time that as long as the United States was in Europe, two consequences must follow: "Europe couldn't develop organically, and France couldn't lead Europe." As the Iraqi debate unfolded, the French saw that European public opinion was *strongly* opposed to what America wanted to do in Iraq, and thought this was their chance to get out ahead, lead European public opinion, and get the United States out of Europe. Before the cold war ended, France would never have challenged the United States directly because of the Soviet Union, "[a]nd now there is no reason not to," Scowcroft said.

The British were on the other side of this European coin; only the British were saying, "Don't pay any attention to the French, we are the ones who can control the European Union—this 800 pound gorilla across the Atlantic—we are the natural leaders of Europe, we are the bridge between continental Europe and the United States." "I really think that [the French-British leadership tussle] was at the heart of this rift," Scowcroft told me.

Fifty years of creating "an ever closer Union" had also changed the way the Europeans approached the resolution of crises. Creation of the European Union had taught them the benefits of giving up pieces of their sovereignty to create a more powerful whole; centuries of warfare in Europe had been eliminated. During his presidential campaign, Nicolas Sarkozy lauded the virtues of the European Union by pointing out that the 50 years of the European Union reflected the only half century in European history that there had not been a major war in Europe.

Further, as America rolled out its so called War on Terror and ordered Europeans to march in single file behind it, the United States simply did not appreciate that recent European experience meant the word "war" signified two different things on either side of the Atlantic. The European Union's erstwhile ambassador to the United States, Hugo Paemen, put it this way.

For the majority of the Americans, Paemen explained, war is a kind of heroic event. Courageous young men go to a faraway land to fight for what they consider to be the good cause, with all the technology and moral support the nation can muster and is determined to show the rest of the world what these young men are capable of. They return victorious, they are celebrated; even the families of those who were killed are proud that these men and women sacrificed their lives for the nation.

"But for most Europeans war is synonymous with seeing your own city destroyed and a lot of innocent victims, often your own family killed. It is not a heroic event at all," Paemen said. This threat of a war and all its horrors without a clearly defined target, "[s]hifting from Osama Bin Laden to Al Qaida to Iraq, and possibly to other countries. It made the Europeans somewhat suspicious as the perception grew that there was no clear American agenda," he said.

With this perspective on the state of the transatlantic alliance when 9/11 took place, let me offer three areas of impact on war and politics resulting from the terrorist attacks of 9/11 and their aftermath: The European Union will become stronger and more cohesive, the North Atlantic Treaty Alliance (NATO) will tread water, and in the absence of a brand new approach to rebuilding the transatlantic alliance, the relationship will deteriorate. (The business relationship between the EU and the United States is stronger than ever; as mentioned earlier; my chapter focuses solely on the political and military part of the alliance.)

A Stronger, More Cohesive European Union

External shocks have lubricated Europe's integration at many critical milestones. These shocks have come from American actions that were perceived by Europeans as contrary to behavior by a close ally.

In 1956, Egypt nationalized the Suez Canal, in which Britain and France were sizable investors, and for whom the loss of this passageway had serious geopolitical consequences. The two European powers labeled Egypt's action an act of war and invaded Egypt to forcibly take back the Canal. The United States disagreed with the British-French action, publicly voiced its disapproval, and forced a reversal of their invasion. That America would act against two of its closest allies, and force them to reverse a decision they considered to be in their national interest was a rude awakening for Britain and France, and Europeans in general. The landmark treaties resulting in the European Atomic Energy Community and the European Economic Community were signed the very next year in 1957.

Mounting American budget deficits, a stagnant economy, inflation and the dollar's gyrations played havoc with European currencies in the early 1990s. Since the trade of most European states is with one another, these currency fluctuations were hugely damaging to European economies. The realization that even America could so badly manage its economy and that this mismanagement could affect Europe's many, relatively smaller, currencies and markets was the impetus for the agreement on European monetary and economic union, the centerpiece of the Treaty of Maastricht in 1993. To minimize future currency shocks, Maastricht created a Europe-wide financial market with a powerful single European currency to try and offset the global influence of the dollar.

The Cuban missile crisis of the 1960s had already shown the Europeans that seemingly isolated developments in the American hemisphere had the potential to drag Europe into a nuclear war with the Soviet Union. In 1962, the Russians had secretly installed nuclear missiles in Cuba and the United States had given an ultimatum to Russia that if the missiles were not removed, the United States would bomb Cuba. Had that happened, the Russians would have retaliated by bombing a major European city, probably West Berlin. Under NATO agreements an attack on Europe would trigger an immediate American missile attack on the Soviet Union, which would then have launched a massive missile attack on the United States and Europe. Fortunately for the world, the Russians backed down in Cuba. But the lesson was not lost on the Europeans.

The 2003 unilateral American invasion of Iraq has generated virtually universal European opposition, and is the latest reminder for Europeans that they need to begin controlling their own security and foreign policy. To achieve this, the Europeans aim to set up the equivalent of a European State Department, or Foreign Office, within the European Commission, complete with a diplomatic corps and the equivalent of the European Union's first foreign minister, called the EU High Representative for Foreign and Security Policy. Once these changes are implemented, the political developments in the European Union will balance the significant economic, financial, and business clout of the EU. This step is not an easy one for the Europeans—witness the debacle of the European Constitutional Treaty, and its successor, the Reform Treaty. But, given the EU's successful record over 50 years, these changes will take pace, and I believe, sooner rather than later.

A NATO that Continues to Tread Water

Can there really be a major divide between Europe and America when NATO still exists? Unfortunately the answer to that question is, "yes." Not only does the divide exist in spite of NATO, but the attempt to remake NATO as a global fighting machine makes the divide worse. NATO has become a source of continuing friction in the European-American relationship because it has no agreed mission any more, and because it is being forced to take on a new mission—operating anywhere in the world—for which it is singularly unqualified.

There is also the long-forgotten close connection between NATO and the United Nations—an organization not held in great esteem by many Americans, but considered by Europeans and much of the rest of the world to be the basis of international law. The United Nations was barely two years old when NATO was created, and the designers of the treaty went out of their way to ensure the United Nations' umbrella of legitimacy covered their newly minted Western alliance. Witness the opening sentence of the treaty's preamble: "The Parties to this Treaty reaffirm their faith in the purposes and principles of the *Charter of the United Nations* [emphasis in the original] and their desire to live in peace with all peoples and all governments."

The drafters and signatory countries were careful to thread the United Nations, especially its Security Council, into the fabric of the treaty as article 7 demonstrates: "This treaty does not affect, and shall not be interpreted as affecting in any way...the primary responsibility of the Security Council for the maintenance of international peace and security."

Try to reconcile article 7 with the post-September 11 American appointment of itself as the guardian of world peace and security, or with the American invasion of Iraq that was carried out in blatant disregard of the Security Council, and the reason for NATO's irrelevance today comes into focus. Without a consensus to use force among the United States, the European Union, and the United Nations, NATO cannot be used. And the United States has stepped away from operating in this collaborative fashion because the guiding principle for American policy today is: you are with us, or you are against us, but you have no say in what we decide. This policy is fundamentally at odds with NATO's.

I recognize that the Obama administration in the United States will attempt a different, much more multilateral, rooted in old alliances, approach. But, in the absence of a basic agreement between Europeans and Americans on when and how force is to be used, old-fashioned multilateralism will not have the impact it used to have. Recall that Senator McCain (who lost the 2008 American presidential election, but still got 46 percent of the vote) was ready to use NATO to teach Russia a lesson during the 2008 crisis between Russia and Georgia. The Europeans wouldn't have any of it. Similarly, in March 2009, when new American vice president Joe Biden asked the Europeans for more NATO troops for Afghanistan, he was promptly told there would be none provided. And, in a quote that underscores my point about the need to agree on when and how force may be used, Agence France Press, on March 10, 2009, quoted Solana, the EU's foreign policy chief as saying "The situation in Afghanistan is not going to be resolved only militarily. There are many things that can be done in Afghanistan that are not exclusively increasing the number of troops."

"Your point about the closeness of NATO and the United Nations is a very good one, because we have lost, if we ever understood the connection between those two organizations," former senator Chuck Hagel of Nebraska (now chairman of the Atlantic Council in Washington, DC) and one of the most astute foreign policy players in the United States Senate told me during the conversations I had for my earlier mentioned book.

Hagel is right on the mark with his observations. A part of the answer to the question of whether there can really be a divide between Europe and America while NATO still exists lies in facing the reality that NATO functioned when Europeans and Americans played by the same rules of global engagement. There was broad agreement between them on who the common enemy was and when and how military force could be used. These rules of engagement—at the heart of NATO—were demolished when the United States chose to act preemptively by invading Iraq without Security Council authorization and in the face of opposition from leading European countries. Under America's new rules of engagement, America, all by itself, could decide who the enemy was, declare war, and attack preemptively anywhere in the world. The rest of the world simply had to accept America's verdict. "You are with us, or you are on the side of terrorism," President Bush had declared. France, Germany, and Russia had begged to disagree and blocked any participation in the Iraq War by NATO.

Without consensus between the Europeans and Americans on how force is to be used, isn't NATO today more like a corpse on a horse, rather than the powerful knight in shining armor it is still presumed and portrayed to be?

NATO's impotence was again on display in April 2004. The United States had by then already become bogged down in Iraq in a guerilla war on its way to becoming a communal-civil war, and increasingly found itself without the necessary military manpower to confront the deteriorating situation. To overcome this shortage and to put an international face on the Iraq War, United States Secretary of State Colin Powell urged NATO to become involved in Iraq by sending European troops under its auspices. In an almost immediate rebuff to the United States—NATO's supposed leader—both France and Germany challenged Powell's decision to ask NATO for help without first getting United Nations approval, and the secretary's request was stillborn.

The Europeans had again served notice that for NATO to be invoked as a mutual security alliance, the United States had to play by the established rules. These rules placed the Security Council at the center of the world order and required its approval before force could be used against a sovereign state.

A Weaker Transatlantic Alliance, Unless...

The darkest legacy of 9/11 and its aftermath has been the rupture of long-standing, common political and military interests that tied the United States and Europe together. Count me on the side of those who believe the transatlantic alliance is today more necessary than ever.

In my opinion, the most pressing need for Europeans and Americans now is to agree on when and how to use military power. There is a huge gulf between the two in this regard and it must be bridged going forward to permit the two sides to deal with anything else.

For the alliance to function effectively again, Europeans and Americans must reach a compromise on the fundamental issue of when and how to use military power. Peter Jay, a former British ambassador to the United States, succinctly captured this thought in our conversation. "Until we, the United States and Europe, sort out agreed basic premises about the rules of the global game, it will become increasingly difficult to resolve, or even indefinitely to fudge the day to day issues that confront us," he warned.

It would have been impossible for the outgoing Bush administration with its neocon baggage to engage Europe in discussing such a fundamental issue, even if the administration had been so inclined, which it was not . But now, with the lessons from Iraq and Afghanistan staring both sides in the face, and with the Obama administration, it is a different story. America must realize it cannot succeed in its quest for a more peaceful and stable world without its traditional European partners and they in turn must recognize the costs, to themselves and the world, of an untethered America. Both sides undoubtedly have a whole new appreciation of the value of the alliance, the need to rebuild it, and the obstacles to doing so.

To move forward with the goal of a European-American agreement on the use of force will require a dialogue on two key issues. First, there must be agreement on the universal values that transcend cultures because Europe and America may have to fight for them. Second, there must be agreement on the use of force: when is it justified and how should it be used, given that America and Europe do not share the same vision about this.

Even though it created some frustrations, the hegemony of the United States used to be tolerable for Europeans; and, by and large, they were willing to live with it. But, after seeing American behavior after 9/11, I don't believe the Europeans are willing to accept this hegemony any more, even with a President Obama.

With their longer historical perspective, Europeans know the United States dominated unipolar world of today will not stay that way forever; in fact a case could be made that America's global military dominance is already waning: Using all the power that the United States possesses it has not been able to subjugate Iraq or Afghanistan, third-rate powers, after wars that have already lasted for five and seven years respectively.

America should also let the Europeans know that negotiations on the use of force issue, but also any others that might come up, will be handled as between equals: meaning the United States will henceforth deal with the European Union as an equal partner across the negotiating table, and will be prepared to begin this involvement with full partnership in formulating future strategy for the entire region that stretches from Iraq through central Asia through Afghanistan.

The Bush administration would never have countenanced such a move, but American voters have created a whole new reality with the clear mandate given to President Obama, in the 2008 presidential elections, to dramatically change the direction of American foreign policy. The new administration should move aggressively to change tack and begin to renegotiate a new transatlantic alliance.

This approach has the added advantage of correcting what is in my opinion, the historically damaging tilt of American foreign policy toward Britain. I firmly believe that the "special relationship" between America and Britain needs to change to a "special relationship" between America and the European Union. Direct negotiations with the European Union will force Britain to work within the EU. If it chooses not to be a part of the European negotiating team, it will have no place at the table.

The Europeans, on their side, will then have to come up with a common negotiating position. Will they be able to do that? My hunch is they will, especially with their proposed new High Representative for Foreign and Security Policy. An American initiative as described above may even help the European Union crystallize the role and limits of its new foreign minister more speedily because he or she would undoubtedly spearhead the coordination of this project on the European side.

And who knows what this sea change in European foreign and security policy formulation may mean for the United States? "The Europeans are in the process of trying to forge a common understanding about security and foreign policy," former President George H. W. Bush told me. "So it's important for the United States to participate in the dialogue from the beginning, which will ensure that America is treated as the ally that it is and not a competitor." Sound words from a Bush who knows the value of alliances, and undoubtedly knows what a reinvigorated transatlantic alliance will mean for global stability in the twenty-first century.

Note

Note on my book, extensively referenced in the essay: *America and Europe After 9/11 and Iraq: The Great Divide*, by Sarwar A. Kashmeri. Originally published in hardcover by Praeger Security International, Westport, CT, Copyright 2007 by SAK (two printings). The book was subsequently revised and updated. This edition was printed in paperback in 2008 by Potomac Books, Dulles, Virginia. Copyright SAK.

Chapter 17

The Impact of 9/11 on U.S. Relations in Asia

*Takuya Murata**

This chapter focuses on the impact of 9/11 on Japan, India, and China, and their relations with the United States. Long-term trends linked to 9/11, the War on Terror, and U.S. policy are considered along with long-lasting issues for Japan and India. Direct international relations between India, China and Japan, however, are beyond the scope of this chapter.

Japan in the U.S. Reaction to 9/11

The attacks on September 11, 2001, were a major terrorist incident that killed thousands of Americans and foreign citizens working in the World Trade Center. The 9/11 attacks brought down the World Trade Center that symbolized American economic might. They also caused minor damage to the Pentagon, the center of U.S. military power. Further, a stymied attack planned for Capitol Hill showed that 9/11 also targeted the U.S. symbol of democracy. Thus the 9/11 attacks were understood to be an assault on institutions that represented core U.S. values: democracy and the free market as well as the American military might that supported these values through the cold war. In this way, the 9/11 attacks were interpreted to be a profound attack on American nationhood. The ensuing War on Terror came to be defined as a conflict between the West and Islamic fundamentalism, a conflict between good and evil that was to be waged on a global basis. This became the Bush administration's number one priority.

---

*Takuya Murata completed graduate work in political science at the University of Hawai`i.

In the aftermath of 9/11, the United States tried to make sense of 9/11 primarily through the lens of World War II, specifically the Pacific War against Japan. The 9/11 attack was compared with Pearl Harbor countless times as a surprise attack that shook America, against which Americans united and prevailed. Both 9/11 and Pearl Harbor were often described as unprovoked attacks on innocent Americans that struck at Americans' sense of safety. Other parallels include the view that fascist Japanese and Islamic fundamentalists were evil and must be brought to justice by America. The interpretation was further strengthened as the iconic photograph of three New York City firefighters raising the American flag over the rubble of the World Trade Center was continuously compared by the mass media to the famous photograph taken on Iwo Jima where U.S. soldiers planted the American flag upon victory over the Japanese military stronghold.

This powerful and nationalistic manner in which the United States experienced 9/11, used World War II as the model despite the fact that the it occurred less recently than the cold war. By starting with 9/11 (Pearl Harbor in December 1941) and celebrating the heroic firefighters at Ground Zero (Iwo Jima in February 1945), post-9/11 America went from the start of battle to victory in a matter of days. This was almost one month before the war in Afghanistan was launched—keep in mind that the wars in both Afghanistan and Iraq still go on as of this writing. Perhaps one could venture to ask whether invoking the parallel with Iwo Jima in the immediate aftermath of 9/11 was somewhat premature.

The choice to understand 9/11 through comparisons with World War II, rather than the more recent cold war, may have come as a surprise to some. Pearl Harbor took place more than 50 years ago, and many young Americans have experienced Japan only as an ally in the cold war. The visceral reaction of both U.S. politicians and the American public to make sense of 9/11 through Pearl Harbor seems to imply that Japan is still the archetype of the enemy in American hearts and minds. This line of thinking appears to fit with U.S. hesitation to push Japan to go nuclear as a counterweight to a nuclear and rising China. But clearly the United States does not seek to return U.S.-Japan relations to what it was in 1945, just because 9/11 reminded Americans strongly of Pearl Harbor. The past is often invoked to understand the present, and clearly Japan is not to be blamed for the 9/11 attacks in any way.

One possible explanation may be the lack of heroic images of victory from the cold war; for example, there are no photos of Americans planting the Star Spangled Banner in Moscow. The Cuban Missile Crisis was a great achievement in a disaster averted, but it was not a heroic victory that brought significant advantage to the United States. The cold war was primarily fought at a state-to-state level with missiles pointing to enemy targets, and it was not a war where citizens fought at a personal level. The major hot war during the cold war was the Vietnam War, which is primarily understood by the U.S. public as something other than a victory, something that divided America rather than brought her together. If the United States had viewed 9/11 through parallels with the Vietnam War, President Bush could have faced more difficulty in rallying American support for the War on Terror in Afghanistan. Thus, in the days after 9/11, when images that invoke a sense of victory and greatness were sought in face of adversity, it was images from World War II that inspired Americans. Perhaps these comparisons also worked in favor of the Bush administration who sought to mobilize the U.S. public to go to war in a far away place called Afghanistan that few Americans could find on the map, as FDR had led America to fight Japan that was hardly known to Americans at that time.

Although, in the aftermath of 9/11, the United States was reliving the conflict years of 1940s fighting against Japan, following September 11, 2001, Japan acted swiftly in support of the United States It seemed as if Japan was offering its support when the United States needed it and the alliance was functioning smoothly. But the United States was not the only country making sense of the present using frameworks from the past. Japan was also drawing heavily on the past to make decisions in the here and now. In the Gulf War, Japan was heavily criticized by the international community for its checkbook diplomacy—for not putting Japanese citizens at risk of war but only contributing to international stability by sending money.

The Koizumi administration was determined not to make the same mistake, and Prime Minister Koizumi promised the Self-Defense Forces (SDF) and aircraft carriers for logistical and reconstructive support in the War on Terror. Although ultimately the Japanese parliament did not support legislation allowing the full package, Koizumi managed to get an emergency Anti-Terrorism Special Measures Law and deployed the SDF to the Indian Ocean to provide logistical support. Prime Minister Koizumi and President Bush were known for their friendship and Secretary of Defense Donald Rumsfeld thanked Koizumi for Japan's contribution to the War on Terror. Yet beneath the surface, there were seeds of misstep in the U.S.-Japan relationship. That is, while it may seem as if Japan was coming to America's aid, Japan was actually trying to avoid international criticism that its old policy had caused. Although 9/11 did not remind Japan of Pearl Harbor, it was using a very different historical event, the Gulf War, to impel it to support the U.S. position.

End of the U.S.-Japan Alliance

Emerging issues that had the potential to weaken the U.S.-Japan alliance existed even before 9/11. However, 9/11 played a crucial role in consolidating these possibilities into long-lasting trends. This set of trends pushes the alliance toward its end, and to create a new future unlike the decades of U.S.-Japan alliance of the cold war years. Even today, the alliance plays an important stabilizing role in Asia, the fastest growing area of the world. The

U.S.-Japan security alliance is a key anchor of the hub-and-spoke security system in currently predominant in the Asia Pacific region. This is a volatile region that contains many nation-states with historical rivalries and shifting power balances. The 9/11 terrorist attacks undoubtedly changed many things, and even things such as the U.S.-Japan alliance that seems to be unrelated to 9/11 were affected.

First of all, 9/11 marked the beginning of the period defined by the War on Terror that solidified the divergence of American and Japanese core interests. The uncertain years after the end of the cold war era had ended. The Bush administration defined West-against-Islam and made it America's top priority. Japan is neither Western nor Christian, and has had little reason to fear Islamic terrorism. Rather than decreasing any terrorist threat to Japan from cooperating with the United States, Japanese involvement in the War on Terror may change Japan from a nontarget to a target. Further, the West versus Islam worldview broadcast by the United States was very inconvenient for Japan, which needed both the West, for its export markets, and the Middle East, from which to import oil. In this way, 9/11 inserted a large gap in priorities between the United States and Japan. Positive interests supporting the alliance faded, and the negative threat from the U.S.S.R that bonded Japan and the United States had already disappeared when that Communist superpower collapsed.

Second, the long military engagement in Afghanistan and later Iraq brought doubts about U.S. military capability. News from the Pentagon described a U.S. military that was exhausted and overstretched. As the United States redeployed military staff from East Asia into the Middle East, doubt spread about U.S. ability to assist Japan in case of an attack from North Korea. These questions about U.S. capability compounded preexisting and growing doubts about U.S. willingness to come to Japan's rescue. The potential North Korean threat had changed from a frontline of the global cold war into a local conflict that does not affect the United States.

Third, the United States decided to go it alone. When 9/11 occurred, the United States was the sole superpower. Given the importance of achieving retribution to the Bush administration, perhaps isolationism seemed most expedient. From the onset of the war in Afghanistan to the beginning of the war in Iraq, overwhelming American power appeared to be all that was needed to secure its goals. The United States did not need allies, and did not want allies that would slow down the decision-making process. Perhaps the United States needed to feel invincible again after the deep sense of vulnerability the nation experienced at 9/11. Either way, the Bush administration did not pay attention to its allies. Effective alliances can facilitate the achievement of U.S. goals, yet at the same time they pose challenges. Allies will not cooperate if they cannot meet their goals, or they may sabotage the alliance if the U.S. demands run counter to the ally's core interests. The sole superpower did not want allies, perhaps loyal yes-men but not allies, and it made that clear. Ironically at that time, Japan was seeking a more equal alliance as its one-sided dependence on American protection had ended with the cold war.

Fourth, the Liberal Democracy Party (LDP) of Japan, which has been staunchly pro-United States, lost its grip on power. The LDP was formed in 1955 and since its inception it had upheld Japan's alliance with America as a key tenet of its cold war policy. The LDP had formed the ruling government for most of the past 50 odd years; however, public support for successive LDP cabinets has become consistently low with the exception of that of Koizumi. The era of LDP-dominated pro-America politics is coming to an end whoever increases their influence—whether the DPJ, independents, or other parties. The 9/11 attacks also reinforced this important trend. Former prime minister Abe had made the War on Terror his first priority even though the public was deeply troubled by domestic issues such as rising inequality and problems in the pension and healthcare systems. The Democratic Party of Japan took control of the Upper House in September 2007, and this was a major setback for the LDP. It also represented a severe decline in U.S. influence in Japan.

The 9/11 Attacks and India

In comparison with cooling U.S.-Japan relations, U.S. relations with India warmed up in the years following 9/11. Before 2001, the two countries were distant as India was pro-Russia and tensions arose from India's nuclear weapons program. Yet 9/11 changed many of these factors. The subcontinent became important to the U.S. policy objectives, and India was so much bigger than all of its neighbors that it was a key player in south Asia by default. At the same time, India started to become important economically as a fast-growing emerging market.

The United States had conceptualized terrorism before 9/11 as a distant threat: something that could happen to states in the developing world, possibly affecting U.S. embassies in developing countries, but not the U.S. mainland. However, in the post-9/11 world, the United States has also been shown to be vulnerable to terror attacks and the Bush administration decided to take preemptive action. The 9/11 assault flattened the playground. In the immediate aftermath of 9/11, no one knew whether a city located in a conflict region or an American city was the more likely target.

India also experienced vulnerability from terrorism. But after both India and Pakistan went nuclear, its option to take preventative action was severely constrained. Thus India was very supportive of U.S. determination to stop terrorism. There was optimism that the United States would take on all terrorists in a big way, as it was dealing with its own problem unlike before, when it was benevolently helping developing countries in need of protection. New Delhi respected U.S. military prowess and hoped that the U.S. War on Terror would result in decreased terrorism in general, particularly terrorism affecting India. It was this perceived strategic convergence that pushed India toward the United States in the aftermath of 9/11 when India made clear statements in support of the United States.

Yet 9/11 was followed by several attacks on India. There were attacks on Srinagar in October 2001, and a bomb attack was launched on the Indian parliament in December. Further terror incidents occurred in New Delhi in 2005, and in July 2006 a series of bombings took place in Mumbai. The latter attack was reportedly characterized by al Qaeda-style and responsibility was claimed by Lashkar-e-Taiba.

These developments seemed to imply U.S. involvement in the region might be intensifying terrorism against India rather than decreasing it. It was reported that al Qaeda operatives in Iraq had linked with Pakistan-backed groups that were planning attacks on India. The increasing insurgency in Iraq, U.S. support for Islamabad, and the terror attacks in Mumbai appeared to be connected. The War on Terror that ostensibly sought to reduce terrorism was increasing it for India. Perhaps nonstate actors backed by Pakistan were not terrorists by the American definition, but this was a main terrorist group for India. This tension in defining the enemy was ironic as the December 1999 Indian Airlines Flight 814 was often compared with 9/11, which implied that perhaps a similar group was behind both attacks.

Perhaps the War on Terror was a success for the Bush administration in so far as al Qaeda operations are primarily fighting the United States in Iraq, thereby reducing the direct threat to the U.S. territory. History shows that the United States has avoided major terrorist disasters since 9/11. However, strong rhetoric used by the Bush administration against Islamic fundamentalism did not help to moderate Indian domestic tensions between Hindus and Muslims manifested by events such as the conflict that took place in Gujarat in 2002.

Yet even as U.S.-India interests began to diverge on the War on Terror, the initial rapprochement between the two countries in the aftermath of 9/11 kept developing. Better relations seem as if they are here to stay, although India's closest ally remains Russia, which has been restoring its power swiftly. The Bush administration was supportive of India's ambition to grow into a major economy armed with nuclear weaponry, as U.S. business interests seek Indian markets and U.S. foreign policy seeks a counterweight to rapidly growing Peoples' Republic of China (PRC).

Impact of 9/11 on U.S.-China Relations

Relations between the two countries had grown cold starting with the 1989 Tiananmen Incident, which slowed trade, investment, and other economic interaction. Subsequent events such as the bombing of the Chinese embassy in Belgrade in 1999 and the aircraft collision in April 2001 did not help to bring China and the United States closer. Despite the end of the cold war, relations between the victorious Capitalist power and the remaining most powerful Communist nation did not improve. The general consensus was that China was the main threat in a post-Soviet world that still viewed communism as the primary hostile ideology.

The events around 9/11 fundamentally altered the top spot in the list of America's main threats. Communist China was definitively replaced with Islamic terrorism. Rather, as a strong state willing and capable of acting to suppress nonstate actors, the PRC quickly moved to fill a cooperative position in the U.S. War on Terror. In this way, 9/11 was an important turning point that firmly consolidated emerging trends pointing to better U.S.-China relations, such as successful negotiations for China's entry into the World Trade Organization (WTO).

The 9/11 attacks effectively served to alter the paradigm from U.S.-China competition to cooperation in the War on Terror by placing emphasis on threats from Islamic terrorist or separatist movements. As the share of Chinese energy imports increased from central Asia and the Middle East transported through sea lanes in Southeast, stability in these regions increased in importance for China. Further, Beijing had been concerned about the potential threat to national integrity posed by separatist movements in Xinjiang networking with organizations in central Asia, particularly Afghanistan, before 2001. Thus, cooperating with the United States and other countries to ensure stability in these areas was compatible with Chinese interests. Further, as stability and peacekeeping took higher priority over human rights, an area of friction between the United States and China, the ideology driving the Bush administration's post-9/11 War on Terror created an environment that facilitated improvements in U.S.-PRC relations.

The U.S. focus on security issues in Afghanistan and Iraq has also shifted U.S.-China relations toward cooperation. The Bush administration has chosen Pakistan to be a key ally in its War on Terror, and historically Pakistan has been China's ally as well. Perhaps equally importantly, this takes the pressure off Taiwan, which is a historical point of contention. Further, the key role that Beijing played in the six-party talks has pushed the PRC toward being perceived as a responsible international player who contributes to stability. This has permitted Washington to avoid a major confrontation in Northeast Asia so far, allowing the United States to keep its focus on the Middle East.

Yet despite these positive developments in bilateral relations, there is a limit to the extent that U.S.-PRC relations can be expected to improve. As with Japan, it does not serve Beijing's interests to be perceived by Muslim countries to be participating on America's side in a conflict that is increasingly cast as a West-Islam clash. Further, too much success by the United States in central Asia, Middle East, or South Asia could threaten to displace Chinese interests in these regions. However, the loss of the U.S. military base in Uzbekistan and the setbacks Washington have suffered in Iraq assuage

Chinese concerns of being overtly exposed to U.S. bases in Uzbekistan and Kyrgyzstan on their western border, and from Korea and Japan to the east.

Perhaps more importantly, the realignment of interests leading to better relations between the globally dominant United States and rising China in the aftermath of 9/11 is primarily short to medium term. Events around 9/11 do not change the long-term conflict of interest that is expected to emerge between Washington and a potentially revisionist Beijing. Although the PRC is already part of the UN Security Council, Beijing has been expressing discontent about the predominant role of Organisation for Economic Co-operation and Development (OECD) countries, particularly the United States, in controlling key global institutions such as the G7, IMF, and the World Bank. Beijing is actively pushing for forums like G20 where developing countries have more say. As Chinese power grows quickly and reduces the gap between its economic influence and that of the United States, the potential for more friction increases unless the United States is willing to give up some control of Bretton Woods institutions in favor of emerging economies.

Before 9/11, the United States had looked at China as the upcoming threat. While this may not have changed in the long term, 9/11 and its aftermath brought a short-term window when the interests of the United States and the PRC aligned allowing greater communication and cooperation. This creates an important window of opportunity that may allow Washington and Beijing to find a medium-term solution before long-term tensions arise. This is especially true as the two nations' economies increasingly become interdependent and other common areas of interest develop.

The 9/11 assault and its aftermath facilitated a dramatic change of status for the PRC from United States' main threat into a cooperating state. The current financial crisis is reinforcing this trend, opening this short-term window wider. Problems of the United States and its global economic order are fundamentally altering its relationship with China, with the PRC acting as a helper who is propping up the global economy through expanding domestic demand and as a partner whose economy is deeply integrated with the global economy. The end of the Bush administration may mute the West-Islam dichotomy despite the persistence of the conflicts in Afghanistan and Iraq, but the developments ensuing 9/11 make it rather unlikely that the United States will enthusiastically put China back in its old position of the foremost potential enemy.

The Resurgent Nation-State

Beyond bilateral relations, 9/11 had an important impact at a systemic level—its reinforcement of the nation-state. The 9/11 attacks set up a parallel and powerful framework for conflict between the state and nonstate actors, alongside its construction of a West-Islam conflict.

As the United States pursued al Qaeda, traditional allies such as the United Kingdom and Japan offered their support. Further, undemocratic countries such as Russia, China, and Uzbekistan offered support, and enemy states like Iran quietly offered help to U.S. soldiers who may seek refuge on the Iranian border once the U.S. decision to enter Afghanistan was made. Almost all nation-states came together against this new threat with the serious realization: if even the United States is vulnerable to terrorist attack, they all are. This effectively but temporarily damped interstate competition, creating an alliance of nation-states.

The power of the nation-state that had been eroding under globalization, regionalization, and localization was rapidly restored. Power shifted from civil society, international and regional organizations to national institutions like the presidency and the military. Borders that had become increasingly permeable were closed down in the name of security. Humans are marked by nationality and checked whether they are citizens. National identifiers are placed onto global citizens, and goods stopped and screened for precaution.

The 9/11 attacks signaled a major shift in U.S. policy from supporting self-determination to fighting the War on Terror. Encouraged by this change, countries with Muslim minorities such as Russia and China increased operations to pacify their own Muslim communities, with significantly less regard to international public opinion. Secular states ruling Muslim majority populations, such as Uzbekistan, took strong measures for counterterrorism and for curbing extremism. A strengthened state apparatus and a decrease in civil liberties was a key result, whether through Homeland Security in the United States or India's antiterror law passed after the December 2001 attack on its parliament.

The United States enjoyed unprecedented leadership and cooperation in the aftermath of the 9/11 attacks. However, with the Bush administration's Operation Iraqi Freedom, this support rapidly diminished and the publics and civil societies around the world protested against their governments' support of U.S. policies. This experience of an American unipolar world where the United States was perceived to act unilaterally and unethically created a lasting impression on the world. Even in countries like Japan and Britain that were firmly in the American camp during the cold war and sought to create an U.S.-led world; the public expressed strong anti-American sentiments; and support visibly weakened for their pro-Bush governments. This dramatic shift in the desirability of an U.S.-led future will have important tertiary effects as the European Union (EU), China, India, Brazil, Middle East, and Russia increase their power. The ability of the new U.S. president in 2009 to create a desirable U.S.-led future and to separate it from negative images of a Bush administration-led future may have important effects on U.S. power.

With the ensuing war in Iraq and the erosion of many countries' support for the United States, this fortification of the nation-state was channeled into programs that enhance narrow national interests. This was true for a diverse range of national governments from Russia's pacification of Chechnya and reassertion of Moscow's control over its natural resources, to Abe's remilitarization of Japan, and North Korea and Iran's nuclear programs. There is a tendency to strengthen national militaries that are seen by the public to be more acceptable in times of emergency and war. The first phase of interstate alliance led by the United States shifted into a second phase without an obvious leader; international competition has returned with a vengeance.

Asia is quite unlike North America, which consists of only three states regionalized through North American Free Trade Agreement (NAFTA), or the recently established EU. With the small exception of Association of Southeast Asian Nations (ASEAN), Asia is a region of nations, many of which, after decades of colonization, resist relinquishing sovereignty. In many ways, the return of nation-state-based international relations on a global scale is important to this region as it means that these nations are more in line with global trends, and they are less subject to globalizing forces penetrating into their independence. Of course, the resurgent nation-state has important ramifications for the United States as well. Even though the it can act unilaterally, stronger national polities make it more challenging for U.S. power to penetrate into other countries.

The 9/11 terrorist attacks set off a potent resurgence of nation-states in alliance, and the war in Iraq played an important role in creating a world of competing nation-states. It appears that this trend of competitive and resurgent nation-states has become a dominant future-shaping trend.

Conclusions

This chapter discussed several important long-lasting issues relating to 9/11. First, the trends strongly discouraging the continuation of the U.S.-Japan alliance implies major changes for the security arrangement in Asia. The power balance is expected to shift, as United States focuses its power in West Asia and Chinese influence keeps expanding in East Asia. Second, U.S.-India rapprochement seems to be in process in many fronts, despite continued contention around the War on Terror because of the subordination of Indian interests to U.S. objectives. Third, U.S.-China relations improved despite the endurance of the possibility of long-term tensions. Finally, the global resurgence of nation-states has strengthened the status apparatus at the expense of civil liberties and international mobility. It also allows Asian nation-states to fortify their executive and military functions, and be less subject to dampened forces of globalization. These are some of the key long-term trends that were set in motion by 9/11 and are still important in shaping the future.

Chapter 18

The New Strategic Importance of Africa

J. Peter Pham*

Before the terrorist attacks of September 11, 2001, on the United States, Africa seemed destined to remain at best peripheral to the strategic landscape as most Americans perceived it. Promising a realist-oriented foreign policy while campaigning for the presidency in 2000, George W. Bush responded negatively to a question from PBS's Jim Lehrer about whether Africa was a significant factor in his geopolitical calculus: "At some point in time the president's got to clearly define what the national strategic interests are, and while Africa may be important, it doesn't fit into the national strategic interests, as far as I can see them."[1] After 9/11, however, reversing course and deeming Africa as an increasingly important "second front" in the "Global War on Terror" (GWOT) through whose optic many of them now viewed the world, U.S. policymakers from the president down began building entirely new framework for engaging the continent through overlapping networks of ties that will have profound political, economic, and military implications for years to come.

The Strategic Context

Princeton Lyman, a former assistant secretary of state who has also served as U.S. ambassador to South Africa and to Nigeria, has observed that, as galling

* J. Peter Pham is Associate Professor of Justice Studies, Political Science, and Africana Studies and Director of the Nelson Institute for International and Public Affairs at James Madison University as well as Senior Fellow in Africa Policy Studies at the Foundation for the Defense of Democracies. The author of three books and over two hundred articles on Africa, Dr. Pham has advised both the U.S. government and private sector on political and security issues affecting relations with the continent.

as Bush's comment about Africa's strategic insignificance might have been to Africans, African Americans, scholars of Africa, development advocates, nongovernmental organizations, and other members of America's small constituency for the continent, the judgment behind it nonetheless reflected "what had in fact been the approach of both Democratic and Republican administrations for decades."[2] With the exception of cold war era concerns about Soviet attempts to secure a foothold on the continent, American interests in Africa have historically been framed almost exclusively in terms of preoccupation over the humanitarian consequences poverty, war, and natural disaster, rather than strategic considerations. In international relations, however, moral impulses rarely have the staying power to sustain long-term commitments—and such was certainly the case with U.S. foreign policy toward Africa.

This analysis was turned upside down in the wake of 9/11. While emphases may change with a new administration taking office, the fundamental outlines of U.S. security policy for the foreseeable future will remain largely determined by the strategic contours of the GWOT, the "Long War," or whatever the term adopted by official Washington to designate America's worldwide conflict with extremist Islamist violence happens to be. After the attacks on the American homeland, concerns were raised about the potential of the poorly governed spaces of the continent to provide facilitating environments, recruits, and eventual targets for Islamist terrorists since, as the 2002 *National Security Strategy of the United States of America* noted, "weak states...can pose as great a danger to our national interests as strong states. Poverty does not make poor people into terrorists and murderers. Yet poverty, weak institutions, and corruption can make weak states vulnerable to terrorist networks and drug cartels within their borders."[3] With the possible exception of the Greater Middle East, nowhere was this analysis truer than in Africa where, as the document went on to acknowledge, regional conflicts arising from a variety of causes, including poor governance, external aggression, competing claims, internal revolt, and ethnic and religious tensions, all "lead to the same ends: failed states, humanitarian disasters, and ungoverned areas that can become safe havens for terrorists."[4] The attacks by al Qaeda on the U.S. embassies in Dar es Salaam, Tanzania, and Nairobi, Kenya, in 1998, and on an Israeli-owned hotel in Mombasa, Kenya, and, simultaneously, on an Israeli commercial airliner in 2002 only reinforced the analysis of Africa's susceptibility to terrorism,[5] as have the more recent "rebranding" of Algerian Islamist terrorist organization Salafist Group for Preaching and Combat (usually known by its French acronym GSPC) as "Al-Qaeda in the Islamic Maghreb" (AQIM)[6] and the ongoing activities of al Qaeda-linked Islamists in the territory of the former Somali Democratic Republic.[7]

In tandem with preoccupations about terrorist threats, a second important group of considerations also worked to heighten Africa's relative importance in calculations of America's strategic interests in the aftermath of the events of 9/11. In his 2006 State of the Union address, President Bush called for the United States to "replace more than 75 percent of our oil imports from the Middle East by 2025" and to "make our dependence on Middle Eastern oil a thing of the past."[8] In 2008, according to data from the U.S. Department of Energy's Energy Information Administration, African countries accounted for more of America's petroleum imports than the states of the Persian Gulf region: 916,727,000 barrels (19.5 percent) versus 868,516,000 barrels (18.4 percent).[9] Moreover, most of the petroleum from the Gulf of Guinea off the coast of West Africa is light or "sweet" crude, which is preferred by U.S. refiners because it is largely free of sulfur. While production fluctuates, the significance of Africa for America's energy security cannot be underestimated.

While African hydrocarbons, especially those from the West African producers along the Atlantic Ocean, are particularly attractive to American companies for a variety of reasons, not least of which is the higher marginal profit rates to be made per unit, both because of ease in extraction and transport and because, in the case of oil, the quality of the crude is particularly adapted to U.S. refineries,[10] access to the resource is not without its risks. Sporadic attacks by just one small group with localized grievances, the Movement for the Emancipation of the Niger Delta (MEND), have nonetheless succeeded in cutting oil production by America's fifth largest supplier, Nigeria, by an estimated 500,000 barrels per day, or approximately 25 percent, since the beginning of 2006.[11] David Goldwyn, who served as assistant secretary of energy in the Clinton administration, for example, has testified before the U.S. Senate: "While the region's geological prospects are good, the risk of an oil supply disruption from the region is rising from internal and external sources. We are in no position to endure a serious oil disruption from the Gulf of Guinea today. The global oil market is stretched to capacity."[12] And it goes without saying that U.S. analysts have not been oblivious to the fact that other countries, including China and India, have been attracted by the African continent's natural wealth and recently increased their own engagements there.[13]

Regional Security Initiatives

With concern both for integrating Africa into the struggle against terrorism and securing access to its strategic resources driving the reevaluation of the continent's position in U.S. foreign policy, it is not surprising that security initiatives have played a prominent role in Washington's recent courtship of African partners, even in programs not managed by the Department of Defense. In late 2002, concerned that terrorist organizations might establish a foothold in the vast spaces between the Mediterranean littoral of North Africa and Gulf of Guinea, the State Department launched the Pan-Sahel

Initiative (PSI), a modest effort to provide border security and other counter-terrorism assistance to Chad, Mali, Mauritania, and Niger using personnel from U.S. Army Special Forces attached to the Special Operations Command Europe (SOCEUR). Funding for PSI was modest, amounting to under $7 million in fiscal year 2004, most of which was spent on training military units from the four partner countries. U.S. Marines were also involved with certain aspects of the training and air force personnel provided support, including medical and dental care for members of local units as well as neighboring residents. The program's modest funding was stretched to provide nonlethal equipment including Toyota Land Cruisers, uniforms, and global positioning system (GPS) devices for participating military forces.[14] The first test of both PSI-trained units and the regional interstate counterterrorism cooperation that Washington tried to encourage came in early 2004 when a band of fighters from the GSPC were spotted moving in a convoy of Toyota SUVs and were waylaid by Algerian military forces in the deserts of northern Mali. Those fighters who were not slain were tracked by U.S. personnel who passed the information on to the PSI partners. As a result, Chadian forces, backed by Nigerian units, caught up with the fugitives in northern Chad and wiped the party out, killing nearly four dozen terrorists. Subsequent investigations revealed that the dead GSPC fighters included nationals from several Sahelian states, confirming the PSI's underlying presupposition that there was a radical movement that bridged the harsh Saharan divide.

As a follow-up to the PSI success as well as to overcome what the then Deputy Assistant Secretary of Defense for African Affairs Theresa Whelan called its "Band-Aid approach,"[15] the State Department-funded Trans-Sahara Counterterrorism Initiative (TSCTI) was launched in 2005 with support from the Department of Defense's Operation Enduring Freedom-Trans Sahara (OEF-TS). TSCTI added Algeria, Nigeria, Morocco, Senegal, and Tunisia to the original four PSI countries. The new initiative was inaugurated in June 2005 with an exercise dubbed "Flintlock 05," whose goal was to help "participating nations to plan and execute command, control and communications systems in support of future combined humanitarian, peacekeeping and disaster relief operations."[16] The training was "to ensure all nations continue developing their partnerships" while further enhancing their capabilities to halt the flow of illicit weapons, goods, and human trafficking in the region; and prevent terrorists from establishing sanctuary in remote areas."[17] Funding for TSCTI has increased steadily from $16 million in 2005 to $30 million in 2006, with incremental increases up to $100 million a year through 2011. As part of TSCTI (which was renamed the "Trans-Sahara Counterterrorism Program," TSCTP, in late 2007) and in addition to the Pentagon-led train-and-equip efforts, the African countries also receive counterterrorism-related support from State Department programs—especially the Anti-Terrorism Assistance (ATA) program and the Terrorist Interdiction Program (TIP)—and other U.S. government agencies, including

U.S. Agency for International Development (USAID) and the Department of the Treasury.

Similarly, the East Africa Counter-Terrorism Initiative (EACTI), launched in 2003, provides training and some equipment for counterterrorism units, as well as support for legislators and other senior-level decision makers involved with drafting and implementing laws against terrorist financing and money laundering. Since its inception, this State Department-administered program has disbursed more than $100 million in funds to support programs in Djibouti, Eritrea, Ethiopia, Kenya, Tanzania, and Uganda, although the partnership with Eritrea has largely fallen by the wayside with the regime in Asmara's subsequent support for insurgent groups in Somalia.

While United States has historically deployed naval forces to Africa only to rescue stranded expatriates, the U.S. European Command (EUCOM) has taken the lead in maritime engagement in the Gulf of Guinea. In October 2004, EUCOM hosted the first ever "Gulf of Guinea Maritime Security Conference" in Naples, Italy, headquarters of the U.S. Sixth Fleet. The three-day meeting brought together African diplomatic and naval officials from Angola, Benin, Cameroon, Equatorial Guinea, Gabon, Ghana, Nigeria, the Republic of Congo (Brazzaville), São Tomé and Príncipe, and Togo, as well as representatives from the United States, France, Italy, the Netherlands, Portugal, Spain, and the United Kingdom. The conference participants pledged to continue dialogue and cooperation to combat common threats such as piracy, smuggling, and drug trafficking as well as terrorism. As an immediate result of the Naples conference, at the beginning of 2005, the submarine tender USS *Emory S. Land* was deployed to the Gulf of Guinea with some 1,400 sailors and Marines for a two-month training operation involving officers and sailors from Benin, Cameroon, Gabon, Ghana, and São Tomé, and Príncipe.[18] Between May and July of that year, the U.S. Coast Guard Cutter *Bear* was deployed to the same waters on a similar training mission.[19]

Subsequently, in late 2005, the dock landing ship USS *Gunston Hall* and the catamaran HSV-2 *Swift* conducted five weeks of joint drills with forces from several West African nations, including Ghana, Guinea, and Senegal. The drills included live fire exercises, small boat maneuvers, and amphibious landings—the very type of activities that naval forces would be called upon to undertake against pirates, smugglers, and terrorists in those waters. In early 2006, the *Emory S. Land* returned to the region, again with some 1,400 sailors and Marines, to boost maritime security and strengthen partnerships, calling on ports from Senegal to Angola. And in November 2007, the Department of State and the Department of Defense cosponsored a ministerial-level conference in Cotonou, Benin, on "Maritime Safety and Security in the Gulf of Guinea" that included representatives from 11 Gulf of Guinea countries as well as delegates from the United States, Europe, Senegal, South Africa, the African Union, and regional and international organizations.

In late 2007, the dock landing ship USS *Fort McHenry* was stationed in the Gulf of Guinea on an extended seven-month deployment until the spring of 2008 as part of a multinational maritime security-and-safety initiative that partners with West African countries to train teams from 11 African countries along the gulf, helping them to build their security capabilities, especially in maritime domain awareness. The then commander of U.S. Naval Forces Europe, Admiral Henry G. "Harry" Ulrich III, described the *Fort McHenry*'s mission, which he characterized as within "the spirit of AFRICOM and the initial operating capacity of AFRICOM," as "the tipping point for us [which will] move this whole initiative of maritime safety and security ahead."[20] The *Fort McHenry*'s West Africa deployment, where it was joined by the *Swift*, is a new international interagency effort known as African Partnership Station (APS) in which European and African sailors join their American counterparts as well as civilian personnel onboard. It is aimed at enhancing regional and maritime safety and security in West and Central Africa through assistance in developing maritime domain awareness, maritime professionals and infrastructure, maritime enforcement capabilities, legal and regulatory regimes, subregional cooperation, and public awareness of maritime security issues.

Established in 2002, the Combined Joint Task Force-Horn of Africa (CJTF-HOA) is presently the largest American military operation in Africa. Headquartered at Camp Lemonier, a onetime French Foreign Legion post in Djibouti which, in May 2003, became the only U.S. base on the African continent, the approximately 2,000 sailors, soldiers, airmen, and Marines, as well as civilian government employees and contractors of CJTF-HOA have seen their mission evolve considerably since its initial inception as a kinetic antiterrorism operation. As it is currently articulated, CJTF-HOA's mission is to employ an "indirect approach to counter violent extremism," that is, to "conduct operations to strengthen partner nation and regional security capacity to enable long-term regional stability, prevent conflict and protect U.S. and Coalition interests."[21] Thus while U.S. special operations forces are present and actively engaged in action against terrorism in the Horn of Africa—including strikes targeting al Qaeda-linked terrorist leaders in Somalia—CJTF-HOA has more recently focused primarily on indirect activities, aimed at denying extremist ideologies as well as individuals and groups the ability to exploit the vulnerabilities of the nations and societies in the subregion. To this end, CJTF-HOA's commanders stress the importance of interagency collaboration in its "area of interest" as the key to success in achieving U.S. strategic objectives as well as those of other members of the coalition and other partners (military personnel from a number of coalition partner countries, including Djibouti, Egypt, Ethiopia, France, Kenya, Pakistan, Romania, Seychelles, Mauritius, South Korea, Uganda, Yemen, and the United Kingdom have been embedded in the task force's staff and are involved in almost all of its operational phases, including strategic and operational planning and execution.).[22]

On February 6, 2007, President Bush ordered the Department of Defense to stand up the United States Africa Command (AFRICOM) as America's sixth geographic unified combatant command by October 2008 with a mission "to enhance our efforts to bring peace and security to the people of Africa and promote our common goals of development, health, education, democracy, and economic growth in Africa" by strengthening bilateral and multilateral security cooperation with African states and creating new opportunities to bolster their capabilities.[23] The move was not surprising, given that despite the 2006 *National Security Strategy* having proclaimed that "Africa holds growing geo-strategic importance and is a high priority of this Administration,"[24] U.S. efforts on the continent were still handicapped by an antiquated structural framework inherited from times when it was barely factored into America's strategic calculus. For defense-planning purposes, most of Africa—42 of the continent's 53 countries[25]—fell under the aegis of the Stuttgart, Germany-based EUCOM, with the rest being the responsibility of the Tampa, Florida-based U.S. Central Command (CENTCOM),[26] or even that of the U.S. Pacific Command (PACOM), based in Hawaii.[27] With new command slated to embrace all of Africa except Egypt—which will remain with CENTCOM owing to the country's importance to the Middle East, although it will also be involved in AFRICOM-related activities insofar as they relate to Egyptian interests in Africa—U.S. military planners clearly hope to move beyond the disjointed approach that has hindered their engagement with Africa to date as well as developed dedicated resources. While there has been some apprehension about "militarization" of the institutionalization of programs, the initiative "augurs well for a more consistent partnership with the continent."[28]

In addition to the initiatives led by or otherwise directly involving U.S. military personnel, generous grants from the State Department's International Military Education and Training (IMET) program have sought to enhance the capacities of America's African partners. During the 2007 fiscal year alone, approximately 1,400 African military officers and personnel received professional development at U.S. military schools and other training assistance. On a significantly broader scale, under President Bush, the Global Peace Operations Initiative (GPOI), which in 2004 subsumed the Bill Clinton administration's African Crisis Response Initiative (ACRI) as well as the Bush administration's own earlier Africa Contingency Operations Training and Assistance Program (ACOTA), aims at training and equipping 75,000 military troops, a majority of them African, for peacekeeping operations on the continent by 2010.[29] The five-year, $660 million GPOI program, which is administered by the State Department and uses private contractors to do the bulk of the outfitting and training, is especially important not only because of the general reluctance of American public opinion to deployment of troops to conflict situations in Africa in the absence of explicit threats to U.S. interests, but also because it responds to Africans' aspirations to capacity-build their own emergent continental and regional peace and security institutions. One leading scholar of Africa summarized the connection between the interests of both sides of the relationship: "The United States has a vital interest in strengthening the military and intelligence capacity of poor countries like the ones we find in Africa. For their part, African countries could measurably improve their ability to solve the problems of peace and security with the aid of the United States."[30]

Other Evolving Programs

While the "hard power" of its defense and intelligence services has spearheaded America's post-9/11 activism in Africa, this does not mean its operations remain a responsibility of the new combatant command; the implication is that "soft power" instruments,[31] including diplomatic outreach, political persuasion, and economic programs, did not also have their place. In fact, while a military structure, AFRICOM itself pursues extensive links with the State Department, USAID, and other government agencies, than other regional combatant commands. In addition to a military deputy commander, AFRICOM was given a civilian deputy to the commander for civil-military affairs who is responsible for the command's cooperation with the various agencies and directs its health, humanitarian assistance, and security sector reform programs. Because the Africa Command's activities affect those of other government agencies, the then Principal Deputy Undersecretary of Defense for Policy Ryan Henry has argued that while AFRICOM will "be a Department of Defense organization," it should expect to "explore different ways to do the manning, both within the U.S. government and perhaps participation from other governments."[32]

Because of the nature of the American foreign policymaking process in contrast to that of other states, including other democracies, issues of concern to the broader public exercise an important influence on the determination of what constitutes the country's "interests." Thanks to the makeup of the Africa constituency in the United States—a coalition that includes, in addition to the diplomatic and national security bureaucracies, the African American community, religious organizations, businesses, and advocacy groups—while humanitarian sentiments may not be sufficient to sustain policy, the preoccupation with the devastating toll that conflict, poverty, and disease, especially HIV/AIDS, continue to exact across the continent does very much inform Washington's policy. Thus, in a larger sense, foreign aid is strategic, even when the connection between humanitarian concerns and geopolitical stakes is not as explicit as in the case of Sudan where public outrage over the Arab-dominated Islamist government's treatment of the largely Christian or animist South Sudanese and, more recently, its genocidal policy toward the black African inhabitants of the western region of Darfur dovetailed with *realpolitik* worries about the regime's ties to Islamist extremists, including Osama bin Laden, who was sheltered by Khartoum from 1991 until 1996.

Certainly Africa has received more high-level public diplomatic attention since 9/11. George W. Bush journeyed to more African countries during his tenure in office than any of his predecessors, visiting Senegal, South Africa, Botswana, Uganda, and Nigeria in 2003, and returning in 2008 to call on Benin, Tanzania, Rwanda, Ghana, and Liberia. As an envoy for her husband, First Lady Laura Bush made three independent trips to Africa, visiting South Africa, Tanzania, Rwanda, Ghana, Liberia, Nigeria, Senegal, Mozambique, Zambia, and Mali. Special presidential envoys have been used more extensively than in the past as "super ambassadors" to deal with high-stakes regional conflicts like the ones involving Sudan, which have seen the appointment of three successive envoys during the Bush administration: John Danforth (2001–2005), Andrew Natsios (2006–2007), and Richard Williamson (2007–2009).

Africa boasts the world's fastest rate of population growth: by 2020, today's more than 900 million Africans will number more than 1.2 billion—more than the combined populations of Europe and North America—but the dynamic potential implicit in the demographic figures just cited is, however, constrained, by the economic and epidemiological data. The United Nations Development Programme's *Human Development Report 2007/2008* determined that all 22 countries found to have "low development" were African states.[33] While Sub-Saharan Africa is home to only 10 percent of the world's population, nearly two-thirds of the people infected with HIV—24.7 million—are Sub-Saharan Africans, with an estimated 2.8 million becoming infected in 2006, more than any other region in the world.[34] And while the Bush administration's 2003 *National Strategy for Combating Terrorism* argued that terrorist organizations have little in common with the poor and destitute, it also acknowledged that terrorists can exploit these socioeconomic conditions to their advantage.[35]

The Bush administration, working with Congress, consolidated the comprehensive trade and investment policy for Africa introduced by its predecessor in the African Growth and Opportunity Act (AGOA) of 2000, which substantially lowered commercial barriers with the United States and allowed African countries to qualify for trade benefits, including allowing goods made in Africa to be imported to the American market tariff-free, potentially creating millions of jobs in the export-manufacture sector on the continent. As of the beginning of 2008, approximately 39 African countries receive some trade benefits under AGOA. Since 2001, for example, Africa's garment exports to the United States have increased sevenfold. Overall, imports under AGOA have comprised an increasingly significant share of all U.S. imports from Africa. In 2006, AGOA imports were valued at $44.2 billion, or three-quarters of total imports to the United States from Sub-Saharan Africa.[36]

During the Bush presidency, Washington also made HIV/AIDS on the continent a priority with 12 of the 15 focus countries in the President's Emergency Plan for AIDS Relief (PEPFAR) being in Africa, including Botswana, Côte d'Ivoire, Ethiopia, Kenya, Mozambique, Namibia, Nigeria, Rwanda, South Africa, Tanzania, Uganda, and Zambia. With a five-year, $15 billion price tag, PEPFAR, announced in 2003, has been the largest commitment ever by any nation for an international health initiative dedicated to a single disease—and that was before Bush, in his final State of the Union address, called for doubling its funding to $30 billion over the next five years.[37] Since its inception, PEPFAR has supported treatment for 1.7 million people in Sub-Saharan Africa. Similarly, the President's Malaria Initiative (PMI), a collaborative effort of USAID and the Department of Health and Human Services' Centers for Disease Control launched in 2005, has increased funding for malaria eradication by $1.2 billion over five years with the goal of halving deaths due to the disease in 15 African countries: Angola, Benin, Ethiopia, Ghana, Kenya, Liberia, Madagascar, Malawi, Mali, Mozambique, Rwanda, Senegal, Tanzania, Uganda, and Zambia.

The Millennium Challenge Corporation (MCC), established in 2004, is perhaps the Bush administration's most innovative contribution with regard to foreign aid. MCC's Millennium Challenge Account provides assistance to qualifying countries for "compact agreements" to fund specific programs targeted at reducing poverty and stimulating economic growth as well as "threshold programs" to improve performance with an eye toward achieving "compact" status. At the time Bush left office in January 2009, half of the 40 countries worldwide including Benin, Burkina Faso, Cape Verde, Ghana, Kenya, Lesotho, Liberia, Madagascar, Malawi, Mali, Morocco, Mozambique, Namibia, Niger, Rwanda, São Tomé and Principe, Senegal, Tanzania, Uganda, and Zambia, currently eligible for some MCC funding, either through the "Threshold Program" or "Compact Assistance," were in Africa. The two largest MCC compacts so far went to African countries, with Tanzania and Morocco receiving five-year grants worth $698.1 million and $697.5 million, respectively.[38]

One of the key advantages of the MCC approach is the recognition that generous grants of development aid are for naught if the recipients lacked a democratic polity and basic capacity for good governance. It should be recalled that until fairly recently, while most African states were characterized by some form authoritarian rule, only 2 out of the 53 members of the African Union, Botswana and Mauritius, were able to boast of uninterrupted democratic politics since independence.[39] Funding for democracy promotion in Africa has increased steadily during the Bush administration with approximately $175 million spent on such programs in African nations in 2007. By linking eligibility for MCC assistance to demonstrated commitment to policies that promote political and economic freedom, investments in education and health, control of corruption, and respect for civil liberties and the rule of law by performing well on seventeen different policy indicators,[40] the United States put into practice what Nobel Laureate economist Amartya Sen has long argued, "Developing and strengthening a democratic system is an essential component of the process of development."[41]

Looking Ahead

It is no small irony that the Bush administration left office having presided over the numerous initiatives which, cumulatively, result in the United States more engaged in Africa than at any other period in American history. Having entered office doubting whether the African continent really had any significant part to play in America's strategic calculus, it had its geopolitical vision transformed by the attacks of September 11, 2001, and the ensuing global struggle on which it embarked. Thus it became necessary to engage Africa on a series of issues, including counterterrorism, access to natural resources, and broad development agenda that includes political reform, economic growth, and humanitarian relief. The strategic imperatives of the first two sets of issues might well provide the long-term sustenance that the third group of goals had previously lacked. The issue is not whether the administration of President Barack Obama, the first African American to be elected president of the United States, and its successors will continue with the engagement of Africa that has increased exponentially since 9/11—the strategic imperatives are too powerful—but how Washington will strike the balance between the various U.S. interests in such a way as to not allow the demands for energy security and the operational requirements of the worldwide War on Terror to entirely eclipse American ideals about development, good governance, individual freedom, and social welfare.[42]

Notes

1. George W. Bush, interview by Jim Lehrer, *NewsHour*, PBS, February 16, 2000, http://www.pbs.org/newshour/bb/election/jan-june00/bush_2-16.html.
2. Princeton N. Lyman, "A Strategic Approach to Terrorism," in *Africa-U.S. Relations: Strategic Encounters*, ed. Donald Rothchild and Edmond J. Keller (Boulder, CO: Lynne Rienner, 2006), 49.
3. The White House, *National Security Strategy of the United States of America* (September 17, 2002), http://georgewbush-whitehouse.archives.gov/nsc/nss/2002/nss.pdf (accessed March 15, 2009).
4. Ibid.
5. See J. Peter Pham, "Next Front? Evolving U.S.-African Strategic Relations in the 'War on Terrorism' and Beyond," *Comparative Strategy* 26, no. 1 (2007): 39–54.

6. See Guido Steinberg and Isabelle Werefels, "Between the 'Near' and the 'Far' Enemy: Al-Qaeda in the Islamic Maghreb," *Mediterranean Politics* 12, no. 3 (2007): 407–413.

7. See Shaul Shay, *Somalia between Jihad and Restoration* (Edison, NJ: Transaction, 2008).

8. The White House, State of the Union Address by the President (January 31, 2006), http://georgewbush-whitehouse.archives.gov/stateoftheunion/2006/ (accessed March 15, 2009).

9. U.S. Department of Energy, Energy Information Administration, U.S. Total Crude Oil and Products Imports (February 27, 2009), http://tonto.eia.doe. gov/dnav/pet/pet_move_impcus_a2_nus_ep00_im0_mbbl_m.htm (accessed March 15, 2009).

10. See Frederick Cedoz, Robert E. Heiler, William E. Lewis, Tyson King Meadows, and Paul Michael Wihbey, *Breaking the Oil Syndrome: Responsible Hydrocarbon Development in West Africa* (Washington: Congressional Black Caucus Foundation, 2005).

11. See J. Peter Pham, "The Battle for Nigeria," *The National Interest* 88 (March/April 2007): 97–100.

12. David L. Goldwyn, Testimony before the U.S. Senate Committee on Foreign Relations, Subcommittee on International Economic Policy, Export and Trade Promotion (July 15, 2004), http://foreign.senate.gov/testimony/2004/ GoldwynTestimony040715.pdf (accessed March 15, 2009).

13. See J. Peter Pham, "China's African Strategy and Its Implications for U.S. Interests," *American Foreign Policy Interests* 28, no. 3 (May/June 2006): 239–253; J. Peter Pham "India's Expanding Relations with Africa and Their Implications for U.S. Interests," *American Foreign Policy Interests* 29, no. 5 (September/October 2007): 341–352.

14. See Stephen Ellis, "Briefing: The Pan-Sahel Initiative," *African Affairs* 103, no. 412 (July 2004): 459–464.

15. Quoted in Donna Miles, "New Counterterrorism Initiative to Focus on Saharan Africa," *American Forces Press Service* (May 16, 2005), http://www.defenselink. mil/news/newsarticle.aspx?id=31643 (accessed March 15, 2009).

16. United States European Command, "Exercise Flintlock 05 Under Way in Africa" (June 9, 2005), http://www.eucom.mil/english/FullStory.asp?art=565 (accessed March 15, 2009)

17. Ibid.

18. See Terry Burnley, "*Emory S. Land* Completes Gulf of Guinea Deployment," *Navy Newsstand* (March 22, 2005), http://www.navy.mil/search/display.asp?story_ id=17600 (accessed March 15, 2009)

19. See "Coast Guard Cutter *Bear* Kicks off 6th Fleet Deployment," *Navy Newsstand* (June 7, 2005), http://www.navy.mil/search/display.asp?story_id=18620 (accessed March 15, 2009).

20. Gerry J. Gilmore, "U.S. Naval Forces Prepare for AFRICOM Stand Up," *American Forces Press Service* (June 1, 2007), http://www.defenselink.mil/news/newsarticle. aspx?id=46260 (accessed March 15, 2009).

21. U.S. Africa Command, Combined Joint Task Force-Horn of Africa (CJTF-HOA), *Fact Sheet* (February 2009), http://www.hoa.africom.mil/AboutCJTF-HOA.asp (accessed March 15, 2009).

22. See CJTF-HOA, *Defense, Diplomacy and Development in the Horn of Africa* (2007).

23. The White House, Office of the Press Secretary, "President Bush Creates a Department of Defense Unified Combatant Command for Africa" (February 6, 2007), http://georgewbush-whitehouse.archives.gov/news/releases/2007/02/20070206-3.html (accessed March 15, 2009).

24. The White House, *National Security Strategy of the United States of America* (March 16, 2006), http://georgewbush-whitehouse.archives.gov/nsc/nss/2006/nss2006.pdf (accessed March 15, 2009).

25. In Africa, EUCOM's area of responsibility embraced Algeria, Angola, Benin, Botswana, Burkina Faso, Burundi, Cameroon, Cape Verde, Central African Republic, Chad, Democratic Republic of Congo, Republic of Congo (Brazzaville), Côte d'Ivoire, Equatorial Guinea, Gabon, Gambia, Ghana, Guinea, Guinea-Bissau, Lesotho, Liberia, Libya, Malawi, Mali, Mauritania, Morocco, Mozambique, Namibia, Niger, Nigeria, Rwanda, São Tomé and Príncipe, Senegal, Sierra Leone, South Africa, Swaziland, Tanzania, Togo, Tunisia, Uganda, Zambia, and Zimbabwe in addition some 50 Eurasian countries.

26. CENTCOM had responsibility in Africa for Djibouti, Egypt, Eritrea, Ethiopia, Kenya, Seychelles, Somalia, and Sudan, as well as the waters of the Red Sea and the western portions of the Indian Ocean not covered by PACOM.

27. PACOM's African responsibilities included Comoros, Mauritius, and Madagascar, as well as the waters of the Indian Ocean, excluding those north of 5° S and west of 68° E (which were covered CENTCOM) and those west of 42° E (which were part of EUCOM's space).

28. Robert E. Gribbin, "Implementing AFRICOM: Tread Carefully," *Foreign Service Journal* 85, no. 5 (May 2008): 31; also see Sean McFate, "U.S. Africa Command: Next Step or Next Stumble?" *African Affairs* 107, no. 426 (January 2008): 111–120.

29. See Benedikt Franke, "Enabling a Continent to Help Itself: U.S. Military Capacity Building and Africa's Emerging Security Architecture," *Strategic Insights* 6, no. 1 (January 2007): 1–13.

30. Edmond J. Keller, "Africa and the United States: Meeting the Challenges of Globalization," in *Africa-U.S. Relations: Strategic Encounters*, ed. Donald Rothchild and Edmond J. Keller (Boulder, CO: Lynne Rienner, 2006), 13.

31. See Joseph S. Nye Jr., *Soft Power: The Means of Success in World Politics* (New York: Public Affairs, 2004), x.

32. U.S. Department of Defense, Office of the Assistant Secretary of Defense (Public Affairs), "DoD News Briefing with Principal Deputy Under Secretary Henry from the Pentagon," April 23, 2007, http://www.defenselink.mil/transcripts/transcript.aspx?transcriptid=3942 (accessed March 15, 2009).

33. United Nations Development Programme (UNDP), *Human Development Report 2007/2008. Fighting Climate Change: Human Solidarity in a Divided World* (New York: Palgrave Macmillan, 2007), 229–232.

34. Joint United Nations Programme on HIV/AIDS (UNAIDS), 2006 *AIDS Epidemic Report* (2006), 10.

35. The White House, *National Strategy for Combating Terrorism* (February 14, 2003), http://georgewbush-whitehouse.archives.gov/news/releases/2003/02/counter_terrorism/counter_terrorism_strategy.pdf (accessed March 15, 2009).

36. See Danielle Langton, *U.S. Trade and Investment Relationship with Sub-Saharan Africa: The African Growth and Opportunity Act and Beyond*, CRS Report Congress RL 31772 (January 25, 2008).

37. The White House, State of the Union Address by the President (January 28, 2008), http://georgewbush-whitehouse.archives.gov/news/releases/2008/01/20080128-13.html (accessed March 15, 2009).

38. The information comes from the Web site of the Millennium Challenge Corporation, http://www.mcc.gov/ (accessed March 15, 2009).

39. See Larry Diamond, *Prospects for Democratic Development in Africa* (Stanford: Hoover Institution, 1997).

40. See Steven W. Hook, "Ideas and Change in U.S. Foreign Aid: Inventing the Millennium Challenge Corporation," *Foreign Policy Analysis* 4, no. 2 (2008): 147–167.

41. Amartya Sen, *Development as Freedom* (New York: Random House, 1999), 157.

42. See Herman J. Cohen, "In Sub-Saharan Africa, Security Is Overtaking Development as Washington's Top Policy Priority," *American Foreign Policy Interests* 30, no. 2 (March 2008): 88–95.

Part IV

The Future after 9/11

Chapter 19

World Futures: The West, Islam, and Terrorism Futures after 9/11

Sohail Inayatullah*

In this chapter, I (1) revisit scenarios on the futures of terrorism written after the events of September 11, 2001, (2) analyze what has changed and what has remained the same, and (3) conclude with longer-term perspectives on the futures of the world system.

Unpacking Terrorism

The events of September 11, 2001, have been a critical factor in "terrorism" becoming an academic industry. However, generally the debate has not changed dramatically in the last 30 or so years.[1] At the short-term level, strategic discussions are focused on imprisoning the perpetrators and reducing harm to innocent civilians. At a deeper longer-term and systemic level, debates center on the causes of terrorism. Positions and related questions include the following:

1. Is terrorism part of a nationalist struggle and thus must be understood through the lenses of geopolitics (today's prime minister was yesterday's freedom fighter who initially was a terrorist)?
2. Is terrorism essentially a product of inequity and injustice and thus the social, political, and economic conditions that create terrorism must

---

* Sohail Inayatullah is Professor at the Graduate Institute of Futures Studies, Tamkang University, Taipei, and the author of 18 books, including *Questioning the Future* and *Macrohistory and Macrohistorians*.

be dealt as with Tony Blair's famous "tough on terrorism and on the causes of terrorism"?

3. Is terrorism a psychological/criminal aberration and thus solutions come from seeing perpetrators as "mentally ill" and developing indicators or signatures of the future terrorist, including appropriate global criminal courts?

4. Is terrorism part of the revenge of colonies against the former masters, and thus must be seen as part of a normal, though unfortunately violent, process of world systems change?

5. Is terrorism part of the irrationality of the past, particularly the religious past, at this stage being represented by extremist Islam, with science, technology, and commerce as the rational future? Is globalization the only way ahead?

6. Or is terrorism a battle of good versus evil, with the West as good and Islam (or parts thereof) as evil?

7. Certainly the analysis one uses tends to be based on one's particular worldview or ideological positioning. An evangelical Christian or a born-again Muslim is likely to see the issue as that of a good versus evil struggle. Alternatively a more secular social reform perspective would see the challenge as changing the conditions in which terrorism survives and thrives. In contrast, a statesman would look less at ideological differences and more at steps forward that can be taken to achieve peace.

The current context is that individuals and collectivities throughout the world are far from agreeing on the nature and causes of terrorism (and indeed on who are the terrorists—state versus group/wholesale versus retail). There is as well high uncertainty on the futures of terrorism. Defining questions include: Will justice come to the Middle-East? How vulnerable are the United States and Europe to terrorist activities? What new technologies (and what new methods of delivering old technologies) might terrorists use in the future? And at deeper and macrolevels, is this part of a natural pendulum ("nothing new under the sun") or is this part of a foundational transition as the world system moves from a nation-state-based structure to something else?

To begin to map the future, we need to ask what might be the nature of this foundational transition. If not a continuation of the nation-state system, what might it look like? Will it be an empire? And if an empire, *Pax Americana* (economic and cultural) or an Islamic Caliphate, wherein religious views on what is right and wrong define social and economic policy? Or is the future likely to a global governance system—a world government with multiple forms of representation—nation-states, individuals, corporations, professional associations, and nongovernmental organizations? Or is terrorism noise from the suggestion that a new level of superordinate authority is required to deal with problems that cannot be dealt with at less complex national levels? Alternatively, instead of the system reconfiguring itself at a higher and more complex level (empire or world governance/government) are we likely to see a social collapse with terrorism creating a new dark ages with political authority becoming far less centralized?

As an attempt to deal with these sorts of questions, the World Future Society commissioned a series of essays on the world after 9/11.[2] As part of this project, many futurists were asked to develop scenarios of the future. I present below both my initial analysis and the scenarios[3] developed and then provide commentary on them.

Which Defining Discourse

As many others did, I also argued that terrorism should not be framed in the war discourse but instead should be seen as a crime against humanity. As much as possible, strategy against international terrorism should not just be to defeat those who sought to create a new Caliphate through violent means but to strengthen global legal and financial institutions. A strengthened world court moving toward a stronger world governance system could thus become one of the positive unintended consequences of al Qaeda's barbarism. It would also set the stage for placing future criminal activity (environmental, cyber, and genetic crimes, for example) within a jurisprudential framework instead of a war framework. The assumptions underlying this are that with clear systemic rules defining fairness and due process, humans can move forward, even during difficult times. As it turned out, the avenue that was chosen was war—war against the Hussein regime in Iraq, against the Taliban in Afghanistan, and against al Qaeda and al Qaeda-inspired groups throughout the world. Choosing the war discourse has been costly for the United States (2–3 trillion dollars spent on the Iraq conflict[4]) and loss of American legitimacy and goodwill. Moreover, the nation-state model of relations (strategy, military and bureaucracy) has been reinforced.

Along with defining discourses, the argument made in 2001 was that the equation that helped explain the terrorist activities was perceived injustice, nationalism/religiousism, and an asymmetrical world order. I had argued that the perceived injustice part of the equation can be handled by the United States and other OECD nations in positions of world power. This means authentically dealing with Israel/Palestine as well as the endless sanctions against Iraq. Until these grievances are met, there could be no way forward. Concretely this means making Jerusalem an international city, giving the Palestinians a state, and ensuring that there are peacekeepers on every block in Israel-Palestine. It means threatening to stop all funding to both parties (the 10 billion dollars yearly from the United States to Israel, for example, and from Saudi Arabia and others to the Palestinian Authority).[5] It means listening to the Other and moving away from strict good/evil essentialisms. Dualistic language only reinforces that which it seeks to dispel, continuing the language of the Crusades, with both civilizations not seeing that they mirror each other.

However, reflections over the past seven years suggest that perceived injustice has only become worse.[6] The war in Iraq has reinforced views that the United States wishes largely only to secure oil. Battles in Israel-Palestine-Lebanon-Gaza highlight the view that not only has the United States gone the wrong way but also that Western policy makers do not have the cognitive framework or intellectual depth to deal with the complexity of problems there.

The second part of the equation has seen little change—nationalism and religiousism continue, though there appears to be a chance that with an Obama presidency, perceptions may change.

However, the third part of the equation has changed. The world is far less asymmetrical taken as a whole, given the dramatic rise of China with its near two trillion dollar surplus,[7] not to mention India, creating a Chindia of the future and balancing North-South power. Of course, within nations, inequity remains high.[8]

Scenarios

I now quote extensively from the original scenarios. They were first written in September 2001—to map the future, to understand what is possibly ahead, as well to create spaces for transformation. Getting the future right in terms of precise predictions was not the intent.

1. Back to Normal. "After successful surgical strikes against Bin Laden and others, the United States returns to some normalcy. While trauma associated with air travel remains, these are seen as costs associated with a modern lifestyle, i.e., just as with cancer, heart disease and car accidents. The West continues to ascend, focused on economic renewal through artificial intelligence and emergent bio-technologies. More money, of course, goes to the military and intelligence agencies. The Right reigns throughout the World. Conflicts remain local and silent. Over time, the world economy prospers once again and poorer nations move up the ranks just as the Pacific Rim nations have."

This has certainly occurred; normalcy has returned. Terrorism is only part of the big picture Indeed, the bigger story has been geopolitical changes (the rise of Chindia), technological shifts (Web 2.0 and genomics), climate change, and peak oil. Thus it is back to normal but the nature of the normal is no longer business as usual.

2. Fortress United States/OECD. "Australia, for example, is already moving in that direction, with basically a prison lockdown ahead, especially to

newcomers (who desire to enter the fantasy island of the Virtual West escaping sanctions and feudal systems) and those who look different. In the United States this is emerging through tighter visa restrictions and surveillance on foreigners as well as citizens. The carrot is, of course, U.S. citizenship being offered to informants from troubled spots. Of course, once they gain citizenship, freedom is still far away, as they are likely to spend a life time under surveillance (for the State's and their protection).

The response from the Islamic world will be a Fortress Islam, closing civilizational doors, becoming even more feudal and mullahist/wahhabist, and forcing individuals to choose: are you with us or against us, denying the multiplicity of selves that we are becoming. The economy—oil—will remain linked but other associations will continue to drift away."

This scenario has been mixed. Certainly a fortress mentality did occur and leaders used the image of the fortress to gain political advantage as the case of John Howard in Australia, George Bush in the United States, Vladimir Putin in Russia, and most recently Nicolas Sarkozy in France. Surveillance in airports and other vulnerable points has increased dramatically, as has police/military presence in the Islamic world. There has been no rapprochement of understandings between Muslims and the West (and of course of Muslims living in the West). But fortress is too strong of a metaphor as economic and cultural globalization continues.

3. Cowboy/Jihadi War—vengeance forever (with soft and hard fascism emerging). "Bush has already evoked the Wild West, and the Wanted—Dead or Alive image, indeed, even calling for a 'crusade' against the terrorists."

This preferred scenario for bin Laden et al. did not occur. He had hoped that Bush's response to 9/11 would lead to destabilization in the Arab world, leading to extremists in Islamic nations rising up against modernists. A nuclear accident or some other unknown event could only help his cause. Instead, while individuals may prefer bin Laden over the leaders (owing to his charisma and willingness to stand up),[9] the modernist project has not been rejected. National leaders wish to stay elected and alive. Moreover bin Laden promised revolution, not rebuilding. And his imagination of the Caliphate was overly influenced by glories of the past, not by the daily needs of citizens for sustenance and sustainability.

Looking back, the two main mistakes from the viewpoint of their stated goals were: (1) The American war on and in Iraq (as this did not decrease terrorist activities); and (2) al Qaeda moving the war from an attack on U.S. military and business positions to attacks on Muslims (in Pakistan, Indonesia, and throughout the Islamic world) and on other innocents. Muslims saw that this was not an attempt to create a new world but return the world to an Arab monarchy. The brutality of it was too chilling even for conspiracy theorists.[10] The assassination of Benazir Bhutto tipped the scales in Pakistan as did the terrorist attack on the Sri Lankan cricket team playing in Lahore in 2009.

Iraq, for all, has become the disaster—the unwinnable war—and moreover, the United States' strategic error has allowed the return of the Taliban,
in Afghanistan and Pakistan. However, while these wars continue, the war
of eternal vengeance appears to be dying out. As in the recent elections in
the Northwest Frontier Province in Pakistan suggest, individuals asked for
rebuilding and not more suicide bombings.[11] This is not to say vengeance and
cowboy wars cannot return, given the ubiquity of mistrust. Indeed, given
that the various parties and related civilizations have entirely different con-
structions of self, society and the Other, it would not take too many events for
the cowboy-jihadi scenario to return (as in Swat Pakistan in 2009). Indeed,
this is the preferred future for al Qaeda et al. and for domestic political leaders if their electoral futures sag.

Let us turn to the last scenario, which was the most idealistic.

4. Gaian Bifurcation. "A Gaia of civilizations (each civilization being incom-
plete in itself and needing the other) plus a system of international justice
focused not only on direct injustices but structural and cultural. This would
not only focus on Israel/Palestine (internationalizing the conflict with peacekeepers and creating a shared Jerusalem) as well as ending the endless sanctions in Iraq, but highlighting injustices by third world governments toward
their own people (and the list here is endless, Burma, Malaysia's Mahathir,
India/Pakistan/Kashmir). The first phase would be far more legalistic, developing a global rule of law system in the context of multicultural globalization
(with an understanding that there are differing ways of justice and process).
The second phase would have a hard edge, developing a global police force
and a military force. The third phase would be values driven, moving from
military to peace keeping to anticipatory conflict resolution. In this phase,
this future, the United States would move to authentically understanding
the periphery, seeking to become smaller (in terms of its imperial reach) and
globally democratic. This means transforming the world system, focusing on
a post-globalization vision of the future, and moving to world governance.
Specifically, this means[12]

- human and animal rights;
- indexing of wealth of poor and rich on a global level, that is, economic
  democracy – employee ownership;
- *prama*-based:[13] creating a dynamic balance, between regions, rural/city,
  seeing the world economy through the ecological metaphor but with
  technological innovation;
- self-reliance, ecological, electronically linked communities (becoming
  more important than states);
- gender partnership;
- and a transformed United Nations, with increased direct democracy,
  influence of the social movements and transparency within multinational corporations."

We are ever far from this scenario, perhaps even further now that when it was written in 2001. However, this is not say this future is impossible. The outlines of this scenario appear to be generally shared by the cultural creatives, an emerging demographic category in the West (www.culturalcreatives.org), almost 25 percent of the representative population. In the non-West also there is a desire to move away from feudal structures but retain spiritual heritage, to be "modern" but in a different way. This is the image of alternative modernities. Indeed, Riaz Hussan of Flinders University, Australia, argues that Muslims are having a renaissance in increased religiosity, and thus far less interest in extremist political positions.[14]

Still, the systemic changes have not occurred and those wishing for a different future are not in positions of political leadership, nor are citizens ready for this type of transformation given the politics of mistrust. Moreover, moving toward this future requires personal depth and for strategy to not just focus on the litany of terror (headlines) but on the social, worldview causes and mythological causes, that is, a multilayered complex view of reality.[15] Thus, it means challenging violence, but also developing mediation training in schools throughout the world. It means leaders acting in ways that represent the future they wish to see. To move toward this direction, ultimately means far more of a Mandela approach—what Johan Galtung is doing via the transcend (www.transcend.org) network—than the traditional short-term "my way or the highway" conflict resolution approach.

Now what are the futures ahead for the Islamic and Western world? Borrowing from macrohistory, the following patterns are foundational: linear, cyclical, pendulum, and spiral.

The Linear Ascent

The first course for Islam is the linear trajectory. Islam, with fits and convolutions, and minor reversals, will follow the Western trajectory. And if not the Western one, the newly created East Asian model: a strong state combined with market forces; centralized political authority with some consultation; and long-term planning with high levels of social control. Essentially, this is the "father knows best" model of governance.

Muslims in this future will emerge from the medieval era and enter a modernist one. Of course, there will be Iranian-style backslides, but eventually the power of the ayatollahs will diminish as making a living, clear air and water, as well as a desire for a better life for one's children and future generations become more significant than past injustices.

The Islamic world will thus leave its medieval paradigm behind and join the European Enlightenment (or create its own similar version). The current crises, seen from a long-term macroview, are minor reactions to this predestined trajectory.[16] Over time, it will be the United Arab Emirates

(UAE), Turkey, and Malaysia that will lead—those who can create wealth (and not just from oil), innovation, and maintain religious traditions will be remembered.

Of course, seen with far less idealistic eyes, the march into a linear, shared global future continues to have major setbacks. First is despotism within the Islamic world, authority with no wisdom. Second is the continued violence in Palestine/Israel.[17] Third, are the divisions of class and gender, and the urban patterns of poverty, alienation and disempowerment found in the Islamic world. And fourth is the lack of any real leader with the charisma of a bin Laden.

Outside of the Islamic world, equally relevant are the following factors: First is uneven globalization, with few immediate and midterm benefits to the poorest in poorer nations. Second is the continued perceived hypocrisy among the Western powers. When they are not walking the talk, as with the Abu Ghraib crisis (where hypocrisy was hidden behind managerialism instead of the apology of honor, so fundamental in feudal and indigenous cultures) legitimacy declines. Third is Orientalism,[18] the cultural construction of the non-West as inferior—that is, direct, structural, and epistemological violence. And, fourth is hypertechnological advancement via robotics, genetics (from gene therapy to germ line intervention), and nanotechnology that make catch-up practically impossible.[19]

In this vision, the Islamic world's future is contoured by the Rise of the West, from colonial empire to developmentalism and now to globalization (with hints of empire next). The Islamic world's trajectory is defined and limited by the West's technological, economic, political, and definitional dominance, and thus joining the West for most is near impossible.

However with restricted parameters, there is still cultural temporal contagion within this trajectory and thus bin Laden and his cohorts can be seen simultaneously as feudal warriors—with a clear leader, clan, relationships, honor—and as globalists and even "netizens."

Further, the forces of globalization and technologization are in conflict with modernist leaders and bureaucrats focused on a secular rational institutionalized industrial state formations. These leaders/bureaucrats are in tension with citizens living in multiple worlds—the scientific, the feudal, the secular, the modernist, and indeed the postmodernist. New technologies exacerbate the possibility of enhanced multiplicities—CDROM, the Web—all remove the power of interpretation from mullah to individual, allowing for far more individualized religiosity.[20] This possibility of more individualism is unsympathetically understood by bin Laden-type traditionalists (even while they use the tools of global technocratism) and national bureaucrats, who paint all attempts of individualistic and syncretic Islam as unpatriotic. He who owns the means of knowledge, the right to define, is at the heart of the battle within Islam, and indeed, the world. And it is the West, particularly the United States that is the defining agent.

Thus, the linear trajectory is far more difficult when there can be only one "king of the hill." And so the decision by many when they cannot join the party is to destroy it. Thus, instead of the linear rise with fits and starts, it could be endlessly the same, a kind of steady state misery where nothing truly changes, just cycles of minor rises and falls. The cycles are leadership-based or a few nations rising and joining the core in the world system but most Islamic nations or nations with Muslim majorities stay on the periphery of the world system.

A Pendulum Shift

A pendulum swing is another future for Islam and the West. If the West enters into decline, caused partly by ageing (witness the demographic destiny with Caucasians moving from 50 percent of the world's population in the 1850s to probably less than 5 percent by 2150),[21] Islam will be on the rise (especially if it can move away from conspiracy to innovation). In this formulation, both West and Islam are in the same field, facing each other with antagonism and fear, but still part of the same unitary relationship. If the West declines (perhaps owing to imperial overreach, global warming, failed genetic experiments, or an inward-looking security state), it may be Islam that rises to fill the world vacuum, as macrohistorian Johan Galtung has argued.[22] While China and possibly India are the most likely candidates for world hegemony, Muslims could use the current crisis to move away from extremism and recover the spirit of tradition without its negative details. Thus, they could step into a vacuum and provide the ethical anchor to the relativism of postmodernism. This means that the South-North axis will change, not that inequality will end. As we know, 43 percent of the South's global trade is accounted for by intra-South trade,[23] and the South does not wish to transform the world system, merely to have a greater voice in political structures such as the Security Council.

Thus a pendulum shift suggests that Western hegemony is likely to end; China and India are likely to rise, and this would generally benefit Muslims and Islamic nations. This does not mean the nature of the world system is changing, that is, toward a Gaian vision, but rather that the center of gravity will shift.

However, along with linearity, the cycle and the pendulum, there is the spiral. What might a spiral future look like?

A Virtuous Spiral?

This last trajectory is similar to the Gaian bifurcation but with a more realistic frame. This recovery of the past in the context of future-oriented progress is the virtuous spiral. This future is the most hopeful for Islam and the rest of the world. In this alternative trajectory, after a brief foray into postmodernism—endless consumer choices but no ground of reality—a new global ethics may emerge. This is a soft, multicultural Islam engaged in dialogue with the West and East Asia, confident of its dignity, creating an alternative science like that imagined by leaders such as Anwar Ibrahim.[24] Many of Islam's ideas—environmental protection, concern for poverty, Islamic economics, and Islamic science— will become part of the global agenda.

Islam's spiritual history, far less challenged by modernity—coming after the West's entry into it—will be far less problematic (secularism will no longer be the benchmark of the good society) and will help in the creation of a post-postmodern era, a postscarcity, spiritually balanced society with deep sustainability.[25] This is progress with history, an alternative modernity that offers multiple trajectories leading to sustainable development. To create this future a creative minority is needed. The current hijacking of Islam is the shadow response to the paucity of a creative minority. The creative minority offers a new image of the future and practices it. Groups in the United States (progressive Muslims) and in the United Kingdom are working on this,[26] and, hopefully, this can become part of a reformed Islam. Indeed, this was a desired image of the future at an international meeting of Muslim scholars.[27]

Five points were fundamental:[28]

1. An alternative economics to world capitalism
2. Cooperation between the genders based on dignity and fairness
3. Self-reliant ecological communities
4. Use of advanced technologies to link these communities
5. A world governance system that is fair, just, representational and guided by wise leadership

This virtuous spiral model, using aspects of the past to invent an alternative future, is something to be aspired to. The pivotal here, as Zia Sardar argues, is that a reformed Islam can not only transform Muslim society and Islamic thought, but it can also provide a genuine alternative to the dominant mode of doing things globally.[29] Ultimately, this means that even if there are terrorist incidents, almost all the world—all religions, all citizens—will condemn it and challenge it as the conditions that spawn terrorism will have been dramatically reduced.

There Is Life Globally after 9/11

The world for many changed after 9/11. With a distance of more than seven years or so, terrorism, while important, pales in comparison with the events that started the twenty-first century. First came the digital revolution, followed by the demise of the Soviet Union, followed by the mapping of the human genome, followed by the rise of China (its foreign reserves were 18.5 billion dollars in 1988 and now they are 1.7 trillion dollars[30]) and India, followed by the climate change crisis, followed by the peak oil crisis, which in turn was followed by the global financial crisis (potentially leading not only to a long-term collapse but also a transformation of the foundations of the world capitalist system). We are now not only in the midst of these transformations, but are also shifting to an aging planet, at least for the wealthier nations (and eventually for China and India as well in the long run). In the even longer term, 9/11 may be forgotten, though certainly the victims of terror throughout the world should not be.

Of course, the collapse scenario is always there—especially with Pakistan as the weak point in this entire discussion. As we well know, more Pakistanis were killed in terrorist attacks in 2007 than the number of Americans who died in 9/11[31]—and it may be in Pakistan where the world's security issues will be decided. However, other factors—new technologies, demographic shifts, economic shifts, resource challenges—all point to the fact that there is a future after 9/11 after all.

Notes

1. See, for example, Mark Satin, "Twenty-eight Ways of Looking at Terrorism," *New Options* Issue 24 (1986): 1–8 and Mark Satin, "Alternatives to Terrorism: Siding with the World's Poor," *New Options* Issue 28 (1986): 1–4.
2. See Sohail Inayatullah, "Fortress, Vengeance, or Gaia: Three Scenarios," *The Futurist* 36, no. 1 (2002): 21. Also see, Sohail Inayatullah, "After the Terror: Will the World Move Forward," *New Renaissance* 10, no. 4, Issue 35 (2001–2002): 20–21.
3. With minor edits for the purpose of clarity.
4. Joseph E. Stiglitz and Linda J. Bilmes, *The Three Trillion Dollar War: The True Cost of the Iraq Conflict* (New York: W. W. Norton, 2008).
5. Thomas Stauffer argues that the cost to the global community of the Israel-Palestine conflict has been between 6–12 trillion dollars, http://www.wrmea.com/archives/june2003/0306020.html (accessed September 4, 2008).
6. http://pewglobal.org/reports/pdf/253.pdf (accessed September 4, 2008). In the 13-nation Pew world survey on how Muslims and Westerners see each other, they conclude the obvious—that there is a great divide. "Many in the West see Muslims as fanatical, violent, and as lacking tolerance. Muslims in the Middle East and Asia generally see Westerners as selfish, immoral and greedy—as well as violent and fanatical. And: Muslim publics have an aggrieved view of the West—they are much more likely than Americans or Western Europeans to blame Western policies for their own lack of prosperity. For their part, Western publics instead point to government corruption, lack of education and Islamic fundamentalism as the biggest obstacles to Muslim prosperity." In a separate poll, only 4 percent of Pakistanis believed that the United States had a good motivation for the war against terror. http://www.cnn.com/2007/POLITICS/09/11/poll.pakistanis/ (accessed September 4, 2008).

7. http://www.chinability.com/Reserves.htm (accessed September 4, 2008).

8. For more information, see the special issue of *Futures* edited by Jan Nederveen Pieterse and Boike Rehbein. "Emerging Futures," *Futures* 40, no. 8 (2008): 703–776.

9. If this is too difficult to understand, remember that heroes such as Ned Kelly of Australia and Jesse James in the United States were killers, not Gandhian in their actions.

10. Phillip Adams, "Bin Laden Heads for Sin Bin: Al-qa'ida Is in Its Death Throes as Islamists Condemn Its Action," *The Australian*, June 24, 2008, 12. Bin Laden's support, says Adams, citing recent Pew Research Center polls, has dropped from 70 percent approval to 4percent. Approval for al Qaeda has dropped from 33 percent to 9 percent.

11. Associated Press, "Voters in Pakistan's Conservative Northwest Throw Out Religious Hard-Liners," *International Herald Tribune*, February 20, 2008, http://www.iht.com/articles/ap/2008/02/20/asia/AS-GEN-Pakistan-Islamists-Lose.php (accessed February 28, 2008). For example, "They didn't do anything for the people," Bokhari Shah, 65, said of the religious parties. "They have done nothing to help the people, and we are afraid to even come out from our homes because of all these bomb blasts." And: "We voted for the (Islamists) before because they promised to change things, to make life better for us, to end the corruption and to bring a good life. But they didn't," he said. "They just brought restrictions. And look— we are afraid of bombs and rockets all the time."

12. See, Sohail Inayatullah, *Understanding Sarkar: The Indian Episteme, Macrohistory and Transformative Knowledge* (Leiden: Brill, 2002).

13. *Prama* means inner and outer balance. For more on this, see Sohail Inayatullah, *Situating Sarkar* (Maleny, Gurukul Publications, 1999).

14. See Hassan's *Faithlines: Muslim Conceptions of Islam and Society* (Karachi: Oxford: University Press, 2002).

15. For more on this approach see, Noni Kenny, "Unpacking Terrorism Futures'" PhD dissertation, Queensland University of Technology, School of Law, 2008 (to be submitted).

16. For more on this, see "Islamic Responses to Emerging Scientific, Technological and Epistemological Transformations," *Social Epistemologies* 10, no. 3–4 (1996): 331–349; and earlier in *Islamic Thought and Scientific Creativity* 6, no. 2 (1995): 47–68. Also, "Global Transformations," *Development* 40, no. 2 (1997): 31–37.

17. Justified or not justified (Kashmir, Chechnya).

18. Edward Said's work remains foundational. But as important are Ashis Nandy, P. R. Sarkar, and many others.

19. In 1993, just 10 countries accounted for 84 percent of global research and development expenditures and controlled 95 percent of the U.S. patents of the past two decades. The die is cast; technocracy will further create a divided world, with the right to the Net and the right to genetic therapy and modification becoming the battle cry of coming decades.

20. Sohail Inayatullah and Gail Boxwell, eds., *Islam, Postmodernism and Other Futures*, 89–106.

21. For more on this see Sohail Inayatullah, "Waking Up to a New Future," *Journal of Futures Studies* 10, no. 2 (November 2005): 55–62 (special Issue edited by Jordi Serra).

22. Johan Galtung, "On the Last 2,500 Years in Western History, and Some Remarks on the Coming 500," *The New Cambridge Modern History, Companion Volume*, ed. Peter Burke (Cambridge: Cambridge University Press, 1979). See as well Johan Galtung and Sohail Inayatullah, eds., *Macrohistory and Macrohistorians* (Westport, CT: Praeger, 1997).

23. J. Nederveen Pieterse, "Globalization in the Next Round: Sociological Perspectives," *Futures* 40 (2008): 709.

24. See special issue of *Futures*. Anwar Ibrahim, "The *Ummah* and Tomorrow's World," *Futures* 23, no. 3 (April 1991): 302–310. Also see Anwar Ibrahim, *The Asian Renaissance* (Singapore: Time Books, 1996).

25. See www.islamicconcern.com/fatwas.asp for a site on Islam and vegetarianism.

26. There are even Islamic vegetarian societies, challenging the hold of meat as a cultural *doxa*.

27. Organization of Islamic Conference, www.oic-oci.org.

28. Sohail Inayatullah, "Leaders Envision the Future of the Islamic Ummah," *World Futures Studies Federation Bulletin* (July 1996), cover page. See Sohail Inayatullah, "Futures Visions of Southeast Asia: Some Early Warning Signals," *Futures* 27, no. 6 (July/August, 1995): 681–688.

29. Ziauddin Sardar, e-mail message to author, April 2, 2004.

30. http://www.chinability.com/Reserves.htm (accessed September 4, 2008).

31. Mohsin Hamid, "End of a Beginning," *Time* 172, no. 9 (September 1, 2008): 64.

Index

Lightning Source UK Ltd.
Milton Keynes UK
UKOW03n1237230714

235619UK00003B/38/P